13.60

INTRODUCTION TO PHYSICAL EDUCATION

A HUMANISTIC PERSPECTIVE

Leonard Kalakian
Mankato State College

Myra Goldman
Boston State College

ALLYN AND BACON, INC.
BOSTON   LONDON   SYDNEY   TORONTO

LIBRARY OF CONGRESS CATALOGING IN PUBLICATION DATA

KALAKIAN, LEONARD H
INTRODUCTION TO PHYSICAL EDUCATION.

Bibliography: p.
Includes index.
1. Physical education and training.   I. Goldman,
Myra, 1935–   II. Title.
GV341.K28   613.7'07   75-45207

ISBN 0-205-05475-7

Second printing . . . August, 1976

Contents

Preface

This book has been designed as an alternative text for those who have chosen physical education as a career. The focus of physical education is people, therefore, the thrust of this text is people. In support of the deep concern physical education and physical educators must have for people as individuals we have called this book *Introduction to Physical Education: A Humanistic Perspective.*

We have not outlined the history of physical education, nor have we considered the area of teaching methods, or many of the other topics the reader might expect to find in an introductory text. So many of these areas are mechanical and, thus, impersonal. Instead, we have placed the *individual* at the core of all discussions, and have shown how physical education is much more than simply the teaching of skills. Individuals learn the skills that physical educators teach; this text is concerned with what happens to those individuals as they participate in physical education and movement experiences. This text is dedicated to the idea that learning should be fun, and that learning will be more meaningful and useful to the individual when the learning situation is humanistically oriented.

Throughout the discussions are numerous references to the ideas and theories of other writers and researchers. You will also find selected references at the end of each chapter that are concerned with the theme of the chapter. We hope that you will want to read sections of these books, and the articles and studies cited in order to broaden your knowledge and help you to become more fully aware of the many dimensions of what is called "physical education."

This book does not pretend to have all of the answers between its covers. In fact, there may be many ideas and theories with which you will disagree. However, if we succeed in getting you to think about physical education in a slightly different way, and, even if by disagreeing with us you become motivated to read further and perhaps become a bit more humanistic in your own perspective, then this text will have served a valuable purpose.

L.K.
M.G.

INTRODUCTION TO PHYSICAL EDUCATION
A HUMANISTIC PERSPECTIVE

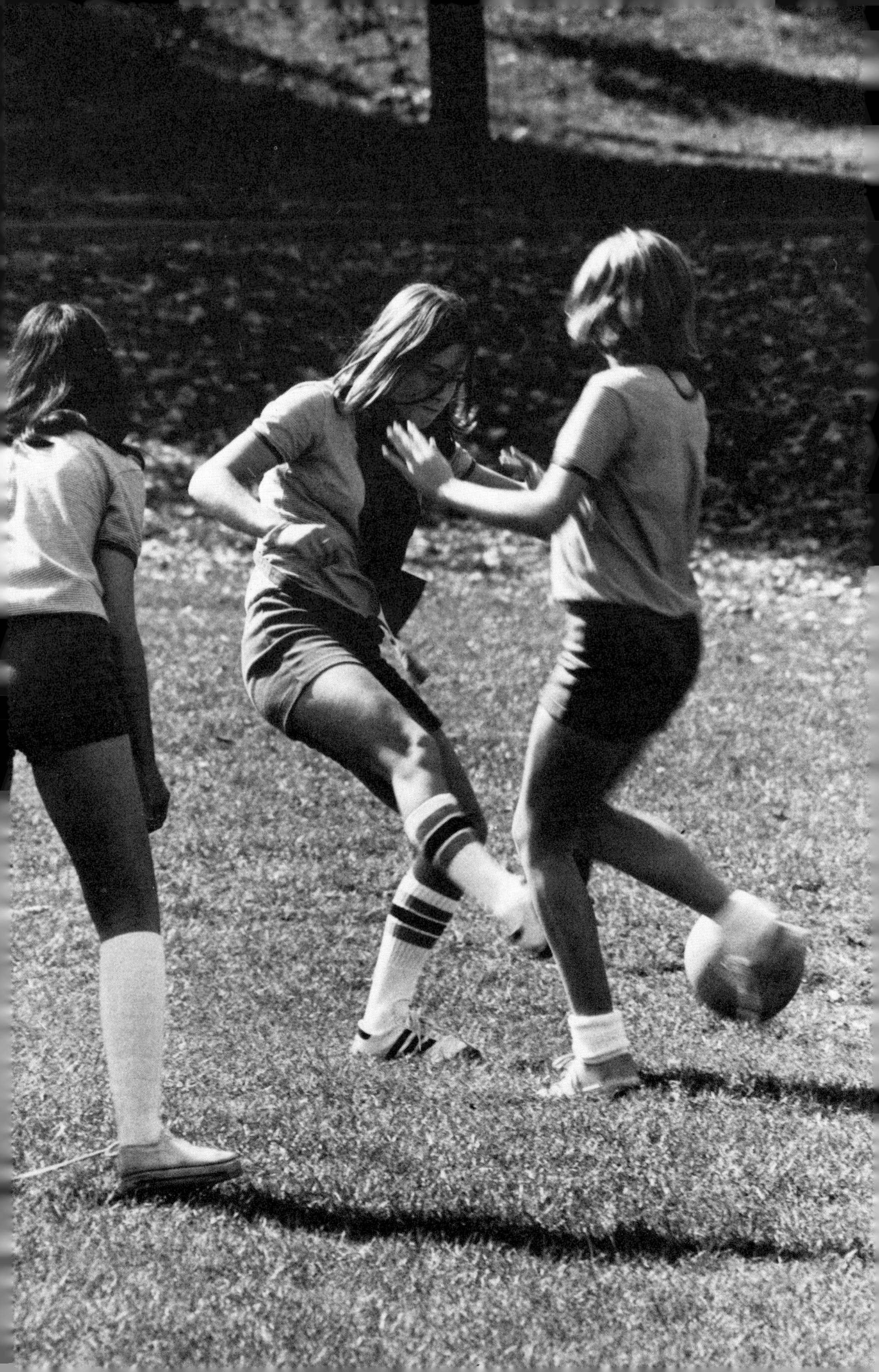

Physical Education: A Modern Concept of Education through the Physical

The modern concepts of the educational field we now call "physical education" have evolved gradually, and have come about because there have been so many different philosophical viewpoints that attempt to define what physical education really is; what physical education ought to be; what physical education ought to do; and how physical education ought to go about reaching its goals.

Over thirty years ago, in an attempt to set down a workable and realistic philosophy of physical education, Jesse Feiring Williams, an acknowledged and highly respected leader in the field, originated the phrase "education through the physical." In a later, more comprehensive definition, Williams, in collaboration with Clifford Lee Brownell, wrote:

' . . . physical education is the sum of man's physical activities, selected as to kind, and conducted as to outcomes.' Since physical education is to be considered as a means of education through physical activities rather than an education of the physical—how absurd the latter—the phrases 'selected as to kind' and 'conducted as to outcomes' assume considerable importance.[1]

1. Jesse Feiring Williams and Clifford Lee Brownell, *The Administration of Health and Physical Education* (Philadelphia: W. B. Saunders Co. 1946), p. 20.

This definition quite clearly supports the importance of the humanistic aspect of physical education. While the education of the *physical* is very necessary, to concentrate on this aspect alone would be a very rigid and extremely narrow view of the value of physical activity. Education of the physical cannot be ignored or disregarded since healthy growth and proper physical development are two desired outcomes of participation in vigorous physical activity.

However, physical educators cannot educate the body while ignoring the mental, social and emotional needs of the individual. Thus, education through the physical asks the question: What will be the effect of a specific activity on the participating individuals? For example, education through the physical is not concerned with how well a youngster plays basketball at the end of an eight-week instructional unit in beginning skills. Rather, education through the physical is concerned with helping that youngster enjoy moving his body in new and different ways, better understand his own capabilities through the use of a particular set of skills, respect and appreciate the varieties of skills exhibited by classmates, and function as a team member as well as an individual. Education through the physical is deeply committed to guiding individuals toward an understanding of themselves, an understanding of others, and an understanding of the "why" of physical activity. Although the phrase "education through the physical" is not a new one, and "the effect of the activity on the individual" is time-honored, both phrases are key concepts in humanistic physical education.

It is possible to trace this humanistic outlook as we reach back into the history of physical education:

> The early Twentieth-Century programs of physical education were still dominated by formal gymnastics, the German and Swedish in particular. They were rivalled, however, by a new concept of physical education known variously as the 'new physical education,' 'natural program,' and 'natural gymnastics,' which was in the process of formation largely through the efforts of a trinity of outstanding leaders in physical education: Dr. Thomas D. Wood, Clark Hetherington, and Dr. Luther Halsey Gulick. It was they who broke with the tradition of formal gymnastics and gave shape and content to a distinctively Twentieth-Century program of physical education, which centers upon the physical as an avenue for promoting education.[2]

Several centuries ago, the term *humanism* applied to both education and physical education. During the Renaissance, the concept of humanism was incorporated into the philosophies and life-styles of the Europeans. According to many historians within the field of physical education as well as other fields during that period, Italy was a world leader in cultural

2. Arthur Weston, *The Making of American Physical Education* (New York: Meredith Publishing Co. 1962), p. 51.

development, and humanism as a philosophy apparently was born and nurtured there and eventually spread to other countries. Humanism of the Renaissance was primarily concerned with the individual—his needs, his interests, his abilities and his general well-being. As to how physical education was viewed:

> The humanists embraced the classical ideal of the 'sound mind in the sound body' as the highest objective of physical education.[3]

It had been the ancient Athenians during the Golden Age of Physical Education in Greece who first truly defined, and then set about finding ways of achieving, the ultimate goal of perfect harmony between body and mind. Unfortunately, physical education during the Renaissance was gradually de-emphasized as other philosophies stressing intellectual achievement came to the fore and flourished. However, humanism in physical education during the Renaissance as viewed by Van Dalen and Bennett is no less descriptive of, and applicable to, humanistic physical education today:

> The humanistic [physical] educators considered how to teach as much as what to teach. Several writers stressed the importance of self-activity, self-expression, individual differences, progressive training, and positive discipline.[4]

Moreover, Baley and Field believe:

> Humanist educators were among the first to be concerned with teaching methods as well as content. They advocated methods which many today believe are new and modern. They discussed individual differences . . . respect for each individual personality . . . encouragement of cooperation among students . . .[5]

The time is apparently right once again for physical education to take a comprehensive look at humanism, and to attempt to adapt this philosophy to meet the needs of present-day students. The task is not a difficult one, for the major objectives of physical education—physical development, motor development, mental development, and personal-social development, certainly encompass both education of the physical and education through the physical. However, to develop a more humanistic physical education, the emphases must be shifted, people-oriented

3. Deobold D. Van Dalen and Bruce L. Bennett. *A World History of Physical Education: Cultural, Philosophical, Comparative* (Englewood Cliffs, N.J.: Prentice-Hall, Inc., 1971), p. 126.
4. Ibid., p. 131.
5. James A. Baley and David A. Field. *Physical Education and the Physical Educator: An Introduction* (Boston: Allyn and Bacon, Inc., 1970), p. 171.

teaching methodologies must be adopted, and activities must be selected with the primary regard based on the positive contributions the activity will make to the student.

In selecting activities, physical educators will find themselves abandoning present curriculums that heavily emphasize team sports while they substitute innovative movement experiences that will have relevance for all students. Physical educators will find that they are redefining not only physical education, but also their own philosophy toward physical education, physical activity, and movement experiences. Redefinition will become a vital part of progress toward a more humanistic physical education. Charles A. Bucher has proposed:

> . . . that the leaders in this field must develop a program of activities in which participants will realize results beneficial to their growth and development . . . that socially they will become educated to play an effective part in democratic group living, and that they will be better able to interpret new situations in a more meaningful and purposeful manner as a result of these physical education experiences.[6]

The preceding discussion has helped to demonstrate that physical education is indeed founded upon a humanistic philosophy, and further that movement experiences are the essence of physical education. Thus, if physical education is to realize the goal of educating through the physical in order to meet humanistic ends, then the vehicle for progress will be curriculums that offer students a wide and diverse variety of movement experiences that have been carefully selected to meet the needs, interests, and capabilities of those students. Let us now more closely examine physical education as it relates to the individual as he experiences movement under the leadership of the humanistic physical educator.

THE INDIVIDUAL AND MOVEMENT-RELATED EXPERIENCES

In any discussion of education through the physical, there emerges an obvious and close relationship to the disciplines of psychology and sociology. Psychology attempts to study behavior, but even more specifically, it studies, and tries to understand, the many ways in which individuals act and react.

Sociology is concerned with the behavior of groups of individuals. Sociology attempts to understand how the interactions among individuals within a particular group affect the structure and function of that group. Human movement is a mode of expression and communication, a primary mode through which the physical education objectives of psycholgical

6. Charles A. Bucher, *Foundations of Physical Education.* (St. Louis: The C.V. Mosby Co. 1972), p. 7.

Introduction to Physical Education

and social development may be attained. Through a humanistic perspective, physical education seeks to discover and develop ways in which movement may be best used to increase the individual's psychological and social awareness.

Self-Knowledge through Movement

A program of education through the physical provides many opportunities for gaining self-knowledge. Further, the individual who is aware of his (or her) capabilities and has set reasonable goals based on self-knowledge will be better able to relate to other individuals and to the environment. Therefore:

> Our attitude about ourself is perhaps the most important in our constellation of attitudes . . . The self-attitude is important because it in part influences our goals and our behavior in reaching these goals. It is important also because negative feelings toward the self will predispose one negatively toward others.[7]

Because man is a physical being, he tends to relate to his environment through physical means. Thus, movement experiences are inextricably involved with the development of man's self-concepts. When movement is used by physical educators in ways that help students to develop positive self-concepts, this is the humanistic approach to education through the physical.

Self-Concept and Efficient Movement

While some data are available that seem to suggest a correlation between a positive self-concept and movement efficiency, the results are far from definitive. In fact, the suggestion is frequently made that a positive self-concept is a prerequisite to efficient movement. From a sociological point of view:

> Studies reveal that socially well-adjusted persons tend to be more successful in athletics, physical fitness and physical education activities than are persons who are less well adjusted socially.[8]

However, we cannot draw from the above statement an implication that physical activity in reality serves to benefit least those individuals who

7. Rainer Martens, *Social Psychology and Physical Activity.* (New York: Harper & Row, 1975), p. 141.
8. Charles C. Cowell, "The Contributions of Physical Activity to Social Development," *Research Quarterly* 31 (May 1960, Part 2), p. 293.

most need to find satisfaction, success, and pleasure through movement, rather:

> . . . everyone consciously or unconsciously sees more than a physiological organism going through motor gyrations or having fun . . . play and exercise have some effect on the behavior patterns of the person.[9]

For years, many of those who have supported the concept of education through the physical have in turn supported the premise that as the individual learns to move more skillfully he also tends to develop a stronger and more positive self-concept. On the other hand, many of those same people also realize that individuals who already possess a highly satisfactory self-concept often achieve a very competent level of movement efficiency because they tend to be highly motivated, have high aspiration levels, and are somewhat naturally aggressive. According to Cratty:

> It has been postulated for a number of years that children learn things in games in addition to the obvious skills they evidence while playing. Some physical educators suggested . . . that a variety of social and personal traits will be improved as a child interacts with his peers on the playfield. Extensive data supporting this rather global contention, however, remain difficult to locate.[10]

There is some research that seems to show a relationship between self-concept and movement efficiency. For example, a recent study by Sonstroem seems to point to a rather high positive relationship between self-acceptance and physical achievement.[11] Similarly, Schendel found that individuals who participated in athletic-type activities seemed to be socially more adept, were socially more mature, and had a more satisfactory self-concept than did nonparticipants.[13] In an earlier study using high school boys as subjects, Merriman reported that those boys who were judged to have high levels of motor ability were more self-confident and had higher levels of aspiration than did boys who were in a lower motor ability classification.[14] Conversely, Leithwood[15] and Hellison[16] have cited

9. Scott, M. Gladys, "The Contributions of Physical Activity to Psychological Development." *Research Quarterly* 31 (May 1960, Part II), p. 307.
10. Bryant J. Cratty, *Movement, Perception and Thought* (Palo Alto, Calif.: Peek Publications, 1970), p. 2.
11. Robert J. Sonstroem, "Attitude Testing Examining Certain Psychological Correlates of Physical Activity" *Research Quarterly* 45 (May 1974): 93–103.
12. Jack Schendel, "Psychological Differences Between Athletes and Nonparticipants in Athletics at Three Educational Levels" *Research Quarterly* 36 (March 1965):52–67.
13. Ibid.
14. Burton J. Merriman, "Relationship of Personality Traits to Motor Ability" *Research Quarterly* 31 (May 1960, Part I):163–173.
15. Kenneth A. Leithwood, "Motor, Cognitive, and Affective Relationships Among Advantaged Preschool Children" *Research Quarterly* 42 (March 1971):47–53.
16. Donald R. Hellison, "Physical Education and the Self-Attitude" *Quest* 13 (January 1970):41–45.

When movement is used by physical educators in ways that help students to develop positive self-concepts, this is the humanistic approach to education through the physical.

data that seems to indicate that self-concept and movement efficiency are not related at all. However, Roberta J. Park has written:

> If physical education is to be responsible to its claim that its programs contribute to the optimal growth and development of children, youth, and adults, any activities ... with which a physical educator deals must be thoroughly infused with the qualitative, inner-directed, means-oriented play element. Sports belong in the physical education curriculum because they contribute to the development of unity and self-actualization for the participant.[17]

Certainly there is need for additional research that will help us to determine more conclusively the extent to which self-concept and movement efficiency are related. The humanistic physical educator must come to the fullest understanding of the human personality that he possibly can if he is going to design and implement a humanistic program of physical education. In the absence to date of highly definitive research concerned with interrelationships between self-concept and movement efficiency, physical educators would serve their students well by heeding the words of Cowell:

17. Roberta J. Park, "Alternatives and Other Ways; How Might Physical Activity be More Relevant to Human Needs in the Future?" *Quest* 21 (January 1974), p. 34.

Much social interaction centers around physical skill. The child lacking motor skills is often barred or not accepted in social participation. Human personality cannot be developed apart from the social group and since our children are destined to live in a highly organized social order, the physical activities of children and youth should be used progressively from kindergarten through high school to develop social learnings and a gradual intensification of social consciousness.[18]

Self-Esteem through Movement

According to Hellison:

Self-esteem is not equivalent to self-concept or other self constructs but is actually an affective self-attitude-i.e., a subjective evaluation of the self having as its basis a feeling of liking or disliking including both direction and intensity.[19]

Everyone has feelings of self-esteem, and depending on certain factors these feelings may run from very negative feelings to very positive feelings. From day to day, an individual's self-esteem may vary depending upon his experiences, his actions, and the outcomes of these actions. Physical education can help the individual to develop a more positive and consistent self-esteem by providing movement experiences in which the individual can experience success.

While it is recognized that different experiences affect different people in different ways, it is generally contended that movement experiences tend to facilitate the development of positive self-esteem. Society generally seems to admire individuals who exhibit a high degree of movement proficiency. The individual who demonstrates superiority in activities held in high regard by society reaps the benefits of positive reinforcement. Positive reinforcement most often occurs in the guise of recognition, awards, and rewards. Such reinforcement facilitates the development and maintainance of positive self-esteem because this type of reinforcement helps the individual to feel satisfied with himself and his accomplishments. When an individual possesses a satisfactory level of self-esteem, this self-attitude becomes a reference point that is used in forming personal and subjective value judgments about the world immediately around him, and about the people with whom he forms social groups. Concerning this very significant part of life Baley and Field suggest:

The physical educator can provide opportunities for the child to experience success by introducing him to activities in which he can find a modicum of

18. Cowell, op. cit., p. 290.
19. Hellison, op. cit. p. 41.

success. He can protect and nourish the child's ego by treating him with respect and affection . . . There are enough opportunities in physical education activities to provide every child with the feeling of satisfaction which comes with achievement. [20]

Self-esteem is thus related to the domain we call "skillful movement" to the extent that man is movement-oriented and tends to relate to his environment in movement-centered ways. Because virtually all cultures value and appreciate the individual who is skilled in movement, the ability to move well contributes to the development of positive self-esteem. This is a highly desired outcome of education through the physical, a nonphysical humanistic outcome stemming from participation in carefully devised movement experiences.

Conformity and Skilled Movement

Some writers have suggested that people's tendencies toward conformity are but one manifestation of the desire to move skillfully and gracefully. Because most people consider skillful movement a desirable human trait, the attempt to achieve movement proficiency is an attempt to conform to the expectations of society. For those individuals who are motivated by a need to conform, participating in movement experiences in a program of education through the physical provides an opportunity for increased acceptance by society. As Seidel and Resnick wrote:

Each person should have an opportunity for self-realization within bounds that society deems desirable. . . . Self-realization has always been an objective in American education . . . Today . . . many people believe that society is going overboard in not only allowing but encouraging everyone 'to do his own thing' . . . The implication for the physical educator, then, is clear . . . He must provide the individual with an opportunity for genuine self-realization . . . by offering a wide variety of activities in his program so that each individual can find at least one in which he can excel. [21]

PHYSICAL EDUCATION AND THE "LESSONS OF LIFE"

Those who support the concept of education through the physical suggest that movement experiences are a reflection of life, and therefore are humanistically oriented. The "lessons of life" include, but are certainly not

20. Baley and Field, op. cit., p. 323.
21. Beverly L. Seidel and Matthew C. Resick. *Physical Education: An Overview* (Reading, Mass.: Addison-Wesley Publishing Company, 1972), p. 130.

limited to, the concepts of fair play, sportsmanship, dedication, cooperation, leadership and followership, loyalty, and competitiveness. Let us look
at each of these concepts individually from the humanistic perspective,
and relate them to education through the physical.

Fair Play

By their very nature, humanistic movement experiences provide opportunities to learn the concepts of fair play since the experiences are designed
to afford each participant an equal chance to succeed. The fair play of the
movement laboratory traditionally has been thought to be easily transfera-
ble to other situations in life that occur outside the domain of what are
purely movement experiences. The underlying premise has been that
individuals who learn the principles of fair play through movement experiences will incorporate fairness and fair dealings with others into their total
life-style. The extent to which the concepts of fair play will transfer from the
movement laboratory to non-movement experiences must remain a matter
of speculation because situations, and the people involved in those situations, vary so much. The factors and variables which affect and determine
human behavior are virtually infinite, and occur in countless combina-
tions. It would, however, seem logical to speculate that individuals are
helped to internalize the concepts of fair play in their associations with
others through participation in those activities specifically designed to
inculcate positive attitudes toward fair play. It would also seem reasonable
to suggest, then, that movement experiences can provide a most viable
way of instilling in the individual a step toward a life-style that encompasses the desirable traits of fair play, honesty, and honorable associations
with others.

Movement experiences are highly appropriate ways fair play may
be practiced, since youngsters naturally and readily relate to movement,
and furthermore, children very frequently identify closely with their physical education teacher. Thus, values which the physical educator attempts
to inculcate in the students through movement experiences tend to have
rather high credibility for those students. If the physical education teacher
is one with whom the students can and do identify, then they will tend to
closely identify with the ideas, ideals, and values of the teacher. Say Nixon
and Jewett:

> Satisfying physical education experiences will contribute to a personal value
> system, a drive toward 'peak experiences' in physical performance. Physical
> recreation should be healthful, joyful, and integrative. [22]

22. John E. Nixon, and Ann E. Jewett. *An Introduction to Physical Education.* (Philadelphia:
W.B. Saunders Co. 1969), p. 77.

As a behavioral concept, sportsmanship is very nearly synonymous with the concept of fair play. However, the term *sportsmanship* is frequently used as much outside the domain of physical education as within. This seems to indicate that society values sportsman-like conduct, and considers sportsmanship in dealings with others a highly desirable human personality trait. The universal use of the word sportsmanship is a tribute to physical education because the word connotes honesty, fairness, and integrity in personal and in group relationships. According to Nixon and Jewett:

> In every game worthy of the name, situations constantly arise which call for appraisal of the contestant, the teammate, or oneself. Participants can learn to appreciate and give proper credit to the skill and ability of the opponent and the cooperation of a teammate. All of these characteristics of learning opportunities in physical education can be utilized to guide the student in understanding and valuing differences among his classmates.[23]

If movement experiences do indeed help to foster the development of sportsmanship and sportsman-like conduct, and these concepts become integrated into the individual's life-style, then the humanistic aspect of education through the physical is being accomplished satisfactorily.

Dedication

When we say that an individual is "dedicated," the implication usually is that the individual persists in an activity or pursuit until excellence is achieved or until a satisfactory conclusion is reached. The things to which individuals dedicate themselves, and the intensity of that dedication, is as variable as are people themselves. Society views dedication as a desirable trait, and judges with great favor those activities that instill dedication:

> There is rather strong agreement today that the focus of the discipline of physical education is human movement. It therefore seems logical that the aim of this area of study is to produce a person who uses his body efficiently and effectively in all movement patterns because he has a cognitive understanding of movement, as well as an affective appreciation of the value of purposeful movement.[24]

The individual learns and conceptualizes dedication by participating in experiences that require devotion and staying-power as prerequisite traits

23. Ibid., p. 28.
24. Siedel and Resick, op. cit., p. 40.

upon which future successful experiences will build. By being given an opportunity to experience successful movement, and through associating that success with the devotion and dedication required to accomplish movement tasks, the individual will better appreciate the worthwhile aspects of dedication. As a concomitant value, the individual will be able to conceptualize dedication to the task at hand as a trait that is applicable to many situations in life.

Cooperation

Certain physical education experiences, particularly team-type activities, help individuals to understand and value the concept of cooperation. If team-type activities are to be successful, then interpersonal cooperative efforts are essential. In any team activity, the individuals involved pool their respective talents so that the group as a whole may accomplish predetermined goals. The team effort is true of life both within and outside of the physical education laboratory:

> Play skills . . . are of major importance in companionship and friendship in the social relationship of children. The physically excellent child has opportunity to lead in games and to learn thereby the very important techniques of leadership and cooperation.[25]

The team concept helps assure that each individual can make a contribution to the group because the respective strengths of each individual are called upon. Outside of physical education, there are many facets of life that operate in team fashion. The family unit is one example, and a physical education department in a school or college is another. All teams, regardless of their differing objectives and purposes, require that individual team members unite in purpose and work toward the accomplishment of a common goal.

Physical education provides opportunities for participants to act cooperatively, and as success is realized from these cooperative efforts, the concept of cooperation becomes a carry-over value that may be applied to other situations. The physical educator has the responsibility for providing such a program:

> The physical education class situation, supplemented by intramural and interscholastic athletic programs, provides for a high degree of interpersonal interaction. The movement activities which typify physical education experiences add another dimension to communication among peers.[26]

25. Cowell, op. cit., p. 295.
26. Nixon and Jewett, op. cit., p. 218.

The concepts of leadership and followership are rather abstract ones. However, participation in movement activities often places the individual in a position where leadership decisions must be made, and certain steps followed in order for the activity to reach a successful conclusion. Where leadership is respected, and the steps to be followed are well-defined and well organized, a satisfactory outcome will be the most likely result. Chaos results when there are too many individuals vying for leadership, or when there is no strong leadership, or no leadership at all. Movement experiences can serve as a vehicle for teaching and practicing concepts of effective leadership and followership. Physical education can help to bridge the gap between the abstract and the concrete. Cowell said:

> Children's insecurities and frustrations show up directly or symbolically in their free play. The aggressive, destructive, unsocial, or antisocial attitudes are acted out in play . . . Games and sports often become substitute responses which redirect behavior . . .[27]

Society considers leadership and followership important. To learn these concepts through direct experience, through the experiences of movement, is education through the physical.

Loyalty tends to evolve out of the close interpersonal associations that form during the course of participation in cooperative group efforts. Such close associations tend to form because the participants realize that they are collectively working toward a common goal. Loyalty as a behavior trait is very close to the trait known as *responsibility*. An individual who can be characterized as a responsible person is very highly regarded as a friend or as a team member. When groups of individuals band together in order to participate in a common cause or some cooperative endeavor, this is group loyalty, or group responsibility, in action. Education through the physical can contribute to the development of a sense of loyalty by providing those movement experiences that can only function satisfactorily when individual members of a team or group have formed a common bond.

It is interesting to note that loyalty frequently extends to those who are not directly participating in an activity. For example, spectators often become very loyal to a particular athletic team, and they vicariously share in the fortunes of that team. The concept of loyalty, then, is built upon affiliation, whether it be actual or vicarious. Because the movement activi-

27. Cowell, op. cit., p. 292.

ties of physical education tend to unite people, these activities have a very humanizing effect upon the individual, and help him to acquire feelings of loyalty and responsibility.

Competitiveness

Participation in physical education activities helps to nurture competitiveness. A certain degree of competitiveness is desirable and necessary if the individual is going to achieve a successful and satisfactory life-style. Competitiveness embodies drive, persistance, and the will to win. A competitive nature is favorably viewed in many parts of the world, as witnessed by almost universal interest in the Olympic Games, for example. Many newspapers devote more column space to sport and the outcome of sporting events than they allot to coverage of international news events. The physical education laboratory is the primary place where the skills of sport are taught, practiced, and refined. Through these programs, an additional ingredient, competition, is added.

That movement experiences are used to nurture the competitive ethic is not without its critics. Some humanists believe that competitiveness and humanism are not especially compatible, since a competitive situation implies that one individual or group is working toward the defeat of another individual or group. However, it must be noted that competitiveness and competition do not necessarily imply the victory of one individual or group at the expense of another, since individuals often compete against themselves to improve a previous time in an event, to improve a score, or to improve the techniques used for a particular skill performance, e.g., mountain climbers, scuba divers, surfers, and sky divers. Such competition is no less vital in physical education:

> We use the term competitiveness to encompass a cluster of motives that predispose an individual to compete or not to compete... Competitiveness... implies a motive to achieve or succeed...[28]

Movement experiences can become a vital part of the means by which individuals can learn to be competitive while still adhering to the humanistic tenets of education through the physical.

SUMMARY

Education through the physical, rather than being a by-product of education of the physical, is an integral part of virtually all learning experiences

28. Rainer Martens. *Social Psychology and Physical Activity.* (New York: Harper & Row, 1975), p. 76.

that occur through the medium of human movement. Physical educators, as movement professionals, are the individuals on whom promotion and facilitation of this unified concept depends. This chapter has shown how movement experiences become vital contributors to education through the physical. As Williams and Brownell so succinctly put it:

> ... One is not to neglect the traditional outcomes in physiological results, in growth and developmental accruals, or in neuromuscular skills, but a proper emphasis in modern education is upon an education in interests and attitudes as well. It is precisely this emphasis that modern physical education is disposed to make. It is convinced that an education in physical activities may mean a real interest in wholesome recreation, that an attitude favoring play, dramatization, and art may touch lives that would otherwise be merely dull and dignified. This conviction is so real that we are ready to cast aside many of the traditional practices in physical education to the end that boys and girls may secure an education that will enrich and deepen life.[29]

SUGGESTIONS FOR FURTHER READING

Anthony, D.J. "Sport and Physical Education as a Means of Aesthetic Education." *The Physical Educator* 60:1–6.

Cohen, H. A. *Humanistic Education and Western Civilization.* New York: Holt, Rinehart and Winston, 1964.

Cratty, B. J. *Social Dimensions of Physical Activity.* Englewood Cliffs, N.J.: Prentice Hall, Inc., 1967.

Sage, George H., ed., *Sport and American Society.* Reading, Mass.: Addison-Wesley Publishing Co. 1970.

Vanderzwaag, Harold J. *Toward a Philosophy of Sport.* Reading, Mass.: Addison-Wesley Publishing Co. 1972.

29. Williams and Brownell, op. cit., p. 21.

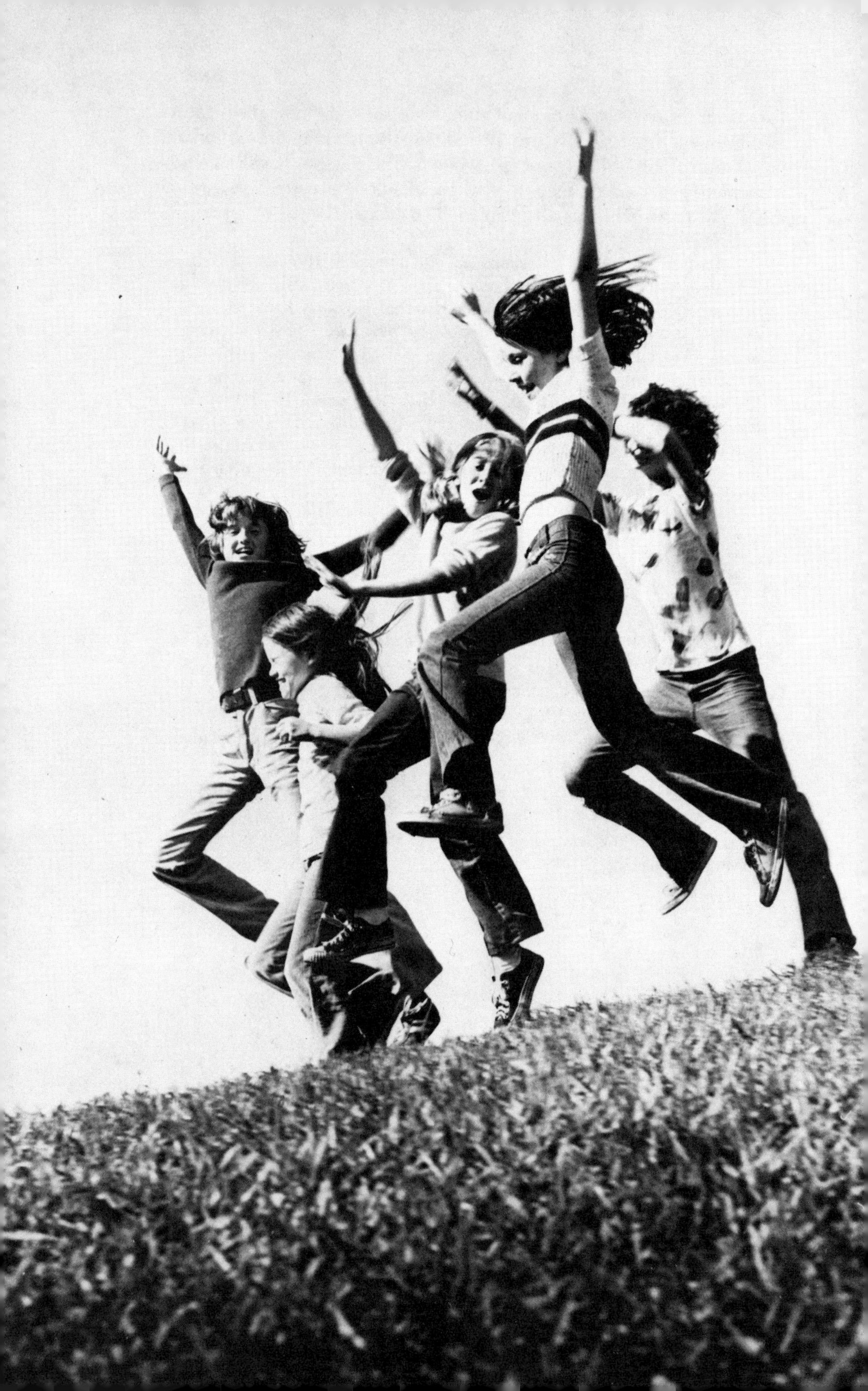

2

Educating the Physical Person

By briefly tracing the history of the humanistic perspective in physical education, and by drawing on the words of highly regarded leaders in the field in the first chapter, we have come to understand a little better the role of physical education in the life of modern man. If we become totally concerned with educating through the physical, however, we might neglect the very important need to learn physical skills. This chapter, which is primarily concerned with education *of* the physical, will outline the ways in which this concept is related to education *through* the physical.

THE IMPORTANCE OF MOVEMENT EXPERIENCES

Movement is a basic component of human existence. Movement aids normal growth and development. The terms growth and development are not synonymous, but they are closely related. Growth is a quantitative measure, while development is more of a qualitative measure.

> Growth *refers to quantitative change, measurable variations of body size and proportion.* Development *is a far more general concept and may refer to quantitative structural changes as well as to a variety of other bio-psycho-social attributes. Reference, therefore, may be made to social development,*

mental development, personality development, motor development and to various other behavioral attributes.[1]

In our modern, technology-oriented world, the movement experiences of physical education are a primary means for stimulating normal physical growth and development. In primitive times, when people had to be continually physically active in order to survive, growth and development were stimulated in a more natural way. Strenuous physical activity was implicit in the struggle for survival. Today, because we are not so concerned with the physical struggle for survival, physical education provides the means for assuring proper growth and development. For some individuals, physical education is the sole dependable source of necessary physical exertion.

In order to educate the physical person, movement experiences must be provided that encompass many areas. The physical education of each individual should include, aside from sports-type skills, the fundamentals of proper mechanical use of the body, experiences in a wide variety of locomotor skills, the techniques of manipulating objects, as well as activities designed to enhance organic fitness and motor fitness.

> *The word* physical *refers to the body. It is often used in reference to various bodily characteristics such as physical strength, physical development, physical prowess, physical health, and physical appearance. It refers to the body as contrasted to the mind. Therefore, when you add the word* education *to the word* physical *and use the words* physical education, *you are referring to the process of education that concerns activities that develop and maintain the human body.*[2]

FUNDAMENTAL MOVEMENT EXPERIENCES

Following, selected basic movement experiences are discussed. While not all-inclusive, these movements are representative of those generally considered to be the essential building blocks for more refined and complex physical skills.

Locomotor Skills

Successful movement is dependent upon the proper development of locomotor skills, which help the body to move through physical space.

1. Bryant J. Cratty, *Movement Behavior and Motor Learning.* (Philadelphia: Lea and Febiger, 1967), p. 107.
2. Charles A. Bucher, *Foundations of Physical Education.* (Saint Louis: The C.V. Mosby Co., 1972), p. 3.

Locomotor skills are classified into two major groupings, those skills that are termed *phylogenetic,* and those called *ontogenetic.* Phylogenetic skills are those which are common to most cultures. This seems to suggest that such skills may be instinctive. In contrast, ontogenetic skills are unique to a culture or cultural group because they are typically invented or created to fill an individual, group, or immediate environmental circumstance. As Corbin explains it:

> The behavioral changes that occur rather automatically with the maturing of the individual are referred to as phylogenetic. It is sometimes said to be of racial origin rather than of individual or cultural origin. This type of behavior includes such activities as grasping, reaching, crawling, creeping, walking, and running. The behavioral changes that depend primarily upon learning are referred to as ontogenetic behavior. These changes will not appear automatically with the maturing of the individual but are learned, or acquired, through environmental experiences. Ontogenetic behavior includes such activities as swimming, skating, riding a tricycle, and driving a car.[3]

A delineation of the ontogenetic skills would most certainly exceed the scope and purpose of this book, because the range and variety of ontogenetic skills is as varied as are the activity needs and interests of humankind. The phylogenetic skills, however, are basic to movement, and indeed would appear to be the foundation for ontogenetic skill learnings. There are ten discrete skills, phylogenetic in nature, that are basic to locomotion. These skills are crawling, creeping, walking, running, hopping, leaping, skipping, jumping, galloping, and sliding. For primitive man, these phylogenetic skills were essential for survival. Today, these skills are the prelude to joyful movement and to all of the benefits that individuals derive from movement. It is worthwhile, in the context of this book, but even more especially in considering the education of the physical person, to discuss separately but briefly, each of the ten phylogenetic skills.

Crawling. Crawling is one of the first relatively effective modes of locomotion. Learning to crawl is a significant event in the life of the infant because it permits the infant to explore his environment. Until the infant begins to crawl, learning experiences are limited, and are confined to those things that are brought to the infant by others. Crawling permits the infant to explore independently and to seek out those things which attract and interest him. Through crawling, the infant becomes an active participant in shaping his own learning experiences. However, in spite of its inherent experience-expanding capabilities, crawling represents a rather limited form of locomotion.

---

3. Charles B. Corbin, ed., *A Textbook of Motor Development.* (Dubuque: Wm. C. Brown Co., 1973), p. 9.

Creeping.   Creeping is a sophistication of crawling, and permits the growing child more latitude as he explores his environment. In crawling, the infant moves along in a supine position using the arms and legs to propel the body. In creeping, the child lifts his trunk from the floor so that the weight of the body is supported by the hands and the knees. Thus, creeping is a more physically demanding skill than is crawling, for the child must contend with an elevated center of gravity, with fewer and narrower points of support for balance, and with the need to support the body weight. Creeping represents a vast improvement over crawling because the increased mobility afforded by creeping serves to increase the environmental area that may be explored. Improved coordination, improved dynamic balance, and increased strength are but a few of the by-products of creeping.

Walking.   Walking is the first of the upright locomotor skills. Learning to walk is a milestone in the young child's development. While walking is initially complex and challenging, it enables the child to move even more freely through his environment. Also, the child's hands are freed, since they are no longer needed as a base of support. The hands become tools for the manipulation of interesting items the child finds and wishes to explore by touch.

Walking is, by far, the most used of the basic locomotor skills. Other upright locomotor skills tend to be more specialized and are not used as much nor are they so generally applicable. Walking is the only basic locomotor skill that most individuals can sustain over relatively long periods of time and over relatively great distances. Walking has long been considered vital for the maintenance of physical fitness. The late Dr. Paul Dudley White, an internationally renowned cardiologist, was an advocate of walking for exercise and fitness. Dr. White felt that a man's overall physical condition was equal to the condition of his legs. He expressed the belief that properly conditioned legs were basic to participation in physical activity, and that walking was one physical activity that could be done throughout life.

Running.   This is the most rapid form of locomotion, and is second only to walking in the extent of its use as a locomotor skill. Running generally falls into two broad categories: running for speed and running for distance. Though the two types of running are the same basic skill, they make very different demands on the body in terms of strength, power, and endurance. The ability to run well is particularly important. Many movement experiences involve running, and the ability to run efficiently and proficiently is a prerequisite to enjoyment, success, and satisfaction in such activities.

Hopping.   Hopping, which involves a one-foot take-off and a landing on the same foot, is not only an important basic movement skill but a safety skill as well. In cases where the individual loses his balance, the execution of a hop is frequently the only way to regain balance efficiently, and to prevent falling. Hopping is an extremely demanding skill to learn in terms of balance and strength requirements. In the case of balance, a challenge is presented particularly because of the relatively small, one-footed base of support. A demand is made on strength because only one limb supports the body weight during the execution of the movement. Because hopping is both a safety skill and a movement skill, children should learn to hop on either foot in various directions.

Leaping. Walking, running, and leaping use essentially similar patterns of foot movement. But while walking and running are basically forward motions, leaping is an upward-forward motion in which the individual attempts to gain height plus distance rather than distance alone. Leaps are used to successfully negotiate obstacles, as in running the hurdles or to catch objects that are thrown too high for the individual to intercept simply by stretching. In the latter instance, the person may run to intercept the object, such as a ball, and then leap in order to make contact. Children should learn to leap comfortably using either foot as the takeoff foot, and should learn to leap in a variety of directions. Leaping adds versatility to the child's catalogue of movement patterns that is not replicated by any of the other locomotor skills.

Skipping. Skipping is a combination of walking and hopping. While skipping is an important skill for true movement versatility, the fact that it is composed of two discrete skills sometimes causes skipping to be the most difficult of the basic locomotor skills to learn and execute properly and confidently. The skip is an important skill for many rhythm and dance activities. It is often used in conjunction with throwing and catching skills in various sports activities. Also, a single skip step is sometimes used as a transitional movement when a rapid change is made from walking to running. When movement circumstances require a skip, the odds are that no other movement will suffice as well.

Jumping. A jump may be executed in combination with any of the basic upright locomotor skills, and is generally used to gain height or distance. Jumping involves taking off from one or both feet and landing on both feet. Jumping affords unique movement capabilities in specific movement situations. An individual may jump to spike a volleyball or to capture a rebound in basketball, or he may jump from the path of the ball in dodgeball. The ability to jump when it is a jumping skill that is specifically called for helps the individual to be adequately prepared to move with efficiency and versatility in a variety of commonly encountered situations.

Galloping and Sliding. Galloping and sliding, except for differences in movement direction, are essentially the same skill involving a step-close-step pattern of movement. While a slide is done in a lateral direction, the gallop is done in any direction *except* laterally. The gallop and slide are uniquely effective because they enable the individual to make graceful and rapid changes in direction. These are particularly valuable skills since they are common to numerous dance activities. Also, they are useful in those games and sports where a player wishes to elude another player or to disguise the intended direction of travel.

These basic locomotor skills represent the foundation of efficient movement. These are the skills that help to give joy and satisfaction to human movement. Each is important in its own right because different movement situations call for the execution of different skills and skill patterns. If a hop, for example, is demanded by the circumstances, then the efficient execution of a hop is uniquely appropriate. When the need arises to rapidly cross a flat piece of ground, for instance, then there is really no effective alternative to running, and when an individual wants to retrieve a moving object that is above head level and just beyond arm's reach, then jumping becomes the most appropriate movement skill to use.

The basic locomotor skills provide the potential for increased movement versatility. The ability to execute each skill, either alone or in combination with other skills, and at precisely the most effective moment, enables the individual to move with greater ease and proficiency. Once learned, these locomotor skills become a passport to fulfillment through movement. Within physical education, where locomotion is the basic learning ingredient, there can be no substitute for providing opportunities for children to gain experience, proficiency, and satisfaction through practice of the basic locomotor skills. The basic locomotor skills represent man's way of responding to an environment where movement is one of the keys to physical well-being.

> Through movement man is able to discover and express his keenest satisfactions, his creative powers and his most rewarding successes; he is able to discover and understand and thereby adapt and control his environment; he is able to explore both self and other awareness.[4]

However, in order for movement to be effective and in order for movement to be sustained as long as it is necessary to do so, the individual must possess more than the desire to move and more than cognitive understandings of the skills and the technical ability to perform those skills.

THE NEED FOR FITNESS

Different activities require different kinds of fitness. Three types of fitness are generally spoken of: physical fitness, organic fitness, and motor fitness.

4. Ginny Studer, "From Man Moving to Moving Man," *Quest* 20 (June 1973): 104.

However, it must be noted that each type of fitness is related to the other, and each is an espect of what is called general, or total, physical fitness. Thus, in discussing one type of fitness, it must be understood that the other types are also implied.

General Physical Fitness

According to Nixon and Jewett:

> . . .physical fitness refers to the organic capacity of the individual to perform the tasks of daily living without undue tiredness and fatigue, having a reserve of strength and energy available to meet satisfactorily any emergency demands suddenly placed upon him.[5]

There are at least eight components of fitness. Each of these components is unique, and in most cases they are mutually exclusive. Successful performance within the parameters of any one component is in no way predictive of successful performance in another component. For example, an individual who is extremely successful in movement activities that require speed is not assured of a high level of performance in an activity requiring highly developed balance skills. Thus, a fast runner will not necessarily be a good figure skater, and activities designed to improve speed will not necessarily help the individual to improve his ability to balance. Therefore, just as different activities call for various fitness components, each specific component can be improved by participation in the specific activities that lend themselves to developing that component. Physical educators must be familiar with the components of fitness, must know the fitness demands of each movement activity, and must have a knowledge of which of the fitness components each activity will foster. These knowledges and understandings will help the physical educator to provide a program which will help students to cope with and respond adequately to physical stresses. These knowledges and understandings will assist the physical educator in developing a program that helps students to become more physically fit while they participate in pleasurable and relevant movement experiences. Let us now examine the eight components of general fitness.

Circulorespiratory endurance. This refers to the ability of the circulatory and respiratory systems to respond to prolonged total, or near total, physical exertion. Circulorespiratory endurance involves generalized maximal or near-maximal bodily effort. Mathews writes that:

> Circulatory efficiency is closely related to respiration, for it is in the alveoli of the lungs that the gaseous exchange of oxygen and carbon dioxide takes

5. Nixon, John E. and Ann E. Jewett. *An Introduction to Physical Education*. (Philadelphia: W.B. Saunders Co., 1969), p. 205.

place. To work efficiently, muscles are dependent upon oxygen more than any other substance. Insufficient amounts of oxygen cause the accumulation of lactic acid in the blood, which impedes the contraction of muscle.[6]

Circulorespiratory activities cause the circulatory and respiratory systems to respond by increasing their output. Because such activities demand that the entire body be used vigorously, highly oxygenated blood is carried to all parts of the body. The effectiveness with which the circulatory and respiratory systems combine to perform this function is a measure of circulorespiratory endurance.

Circulatory-respiratory (C-R) endurance is characterized by moderate contractions of large-muscle groups for relatively long periods of time, during which maximal adjustments of the circulatory-respiratory system are necessary . . .[7]

There are many activities that will require the circulatory and respiratory systems to increase their output. However, these activities must be done vigorously, and the movements must be sustained if maximal output is to be achieved. Representative of these activities are running, swimming, skiing, basketball, soccer, and bicycle riding. The development of attitudes conducive to assuring continued participation in activities that enhance circulorespiratory endurance is the domain of physical education. Our modern society is characterized by labor saving devices and sedentary pastimes, and there tends to be little opportunity to come by circulorespiratory activities naturally. Physical education, sports, and leisure time activities, then, become a primary means through which the circulatory and respiratory systems receive at least minimal exercise for maintenance of their functional integrity.

2. Muscular strength. There are virtually no physical activities that do not require at least minimal amounts of muscular strength. Therefore, muscular strength is a very important component of physical fitness.

Strength refers to the level at which a muscle can function in order to overcome stress imposed by a resistance . . . In most cases, the stronger individual has a greater mechanical advantage in the use of his muscles and is more able to find success in a variety of physical activities.[8]

Many performance failures that are attributed to lack of skill or effort on the

6. Donald K. Mathews, *Measurement in Physical Education.* (Philadelphia: W.B. Saunders Co., 1973), p. 230.
7. H. Harrison Clarke, ed., "Physical Fitness Testing in Schools," *Physical Fitness Research Digest,* series 5, no. 1, January 1975, p. 9.
8. Daniel D. Arnheim and Robert A. Pestolesi, *Developing Motor Behavior in Children.* (Saint Louis: The C.V. Mosby Co., 1973), p. 135.

Every physical educator must have a comprehensive understanding of the methods and techniques for building and maintaining adequate levels of muscular strength.

part of the performer may in fact be caused by strength inadequacies. A lack of strength may result in an inability to perform a skill, and at times may lead to the development of poor performance habits because the individual attempts to compensate for the lack of strength. In either case, a lack of strength needed to perform a particular skill will lead to inability to perform the skill with any degree of success and satisfaction.

Every physical educator must have a comprehensive understanding of the methods and techniques for building and maintaining adequate levels of muscular strength. Some activities representative of those that may be used to help develop strength are circuit training, weight training, running, and selected isotonic and isometric exercises. Armed with all of the knowledge that he can assemble, the physical educator can then plan a program of movement experiences designed to incorporate strength activities that suit the needs and capacities of the students.

3. *Muscular endurance.* Possessing adequate levels of muscular endurance helps to postpone the onset of fatigue during prolonged physical exertion. Many activities in life that are outside of physical education, such as the physical demands of a job, require high levels of muscular endurance. While an individual may possess adequate strength to begin a certain task, muscular endurance is then required if the task is to be brought to a

successful conclusion. An example of this within physical education is the push-up. Strength is required to complete one push-up, but endurance is also demanded if successive push-ups are to be performed to some set criterion. Outside of physical education, the construction trades, in particular, offer many examples where muscular endurance is demanded.

Muscular endurance . . . concerns the ability of a muscle to repeat identical movements or pressures, or to maintain a certain degree of tension over a period of time.[9]

Activities that are designed to bring about increases in muscular strength tend to cause the individual muscle fibers to grow in size. This increases both the size and the strength of the muscle. Weight training, using a set progression of weights, can help to increase strength as can other isotonic as well as isometric exercises. Activities that are designed to bring about increases in muscular endurance tend to increase the circulatory capacity of the muscle. Since muscular strength and muscular endurance are related, the same exercises may be used, but in a sustained manner if the goal is increased muscular endurance.

Muscles generally work at submaximal levels throughout the course of any given day. This creates a compelling rationale for physical education programs to provide movement experiences that will help to increase students' levels of muscular endurance. Effective levels of muscular endurance can help to offset fatigue and help to make prolonged physical exertion a more enjoyable experience.

4. Power. Power becomes an important component of physical fitness whenever rapid, explosive bursts of strength are called for.

Power is the capacity of the body to release maximum force or muscle contraction in the shortest possible time. Power denotes explosive movement, a release of maximum force at maximum speed. Obviously, power is highly dependent upon the elements of speed and strength.[10]

Rapid walking, running, hopping, leaping, skipping, jumping, galloping, sliding, striking, and throwing are all examples of skills that require at least minimal amounts of power. They are also activities that can be incorporated into a program of physical education in order to build power. Power is the primary facilitator of rapid and forceful muscular contraction. Within the physical education program movement experiences can be provided that increase power by placing the requisite emphasis on the development of speed and strength.

9. Barry L. Johnson and Jack K. Nelson, *Practical Measurements for Evaluation in physical Education.* (Minneapolis: Burgess Publishing Co., 1974), p. 112.
10. Evelyn L. Schurr, *Movement Experiences for Children.* (New York: Appleton-Century-Crofts, 1967), p. 191.

5. *Speed.* Most individuals, when talking of physical speed, generally think in terms of a speedy runner, and thus tend to define speed as the ability to traverse relatively short distances as rapidly as possible. In physical education classes running speed is often measured because the ability to run with skill and ease is a critical factor in many movement activities. However, total body speed, as in the context of running, is only one kind of speed. According to Safrit's definition, speed is the

> ... *rapidity with which successive movements of the same kind can be performed.*[11]

We must, then, think in terms of speed of various body parts as they move, and be concerned with providing experiences that will help to improve the various speeds needed for physical movement. Examples of types of speed other than running speed are: speed of arm movement in throwing in order to release a ball quickly; speed of leg movement such as that needed to kick a soccer ball; the speed needed to move the foot from the accelerator to the brake when driving a car, and like skills requiring speed in the many movement activities of life.

The total time required to complete a movement really consists of two phases. The first phase is reaction time, which is generally defined as the time between the receipt of a stimulus and the beginning of the reaction to that stimulus. In driving a car, the change of the light from green to red is a stimulus, and the very start of the reaction is the message to the muscles to being releasing the pressure on the gas pedal. The second phase of movement speed is called movement time, and this is the time it takes to complete the full movement of the foot from the gas pedal onto the brake pedal until enough pressure has been applied to stop the car. Taken together, reaction time plus movement time results in the measure we call movement speed. There are many stimuli in physical education that call for quick reaction times, such as a pitched ball to which the batter must react, or the sound of the starter's gun in track or swimming. Cratty has written:

> ... *reaction time is the time between a stimulus which will impel an overt reaction, and the initiation of that reaction. Thus, reaction time involves no observable reaction on the part of the performer, but is rather the period needed by the nervous system to intercept some kind of stimulus, to integrate the stimulus within the central nervous system, and to transmit the appropriate impulses to various muscular groups.*[12]

Reaction time, unfortunately, is the least improvable of all of the physical skills that are components of general fitness. Because rapid

11. Margaret J. Safrit, *Evaluation in Physical Education.* (Englewood Cliffs, N.J.: Prentice-Hall, Inc., 1973), p. 204.
12. Bryant J. Cratty, *Teaching Motor Skills* (Englewood Cliffs, N.J.: Prentice-Hall, Inc., 1973), p. 32.

movement is of paramount importance in many situations in life, we can, through carefully selected movement experiences, such as weight training, isometric and isotonic exerices, and other activities that also build strength, provide students with proper instruction and sufficient opportunity for practice in tasks requiring speed so that they can realize their potential for developing adequate levels of speed of movement.

6. *Flexibility.* Flexibility is the ability of the body segments to move through normal ranges of motion. Schurr said:

> *Flexibility is the range of movement in a joint. The degree of flexibility determines the extent of extension and flexion of a joint and consequent body action in terms of bending, twisting, and turning.*[13]

Ample flexibility is of prime importance if movements are to be made with ease and comfort. Maintaining a supple and flexible body is dependent on continued participation in the many varieties of movement skills. A generally accepted premise of physiology is that continual use of the body in a variety of ways helps to maintain the needed levels of flexibility. Conversely, lack of use leads to inflexibility. As individuals age, there seems to be a general decrease in flexibility. This may be due in part to decreases in participation in movement activities. This seems to be supported by the observation that many physically active individuals who are beyond middle age tend to be very flexible in comparison with their more sedentary counterparts. Furthermore, flexibility decreases resulting from inactivity tend to foster even more inactivity simply because many physical movements become difficult and even painful to perform where flexibility is low. Thus, the physically less flexible individual gets caught up in a vicious cycle.

Inflexibility may sometimes lead to injury. The inability of body segments to move through normal ranges of motion places undue strain on the body, and damage can result. Such problems can be prevented in those individuals who maintain their flexibility by making movement a habit of life. Any individual, once he has been taught the techniques of static and ballistic stretching exercises in a physical education program, can continue to do these exercises on his own. A flexible body need not be the province solely of the young. A supple body even in advancing years is the return realized from an investment in physically active living. Physical education can serve as the impetus for building good movement habits that will last a lifetime.

7. *Agility.* Agility is the ability to change directions and postions rapidly and effectively. Agility is not only desirable and important in physical

13. Schurr, op. cit., p. 191.

education, but in daily living as well. In any movement activity where effective movement in many directions is required, agility is a prerequisite to successful performance. Dancers, surfers, divers, wrestlers, gymnasts, lacrosse players, and fencers are but a few examples of individuals who must be agile if they are to be successful.

Agility in daily living means being able to change directions effectively on an instant's notice. Being agile helps to avoid accidents and injuries and facilitates movement. The individual needs to be agile in order to drive a car defensively, cross a street, or step onto a moving escalator. Agility can be enhanced with varying degrees of effectiveness. Individuals may become more agile by participating in a physical education program where those locomotor skills which facilitate agility are practiced. Some activities that lend themselves to the development of agility are obstacle courses, rope jumping, slalom-type runs, squat thrusts, and many forms of relay races.

8. *Balance.* Balance is the ability to maintain a proper relationship between the center of gravity and the base of support. There are two kinds of balance: static and dynamic. In static balance, both the center of gravity and the base of support remain fixed. Standing erect or doing a headstand are examples of static balance. In dynamic balance, both the center of gravity and the base of support may be moving, or the base of support may remain in a fixed position while the center of gravity moves. Bouncing on a trampoline or springboard diving are examples of the former, while lifting a weight over the head or doing toe touches are examples of the latter.

> *Balance may be defined as the ability to maintain body position . . . Two general types of balance are commonly recognized:* static balance *is the ability to maintain total body equilibrium while standing in one spot, and* dynamic balance *is the ability to maintain equilibrium while moving from one point to another*[14]

A critical factor in assessing the quality of dynamic balance is whether or not the relative positions of the center of gravity and base of support are such that purposeful movement can be produced and maintained. Executing a cartwheel, for example, requires high levels of dynamic balancing ability. Balance is particularly a problem for the individual since the two-footed base of support is relatively small. This is compounded by the fact that upright forms of locomotion tend to significantly elevate the center of gravity. When the center of gravity is high, and the base of support is relatively small in comparison, balance becomes rather precarious. Good balance may be enhanced through the movement activities of

---

14. Ted A. Baumgartner and Andrew S. Jackson. *Measurement for Evaluation in Physical Education.* (Boston: Houghton Mifflin Co. 1975), p. 166.

physical education. Activities that are especially useful for developing balance include balance beam walking, dancing, many relay activities, hopscotch, rope jumping, and stunts and tumbling. The development of good balance skills will in turn serve the individual throughout the span of a lifetime of pleasurable physical activity.

SUMMARY

The facets of human performance discussed in this chapter are the ones that serve as the foundation for human movement and general fitness. Movement experiences thus have a multiple purpose and a multiple nature. While education through the physical is primarily concerned with the humanistic aspects of movement experiences, we could not hope to accomplish this goal unless we also educate the physical person. This duality of purpose does not conflict with the aims of modern physical education, nor does it imply that the traditional methods of teaching ought to be retained at all costs. What we have attempted to show in this chapter is that the humanistic goals of physical education can be better served. Park has written:

> . . . a major task confronting physical education in the coming decades may be that of maximizing opportunities for individuals to achieve greater self-awareness and actualization through physical activity.[15]

The time for the confrontation to start is now, and the education of the physical person is an initial, critical step in that direction.

SUGGESTIONS FOR FURTHER READING

American Alliance for Health, Physical Education and Recreation, *Annotated Bibliography on Perceptual-Motor Development.* Washington D.C.: AAHPER, 1973.

Arnheim, Daniel D., David Auxter, and Walter C. Crowe. *Principles and Methods of Adapted Physical Education.* Saint Louis: The C.V. Mosby Co., 1973.

Corbin, Charles B. *A Textbook of Motor Development.* Dubuque, Iowa: WM. C. Brown Co., 1973.

Harrow, Anita, J. *A Taxonomy of the Psychomotor Domain.* New York: David McKay Co., Inc., 1972.

15. Roberta J. Park, "Alternatives and Other 'Ways': How Might Physical Activity Be More Relevant to Human Needs in the Future?" *Quest* 21 (January 1974): 34.

Sage, George H. *Introduction to Motor Behavior: A Neuropsychological Approach.* Reading, Mass.: Addison-Wesley Publishing Co., 1971.

Sharkey, Brian J. *Physiology and Physical Activity.* New York: Harper & Row, 1975.

Singer, Robert N. *Motor Learning and Human Performance.* New York: The Macmillan Co., 1975.

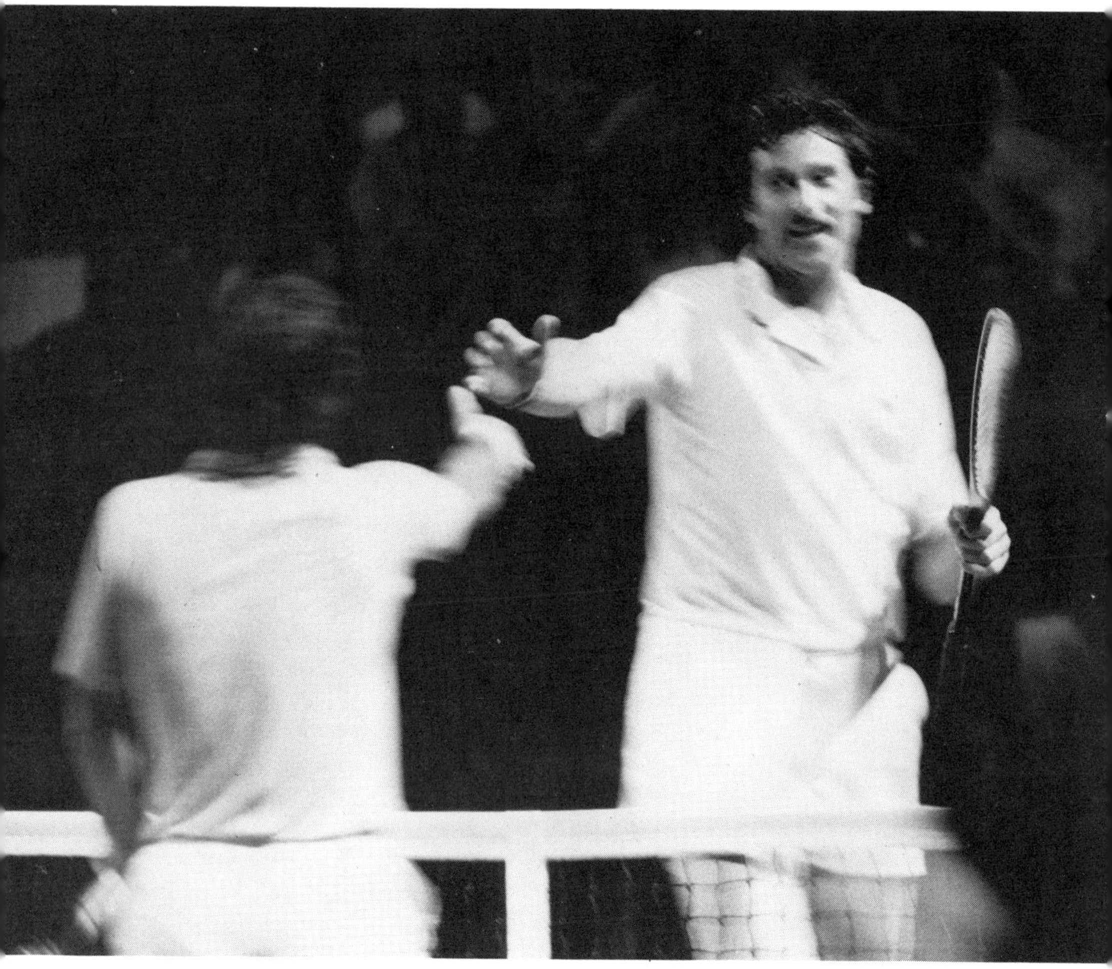

3

Physical Education as a Social Force

Many individuals choose a career without really understanding why they have made a particular choice. Still others set a career goal and find out too late that they have made the wrong choice. Many more choose a goal, set objectives for achieving it, and are content and successful in what they do. Those individuals who decide to become educators must realize that they are not only making a commitment to themselves, but to their future students, the school, and the community as well. The educational process touches everyone, and to choose to become an educator implies an intent to serve through an occupation, rather than be served by a chosen occupation.

Physical educators are educators who have specialized in one particular educational field. Physical educators are educators first, and physical educators second, never the reverse. The same is true of English educators, mathematics educators, and in fact of all educators and of anyone who is connected in any way with education. All educators must have the same commitment—to serve people through education, no matter what their subject specialty.

THE ROLE OF THE PHYSICAL EDUCATOR

In choosing a career in physical education, you are of course making a commitment to yourself. But the most important commitment is the one you make to your students. Physical education is very much concerned with serving individuals, because human movement is one of society's most culturally significant modes of expression and communication. Awareness of the ways in which physical education complements the social and cultural aspirations of people must become an integral part of the physical educator's frame of reference.

The physical educator must have a valid desire to help people as they attempt, through movement, to become healthier, more physically fit, and as they strive toward self-actualization and the development of self-esteem. The physical educator must also realize that he may never see the results of his teaching in terms of human fulfillment, but must realize that he is only a steppingstone on the way to fulfillment. While physical education has admirable aims and objectives, the potential for high levels of achievement and fulfillment is necessarily limited by time, student numbers in classes, and other factors. Students spend relatively little time in physical education class while they are in school, and this obviously limits the influence of the program and the physical educator. However, there can be no doubt that the role of the physical educator is an important one. No other subject in the curriculum is so deeply concerned with the mental, social, and physical well-being of students, and no other subject in the curriculum is in such an advantageous position to help and guide students toward activities that will make their lives more complete and more satisfactory.

SKILLED MOVEMENT AND THE MASS MEDIA

We are living in an age that seems to be marked by a preoccupation, and even perhaps an obsession, with athletic accomplishment. There is an unparalleled pursuit and celebration of movement as a major mode of human expression and achievement. Weekly news magazines frequently devote cover pictures and feature stories to movement, including such diverse forms as ice hockey and ballet. Sports sections in many major newspapers occupy more space than do the international news sections or the financial reports. Also, periodicals devoted wholly or partially to sports are read by millions of people on a regular basis. Radio and television coverage of sporting events is growing phenomenally, and particularly in the case of television, sports have been created simply because viewer demand for new and different events is so great. Even entire movies have been made with themes revolving around sports or the sport hero.

Athletics are popular on the visual media, particularly television, because of their tremendous commercial value. The networks profit from advertisements, while the teams and leagues involved typically receive enormous amounts of money for the broadcasting rights. The viewer benefits only from the vicarious thrills received from watching others as they move skillfully. This is a rather sad commentary to have to make on the growing trend toward spectatorism. However, Felshin has written:

> To the extent that sport can be understood only when it is stylized, popularized, and packaged to appeal to a range of realities of human nature, it [television] serves social ends.[1]

THE PLACE OF PHYSICAL EDUCATION IN THE CURRICULUM

How are we to educate for participation unless we have some means of helping students to appreciate the value of movement? Must physical activity be packaged as a spectator sport in order to get its message across? The answers to these two questions can only be resolved by a re-evaluation and upgrading of physical education programs in the schools. Sadly, although we live in a world that reveres physical prowess, physical attractiveness, and efficient movement, physical education is frequently looked upon as an unnecessary part of school curriculums. Physical education ought to be an important curricular emphasis, but too often this is not the case.

What the Critics Point Out

There are some explanations for the status of physical education in our public schools that may be attributed to those who are critical of the values to be derived from physical education. Some individuals cling to the now disproven concept that man can be divided into two distinct entities: the mental, on the one hand, and the physical, on the other. These same people contend that the primary focus of education must be on mental processes, for they believe that it is the mind of man that has put him into a dominant position. Thus, they seek an education that has an intellectual emphasis, suggesting that progress, innovation, and new technology come from purely intellectual development alone. These individuals do not realize that a productive mind depends largely upon a healthy body.

Still other individuals hold that physical education is frivolous and of no more value than free-play. These individuals regard physical education as a frill and a needless waste of time that could be better given to "academic" pursuits. Many of these people content that a disproportionate amount of time is spent on physical education, including intramurals and

---

1. Jan Felshin, "Sport Style and Social Modes," JOPER 46 (March 1975): 32.

interscholastics, creating a deficit of time to be allotted to classroom subjects.

The practice of attempting to dichotomize man into separate mind and body entities is very questionable. The ancient Greeks believed that there had to be unity between mind and body for man to be able to function at a high level. This concept was particularly important to the early Athenians, of whom Van Dalen and Bennett have written:

> Physical education, which was at its zenith in Athens where it flourished as an integral part of national life, was rooted not only in the utilitarian need to prepare citizens for war, but also in the Greek ideals of beauty and harmony. The objective of education, was not the cultivation of the physical alone, but rather the development of the individual qualities through the physical. The Greeks gave physical education a respectability that it has never since achieved. They accorded the body equal dignity with the mind.[2]

In some ways, as the critics have pointed out, the activities of physical education are play-related. However, this relationship is a positive rather than a negative one, since play is an inherent part of life. Since play is universal, and is so inextricably tied to man's social, cultural, and anthropological heritage, it is a perfect medium for educating the young. Play experiences, as a tool of physical education, are ideally suited for communicating ideas and values.

Play, in an educational context, is anything but frivolous. Play has rightfully been labeled as the business or work of the child, and it is through physical education that the skills of play are learned and refined. Play is equally important in adulthood for play provides the adult an opportunity to increase his social contacts and sustain his cultural heritage.

> The dominant position of social needs will help to put work and play in their proper relationship to each other in our society. The feeling that play is somehow bad and immoral has never been completely conquered. Emphasis on the social values of physical education can conceivably foster an attitude which will not permit the association of guilt feelings with recreational physical activities.[3]

HISTORICAL RELEVANCE OF EFFICIENT MOVEMENT

Almost every culture that is prominent in man's history has held efficient movement and physical prowess in high esteem. Prehistoric man would

2. Deobold B. Van Dalen and Bruce L. Bennett, A World History of Physical Education. (Englewood Cliffs, N.J.: Prentice-Hall, Inc., 1971), p. 47.
3. Marion Alice Sanborn and Betty G. Hartman. Issues in Physical Education. (Philadelphia: Lea and Febiger, 1964), p. 74.

certainly not have survived his harsh and dangerous environment if he had lacked physical stamina. His ability to adapt physically to his environment has permitted us to live and survive into our modern era. It is not mere speculation that causes us to note the cultural significance of skilled motor performances and the worth of physical abilities throughout history. Prehistoric man left his art behind, in the form of cave paintings and pictographs, as a testimony to the worth of physical activity in his life. Many of the scenes are explicit portrayals of people engaged in various forms of skilled movement.

Although life now does not hinge on the same types of survival activities as those of primitive man, we cannot make the assumption that physical activity is any less important for us. Theories of natural selection suggest that in primitive times those individuals who were the most physically skilled and physically able survived to propagate new generations. Conversely, those individuals who could not cope on a physical basis with their environment failed to survive long enough to propagate extensively. Since twentieth-century man is the offspring of an early race that was genetically programmed for movement, it is not surprising that movement activities are a vital and integral part of our social structure and cultural heritage.

Man's need to move through his environment has undergone many interesting and sometimes subtle changes from the era of primitive man to today. Man has changed and grown in countless ways. He has progressed from a being who had to hurl stones in order to kill an animal for food for his dinner to one who can accurately, and repeatedly, safely land men on the moon and bring them home again. Yet, for all the changes in man since prehistory, his appreciation of skilled movement and physical achievement has seldom waned. The focus of movement has of course been different from culture to culture, but it has been the rare society that did not enjoy and desire physical activity in some form.

A Brief Cultural History of Movement

We have already noted primitive man's dependence on movement for survival. In fact, because primitive man had no technology and lived from crisis to crisis, he had time for little else besides survival-centered movement activities. Early peoples eventually began to congregate in communal groups and to share those activities that would help guarantee survival. Group cooperation increasingly led to nonsurvival related patterns of behavior, and these in turn led to socialization. As movement became a tool for ends other than those purely utilitarian, it began to emerge as a pleasurable mode of human expression. The ancient Greeks, who are sometimes characterized as being the first of the civilized cultures, held the functionally sound and structurally beautiful body in awe. The Greek

National Festivals, which have become the Olympic Games of today, were originally designed as events held in honor of the gods worshiped by the Greeks. The form of celebration during the Festivals was centered almost entirely around events that were devoted to physical activity—events that would show the body in motion to its best advantage. The epics and legends of ancient Greece told of men and women such as Helen of Troy, Achilles, and Hercules, who were not only examples of extreme physical beauty, but who were highly proficient physically as well. The Greeks believed in the concept of a strong mind and a strong body being mutually supportive and epitomized the much sought-after quality of human excellence.

While the ancient Romans were a great civilization, they were bent on world conquest, and their primary goal was to develop a society of physically fit citizens who would serve the state as highly efficient and obedient soldiers. The citizens of Rome were indeed highly trained in the arts of war, and were extremely fit physically, but they had little else to fill their lives. It was the Romans, in their pursuit of distraction and entertainment, who first became universally infected with "spectatoritis." Their love of pleasure infected the lands they conquered, most notably Greece, and it was the Romans love of entertainment that helped lead to their own eventual degeneration and downfall as a strong and vital world force. The attitude of the Romans toward the human body also helped to bring about an attitude of negativism toward physical activity.

The early Christian theologians, whose influence rose out of the ashes of the Roman Empire, looked upon the body as a force for evil. They based their philosophy of the human body on the examples of moral degeneration and excess hedonism set by the Romans. The theologians considered the body important only because it housed the soul. To them, the human soul was all-important, and the only worthy pursuits were those designed to prepare the soul for eternity. Any activities of a physical nature, except those performed in defense of the Christian ethic, were unacceptable, indulgent of the body, and morally wrong. These were the Dark Ages for physical activity.

As man progressed toward more modern times, the Industrial Revolution was born, and with it a workday of sixteen to eighteen hours. A frequent occurence was the use and abuse of children as a part of the labor force. Children also toiled for long hours, often in unsafe environments, and for very little compensation. During this era there was little time for recreation or any other nonessential or nonwork-related pursuit. As man moved into the twentieth century, vast changes in life began to occur more rapidly than at any previous time in history. Work hours became shorter, child-labor laws were written, and a technology-based economy began to emerge. All of these combined to give man more time for leisure and recreation. The inherent need for movement began to manifest itself in leisure-centered, nonutilitarian pursuits. This technological revolution, which is not yet one hundred years old, has already revolutionized life in countless and unprecedented ways.

In his book *Future Shock* Alvin Toffler[4] delineates the impact of new technologies on individuals who were accustomed only to those changes resulting from evolution. Toffler divided the past history of man into eight hundred lifetimes, of which the first six hundred and fifty were spent in caves. Since abandoning the caves, and until the end of the seven hundred and ninety-ninth lifetime, man has attempted with varying degrees of success to cope with his environment and its resources. According to Toffler, we are now in the eight-hundredth lifetime, and technology has made man the manipulator, rather than the dependent, of his environment. The author observes, as have others, that ninety percent of the scientists who ever lived are still alive today. Further, Toffler says that man creates resources that were unattainable before, and that he no longer has to accept his environment at face value, but can adapt and adjust it to his liking. The full impact and implications of the eight hundredth lifetime are just beginning to be felt. Toffler asserts that movement-centered, agrarian, earth-oriented man has begun to find himself ill-equipped for the demands of a rapidly changing, sedentary, stress-filled technological society. On the topic of educational facilities, which Toffler says are becoming more and more portable by the day, and thus harder to identify with, he adds this commentary about the sudden impermanence of the portable playground:

> There was a time when a playground was a reasonably permanent fixture in a neighborhood, when one's children, and even, perhaps, one's children's children might, each in their turn, experience it in roughly the same way. Super-industrial playgrounds, however, refuse to stay put. They are temporary by design.[5]

Perhaps twentieth-century man's mushrooming preoccupation with physical activity is an overt manifestation of some subconscious need to reduce cultural shock born of our onrushing technological revolution. The growing allegiance to physical activity as a primary mode of communication and expression is perhaps modern man's way of fulfilling a primordial need for movement as a method of survival in his strange and new environment. As Maslow[6] pointed out, the change of focus which sport and movement have undergone represents a transition from survival

4. Alvin Toffler, *Future Shock*. (New York: Bantam Books, 1970).
5. Ibid., p. 59.
6. Abraham Maslow, *Motivation and Personality*. (New York: Harper & Row, 1970).

to self-actualization. While survival may well be considered man's most basic preoccupation, self-actualization may be considered man's highest level of personal fulfillment. However, until survival has been for the most part assured, man cannot even begin to progress toward self-actualization. Maslow wrote:

> Man is ultimately not molded or shaped into humanness or taught to be human. The role of the environment is ultimately to permit him or help him to actualize his own potentialities, not its potentialities.[7]

No matter in what context movement is sought, be it that of survival or self-actualization or some other reason, movement fulfills a basic human need. Those physical skills that are useful for survival alone are obviously narrow in scope and dimension. But when the purpose of movement is for progress toward self-actualization, then the useful movement patterns are virtually unlimited and multi-dimensional. There is also great joy to be derived from movement that is oriented toward self-actualization.

Skilled movement has another role aside from self-actualization, which implies individualistic, rather independent efforts. Movement has tremendous social significance. Individuals who enjoy physical activity, who move well, or consider themselves to be skillful tend to gravitate toward other individuals with the same positive attitudes toward movement and physical activities. In social situations, these individuals will be at the center of the action rather than retreating to the sidelines as spectators. The enjoyment of physical activity is sometimes a common denominator in the forming of social groups, and it often serves as a strong bond between and among people.

THE RELEVANCE OF PHYSICAL EDUCATION IN CONTEMPORARY SOCIETY

Modern man needs to remain physically active in order to increase his chances for living a long, full, and healthy life. Our modern environment is, in itself, an unnatural one. While twentieth-century technology has brought us to an extremely high standard of living, and has even increased man's expected life span, it has along the way produced pressures that were previously unknown.

Providing for experiences in movement activities through the medium of physical education is a responsibility and obligation of the

7. Abraham Maslow, ed., New Knowledge in Human Values. (Chicago: Henry Regnery Co., 1971), p. 130.

The enjoyment of physical activity is sometimes a common denominator in the forming of social groups, and it often serves as a strong bond between and among people.

schools. Unless the schools assume their proper role in providing high quality programs, the development of movement skills and positive attitudes toward movement will be left largely to chance. It seems almost paradoxical that the curricular status of physical education is sometimes questioned. When we look at the world of movement, we find many individuals offering alternative nonschool programs. While many programs are run under high standards and utilize professionally prepared personnel, there seem to be equally as many who are more highly publicized and more in the public eye who have had little or no formal preparation to teach physical education. The fact that many such individuals are thriving via television programs, in syndicated newspaper columns, and in health spas and figure salons bears witness to the fact that the public often looks to persons other than professionally prepared physical educators for leadership in the realm of movement.

Part of the problem lies in the fact that while many physical educators have claimed professional status for physical education, the field is not yet a profession. A field of endeavor becomes a profession when its practitioners are the sole purveyors of the service the field offers. Thus, only licensed physicians may practice medicine, and only lawyers who have passed the bar may present cases in courts of law. Physical education has achieved only the status of an emerging profession. While most public schools require teachers to be certified in their special educational field, in practice this is not always the case. There are many individuals teaching physical education in the schools who are not certified to teach physical education, but are certified in some other subject field. Most private schools require no certification at all for any teaching position. Also, coaches, who are frequently highly visible to the public, are not always professional physical educators or certified coaches. The standards imposed on physical education, and perpetuated by many directly or tangentially connected with physical education, are but some of the reasons why the field lacks professional status.

According to Morford, physical educators must find out who they are and what it is they are trying to do before physical education can even hope to begin to become a profession. He argues that we have not even developed an appropriate body of knowledge for physical education, and this is but one preliminary step on the way to achieving professional standing. He writes:

> A previous generation of physical education specialists did not see the need to organize a subject area basic to their professional practice. They were adequately prepared to meet the needs of a society in their day. But the physical education of the future, operating in an educationally, intellectually, and technologically advanced super-society, will have to accelerate progress toward a more complete understanding of itself. Only in that way will it be possible to respond as a profession to a society which will tolerate no less[8]

SUMMARY

Man and movement experiences have moved down through history together. For primitive man, movement was inextricably intertwined

8. W.R. Morford, "Toward a Profession, Not a Craft," *Quest* 18 (June 1972): 93.

with survival. Today, movement and survival are still highly dependent, but our conception of the elements of which survival is composed have changed drastically. We have reviewed the important role the school must play in providing quality physical education programs taught by qualified and dedicated physical educators. We have pointed out some of the problems that face every physical educator, and have tried to show how, in spite of the many frustrations, there is still a service to be performed by physical educators.

We have seen how movement can be a social force for both good and ill by citing the examples of the early Greek and Roman societies. Moreover, we have tried to establish the sociocultural place of physical education in man's long and varied history. Finally, we returned to modern-day physical education and tried to determine its status among the professions.

SUGGESTIONS FOR FURTHER READING

"Educational Change in the Teaching of Physical Education." *Quest*, 15, January 1971.

Martens, Rainer, *Social Psychology and Physical Activity*. New York: Harper & Row, 1975.

"Quest for Tomorrow." *Quest* 21, January 1974.

"Teaching Teachers." *Quest* 18, June 1972.

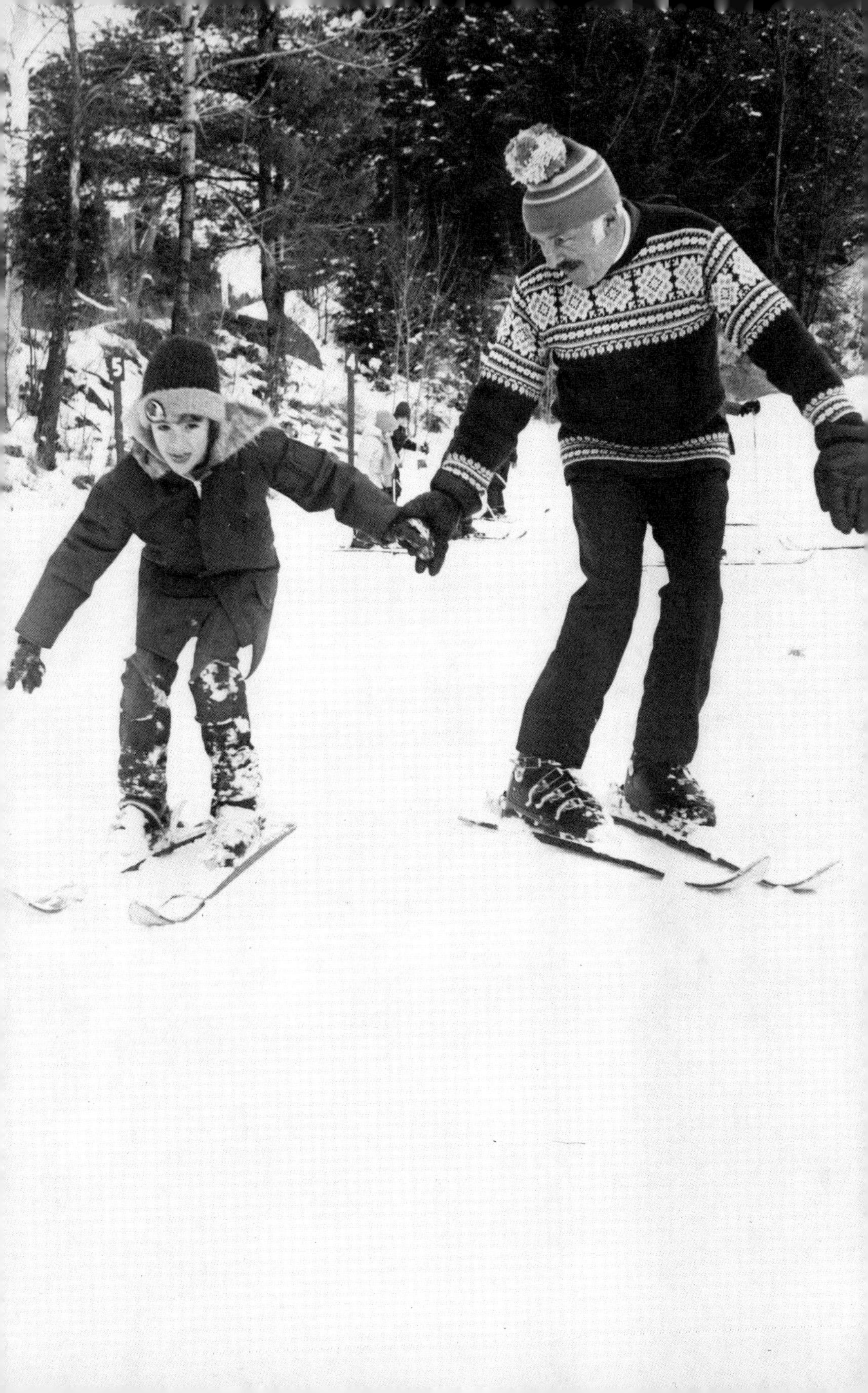
5
4

On Being Physically Educated

4

It is doubtful that a person is ever adequately educated if that person considers education to be simply the product, or sole end result, of formal schooling. The individual who views education in this light also tends to consider learning experiences to be nothing more than bits of data that can be neatly tucked away in the corner of the mind to be called-up if needed, and forgotten or discarded otherwise. Where education is considered to be only a product, it lacks life and vibrancy, and it ceases to advance under its own momentum once formal education has ended. Where education is perceived as a product, learning experiences often begin to fade into obscurity soon after the initial learning experience has taken place. This may be compared to the student who crams for an exam and forgets the material soon after completing the test. The individual who views education in this manner tends not to realize that education is a lifelong, never ending process.

EDUCATION AS A PROCESS

Where both the educational system and the student consider education to be a process, completion of the school years marks the beginning rather than the end of education. When education is a process, it becomes a catalyst which helps to stimulate the continued pursuit and expansion of knowledge, and thus, education never really ceases. The value of education to the learner is limited only by the learner's potential. When education is a process, the person may spend an entire lifetime in the joyful pursuit of new knowledge. Learning becomes an adventure with constant new challenges. In a discussion on the future of education Jewett said:

> Education will be concerned with persons in process; and physical education will be concerned with persons as ongoing, growing, developing beings.[1]

Education happens both within the individual, and to him by means of formal school instruction. The most spontaneous form of education, however, and the most meaningful form, is that which is inner-directed because it has more potential for continued growth and tends to maintain its momentum better. The role of the teacher in the educational process was perhaps best perceived by Gibran who wrote:

> If he is indeed wise he does not bid you enter the house of his wisdom, but rather leads you to the threshold of your own mind.[2]

When students learn principles and are able to form concepts from them, then education is process-oriented. Conversely, the student's ability to conceptualize is hindered when education is product-oriented, that is, when subject matter is presented as isolated, and often unrelated bits of information and facts. Where education is a process, information is better integrated into the student's generalized and readily usable pool of knowledge. Where education is a product, the student has difficulty in generalizing, and the facts he has memorized become limited in value because relationships cannot be readily drawn.

It would be incorrect to imply that the understanding of principles and the ability to form concepts from them is based on something other than facts, or that facts are not important at all. However, where education is process-oriented, facts are merely the building blocks for the understanding of principles and the development of concepts. Facts, in this case, are the beginnings of knowledge rather than the end result of education.

In process-oriented education, the teacher must not simply present facts, but must also assist and guide the students while they assemble these facts into a relevant and effective base of knowledge. This base of knowledge will serve the students well as they continue to become educated. Once a base of knowledge has been formed, students will then be able to become more responsible for their own educations because they will have facts, principles, and concepts at their disposal.

The more responsibility students take for their own education, and the more they actively seek to determine its course and direction, the more

1. Ann E. Jewett, "Who Knows What Tomorrow May Bring?" Quest 21 (January 1974): 70.
2. Gibran, Kahlil. The Prophet. (New York: Alfred A. Knopf, 1956), p. 56.

process-oriented education will become. As much as we might desire students to become equal partners in the educational process, and as much as we might want this to happen right now, there are some definite problems that preclude any instant changes that will be embraced and endorsed by educators. Some of these problems were delineated by Kleine:

> Let's face it, students are not free. They are forced, by compulsory attendance laws, to attend school. They are, for the most part, captives in college-preparatory general education curricula. Even with the advent of the phase-elective program and the inception of mini-courses, students are channeled into relatively regimented courses offered in relatively regimented ways. Considerable lip service is given to 'providing for individual differences' (individual freedom), but too little is done to implement this concept.[3]

PHYSICAL EDUCATION—PRODUCT OR PROCESS?

Physical education currently seems to be closer, on a product-process continuum, to the product end of the line. We make this assumption partly because so many people fall into habits of physical inactivity once they are no longer required to participate in formal physical education classes. It is both alarming as well as an indictment of physical education when we consider the substantial number of people who have given up active participation for a life of spectatorism. For these individuals, physical education was obviously a product whose usefulness ended along with formal education experiences. It therefore falls upon the physical educator—the movement professional—to seek ways to make movement experiences relevant and meaningful so that school experiences in movement will become the base of an ongoing, lifelong process of movement experiences and participation.

> ...physical education... is not limited to the traditional concept of a program of activities set up to teach children a prescribed number of games, dances, stunts and tumbling, gymnastics, and the like, with the hope that certain values such as physical fitness, cooperation, leadership, and similar general desirable characteristics and qualities would result. Rather, physical education is used to indicate not only a program but a process as well—a process in which the product (the student) is the point of focus.[4]

The burden for showing students the continuing, lifelong relevance of physical activity rests with the movement professionals. Because the

3. Glen Kleine, "Let Freedom Really Ring in the Schools," Kappa Delta Pi Record 11 (April 1975): 101.
4. American Association for Health, Physical Education, and Recreation, Knowledge and Understanding in Physical Education. (Washington, D.C.: AAHPER, 1969), p. vii.

student is the consumer and the educator the provider of movement experiences, the assumption must be made that physical educators must, through their programs, initiate a process that will help students to become inner-directed toward continued physical activity. Physical education is the responsibility of physical educators, and credit and criticism alike for physical education programs and their ultimate value to the individual must revert back to the movement professionals to whom the students' future as physically educated persons has been entrusted.

The remainder of this chapter will investigate two areas: (1) how physical education can become more process-oriented and (2) how physical education can help the student to become inner-directed toward physical activity as a life-style. We will establish the concept that the individual is physically educated when he is self-motivated to achieve self-actualization through strong movement programs.

HELPING PHYSICAL EDUCATION BECOME A PROCESS

Ideally, physical education should begin during the early years of life, long before the child begins formal schooling. According to Fait:

> It has long been recognized that children need experiences outside the home before they begin formal schooling to ensure their optimum development and preparation for the tasks of the classroom . . . it is through play experiences that the young child learns about himself: who he is, what he can do, and how he relates to the world around him. It is through play also that he develops his body and motor skills and increases his physical well-being.[5]

When the child is in the formative years, the time is right to begin guiding him into habits of movement that will be of lifetime value to him. By beginning early, an attempt can be made to provide sufficient understandings about physical activity so that later in life intelligent decisions can be made about continuing to be physically active. The child must be helped to realize that physical activity, in the form of movement experiences, is not only fun, but purposeful behavior as well. The acceptance of physical activity as purposeful and necessary behavior is an important part of the educational process. This process must develop a strong base in early childhood so that it will gather momentum throughout life.

The young child's parents in a very general sense, are the child's first physical educators. In a much broader context, particularly during the preschool years, parents are the child's first and most important teachers,

5. Hollis F. Fait, The Physical Education for the Elementary School Child. (Philadelphia: W.B. Saunders Co., 1971), p. 391.

and they become behavior models for the child. Parents who lead an active, healthy life tend to have a positive influence on the activity habits of their children. This seems to be borne out by the research of Snyder and Spreitzer:

An interest in sports is developed at least partly through the parents. Apparently, sports involvement begins in childhood, is reinforced by parental encouragement . . .[6]

Also, there seems to be some evidence that would suggest that fundamental physical skills are learned best early, rather than later, in life:

. . . it is generally agreed that after five or six years of age, on the average, no new basic skills appear in the child's movement repertoire. Rather, the quality of performance in motor tasks continues to improve . . .[7]

The implication is that in early childhood there is a significantly greater propensity for learning and accepting new skills and movement patterns than there is later in life, when movements have been stereotyped and habits of movement formulated. From this, we can make a very strong argument for early and well-planned formal physical education programs.

Orientation of boys and girls to the need for exercise as a way of life should be stressed in order to attain and maintain total effectiveness. Studies . . . have shown the totality of the individual: that physical, psycho-social and mental accomplishments are interrelated.[8]

Strengthening a Weak Link

Young children frequently do not receive the very best physical education experiences. Many early school physical education programs are poorly planned, poorly executed, and suffer from a lack of skilled teaching. This is most unfortunate, because the young child's first formal physical education experience, as we have seen, is the most important one if positive attitudes toward the worth of physical activity are to be developed. Why is the young child, who needs physical activity most, so often the victim of a poor program? The answer lies in many directions, and the finger of blame

---

6. Eldon E. Snyder, and Elmer A. Sprietzer, "Family Influence and Involvement in Sports," *Research Quarterly* 44 (October 1973): 252.
7. Corbin, Charles B. *A Textbook of Motor Development.* Dubuque, Iowa: Wm. C. Brown Company Publishers, 1973. p. 34.
8. H. Harrison Clarke, ed, "Individual Differences, Their Nature, Extent and Significance," *Physical Fitness Research Digest*, series 3, (October 1973), p. 21.

can be pointed at many, including the schools and their administrators, and physical educators themselves.

The School and Administrative Problems

When we think of problems within a school that hinder one program or another, we usually tend to think in terms of class size, facilities, and equipment. There is, however, another aspect that is not considered as often. Many school boards and school administrators feel, within the structure of the elementary school, that any classroom teacher is automatically qualified to teach physical education on the grade level he or she regularly teaches. This kind of logic negates the basic premise that in the early years a strong, well-planned physical education program is so vital and critical to the proper growth of the child. When instruction in physical education comes through an individual other than one trained and qualified as a movement professional, the assumption must be made that physical education has a very low priority in terms of curricular relevance. This is not to imply that the classroom teacher cannot teach some physical education, but that there are people better qualified who will devote full time to this very important aspect of the child's education.

In circumstances where the classroom teacher is the individual in charge of physical education, we must question the physical education frame of reference used by those who are responsible for making curricular and educational judgments. If we assume that these individuals are basing their decisions on what they believe to be in the best interests of children and their education, then it might follow that the decision makers themselves may have been, as children, involved in a product-oriented, rather than process-oriented, educational system. It would follow, then, that their decisions concerning physical education might be based upon their own prior training and experiences. Thus, while they may indeed firmly believe that their decisions are the best, they may in fact not realize the effect of these decisions on the future of the child.

Where physical education is the bottom priority line of the curriculum, the program will not truly be an experience in movement, but will tend to be relegated to a free-play or recess type of activity simply because the classroom teacher does not have the time, or in most cases the training, to plan a real program based upon the real needs of the students. Yet, we are clearly told, and must impress upon those in charge of educational decision making that:

The need for teaching a body of knowledge in physical education appears indisputable, then, if the school accepts its responsibility to assist the individual to develop his potential, by giving him not only the skills but the background for knowing 'how' and 'why,' so that he may continue to grow throughout his lifetime.[9]

Problems within Physical Education

In many respects, physical education and physical educators are to blame for the current low status of physical education within school programs. Sometimes, physical educators have done little to dispel many of the common misconceptions about the nature and worth of physical education as a vital and viable area of study within school curriculums. Where physical education has not been properly presented within a community, long lasting and detrimental effects may result. Today's school children are the parents, voters, community leaders, and school board members of the future. How they will ultimately evaluate and value physical education depends upon the effect of their own physical education experience.

Where physical education is presented as a meaningful, continuing process from the very beginning of the school years, a positive and supportive base is built for the future. Physical educators must understand how to develop a process-oriented program, and they must know and support the objectives of physical education. They must be able to present to their students the purposeful "whys" of the physical education experience so that their students will have all possible opportunity to learn through the medium of movement experiences. However, one tremendous pitfall for physical educators, which is a critical problem as well, was summarized by Berg:

> *Lack of enthusiasm is a problem for many teachers of physical education. After several years of experience, the eager graduate becomes quite efficient in administrative procedures such as handing out lockers, taking attendance, establishing grading criteria, maintaining and storing equipment, and planning instruction, including the choice and sequence of activities, the duration of each activity, etc. Result? The challenge of planning and learning on the job begins to disappear and the once excited young teachers are bored. They've 'done it all.'*[10]

Teaching the "Hows" and "Whys" of Physical Education

Historically, physical educators have exhibited a greater propensity for teaching the "hows" of physical education rather than the "whys." The "hows" of physical education include the skills that are the facilitators of

9. AAHPER, loc. cit., vii.
10. Kris. Berg, "Maintaining Enthusiasm in Teaching," *JOPER* 46 (April 1975): 22.

movement, for example, how to throw and how to catch, how to run, how to swim, how to ski, how to do physical fitness exercises. Instruction in the "hows" to the neglect of the "whys" is product-oriented physical education. Emphasis on the "hows" tends to compartmentalize the skills so that the student never really grows to understand "why" physical activity is relevant and worthy of the time and effort expended. Each student should not only be free to ask the question, "Why do I have to learn this skill?", but he should also receive a meaningful and acceptable answer. When the student receives such knowledge, he will be better able to value his physical education experience, and will be helped to develop a frame of reference for future movement experiences, and their "whys." This is process-oriented physical education in that it is geared not only to "how" but more importantly to "why."

Knowledge of the "whys" gives purpose, meaning, and relevance to the "hows," and knowledge of the "whys" makes the "hows" happen easier and more pleasantly. Further, "whys" give relevance to physical education, and help to precipitate positive attitudes toward a physically active mode of life. The "hows," then, become simply the tools for implementing an active lifestyle. It would seem reasonable to suggest, that more than any other aspect of physical education, that understanding the "whys" best builds the foundation for a lifelong commitment to physical activity and the resultant maintenance of physical well-being.

There are, of course, many individuals who seek physical activity simply because they enjoy it and it feels good. For these people, skilled movement and continued movement experiences are frequently ends in themselves. In other words, because physical activity is satisfying, it is justified, and the participant is motivated to continue this activity because he derives pleasure from it. However, we must also recognize that many individuals are not inner-directed toward movement. If such individuals are to become so motivated, they must be helped to understand that skilled movement can be a means to a desired end rather than being the end alone. It is in this context that the "whys" of physical education take on added meaning and become so critical. The "whys" help the unmotivated individual to understand the ways in which movement experiences become important means to satisfying and important ends.

To suggest that physical educators have been somewhat remiss in neglecting to teach the "whys" is perhaps too mild a criticism. As Ariel points out:

> Presently, physical education remains in its dark ages. Physical education is the only discipline whose goals and objectives are met with improvement of tools. In other words, in order to improve biological efficiency we improve the means i. e., the activity itself.[11]

11. Gideon B. Ariel, "Physical Education: 2001?" Quest 21 (January 1974): 49.

As physical educators we must teach the "whys" along with the "hows." The "whys" are important because they help to explain the relevancy of physical education within the context of education in general. Physical educators themselves tend to understand the "whys" since physical educators use movement as a frame of reference to make skilled movement and continued participation in movement personally satisfying.

While the premise exists that the best performers are sometimes the poorest of teachers, the physical educator who is highly skilled must redouble efforts to empathize with and understand the poorly skilled student, or the student who is not motivated toward activity. Students with low skills, and those who are not motivated need the "whys" of physical activity presented in a manner that they can accept both cognitively and affectively. Physical educators need to develop the skills of presenting the "whys" of physical activity to their students, and they must realize that each student has his own personality, his own potentials, and will be motivated only by the "whys" that suit his own unique needs. Bronson said that:

> People interact with each other and with their evnironment by means of patterns, and the mission of the school is to clarify and reinforce and improve the process of interaction.[12]

A CHALLENGE TO PHYSICAL EDUCATION

The fact that for many people physical education is a product rather than a process seems evident. Over the last several years, the number of spectators at sporting events has increased enormously and new, larger sports facilities are being built to accommodate even more watchers. The number of sporting events televised has also increased and fans continue to demand that they be able to see even more contests on television. Obviously, those who are watching cannot be doing. On the other hand, this decade has also been the era of the jogger, the backpacker and the camper, for example, and many major cities are setting aside areas where bicyclists and joggers can exercise in safety. These latter groups, and those who engage regularly in similar activities, have been well-served by either a process-oriented physical education program or a process-oriented physical educator. Yet on balance it would appear that movement specialists have failed to reach a significant number of individuals, and have failed to dissuade them from a sedentary life-style. This is one of the major challenges to physical education.

12. David B. Bronson, "Thinking and Teaching," *The Educational Forum,* 39 (March 1975): 353.

The benefits of participation in physical activity have both immediate and long range significance for the individual. Depending upon the activity and the participant's frame of reference, these benefits may be social, psychological, physical, or any combination of these. The immediate benefits of participation are usually clear to most people, but sometimes the long range benefits are rather obscure. Thus, the "whys" of physical activity are again a vital factor. If the "whys" are not presented, and the long range benefits not adequately clarified, then participation is apt to decline and finally cease altogether. Lacking an understanding of the "whys," today's participant become tomorrow's spectator. Moreover, physical educators must recognize that many young people will gravitate toward physical activity because of the immediate benefits to be derived from recognition and peer group acceptance. However, by the time these young people have entered the adult world, they frequently discover that adults achieve recognition and acceptance in many ways that often tend not to be movement-related.

Physical education is thus challenged to effectively serve young people through process-oriented programs so that these young people will be guided toward understanding the continued importance of physical activity in the adult world. Physical educators must mobilize so that each program will teach the "whys" as well as the "hows," and so that each program will be process-oriented to serve best those it professes to teach. However, in assuming that change will come quickly and painlessly, we must heed the words of Williams:

> One of the problems from which we suffer in the area of educational thought and behavior is simple-minded utopianism. Salvation will come tomorrow if only we will all adopt behavioral objectives. All learning problems will miraculously disappear if we will simply allow the child to develop naturally. Educational history continuously cautions against such simplistic thinking. It reminds us time and again of the complexity of human and social behavior and of the difficulty in achieving planned change. History shows us that outcome may be quite different from intention.[13]

SUMMARY

Physical education is currently attempting to gain respect by improving programs and seeking to improve on tradition. In this chapter we have tried to show that we must not only revamp our activities, but that we must also help the student to see why a given activity is not only

13. William G. Williams, "Does the Educational Past Have a Future?" Kappa Delta Pi *Record* 11 (April 1975): 103.

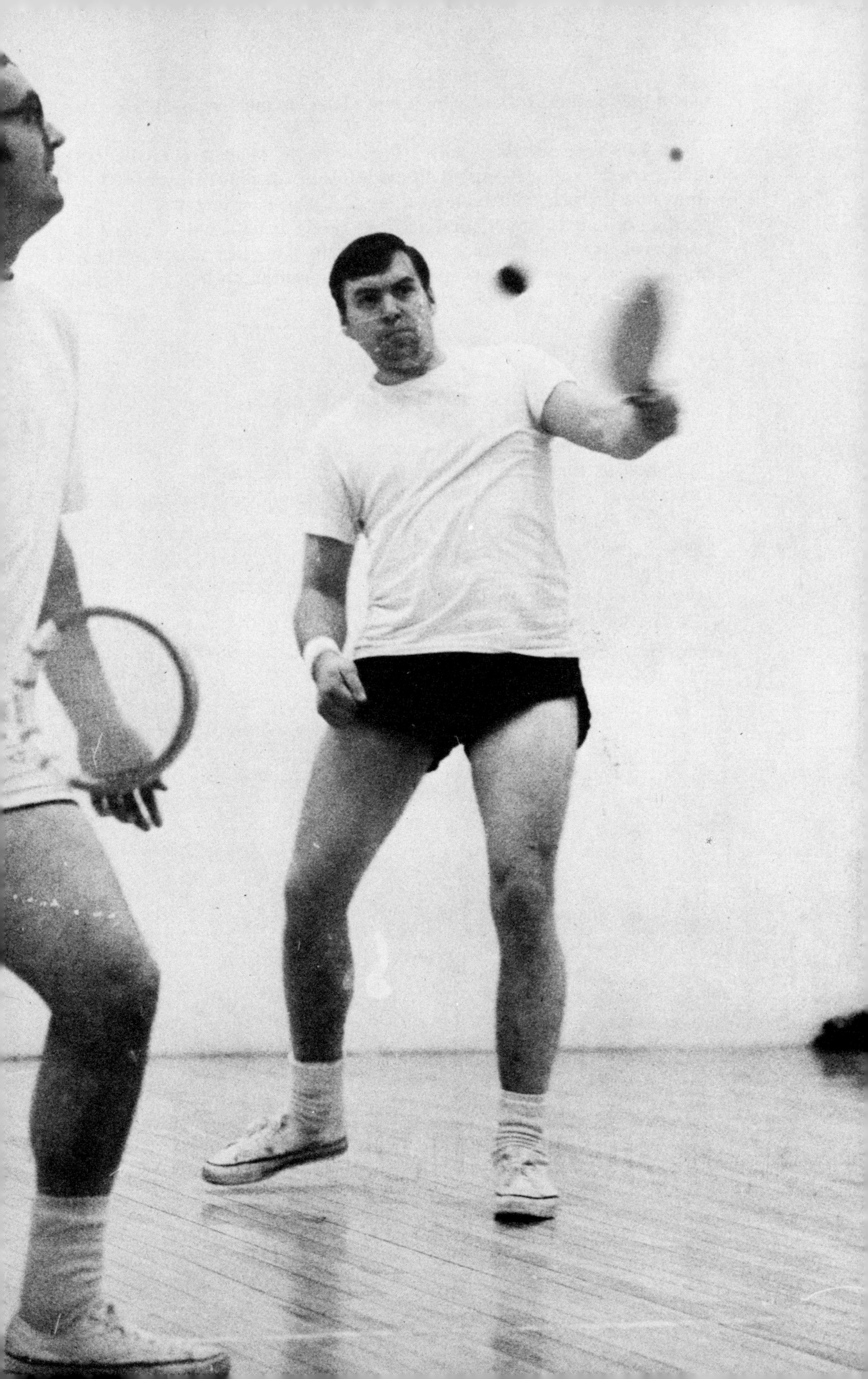

useful for the moment but why it will make life more enjoyable in the future.

We have discussed only a few of the problems and challenges facing physical education, but through this discussion we have tried to show how physical education must become process-oriented so that the product-oriented "how" approach can be de-emphasized. A plea has been made for strengthening elementary school physical education programs, and the need for hiring movement specialists, particularly on this level, has been a major point of emphasis.

SUGGESTIONS FOR FURTHER READING

Cowell, Charles C. and Wellman L. France. *Philosophy and Principles of Physical Education*. Englewood Cliff, N.J.: Prentice-Hall, Inc., 1963.

Crockenberg, Vincent. "Poor Teachers Are Made Not Born." *The Educational Forum* 39, January 1975:189–198.

Feingold, Ronald S. "The Evaluation of Teacher Education Programs in Physical Education." *Quest* 18, June 1972:33–39.

Felshin, Jan. "Sport and Modes of Meaning." *JOHPER* 40, May 1969:43–44.

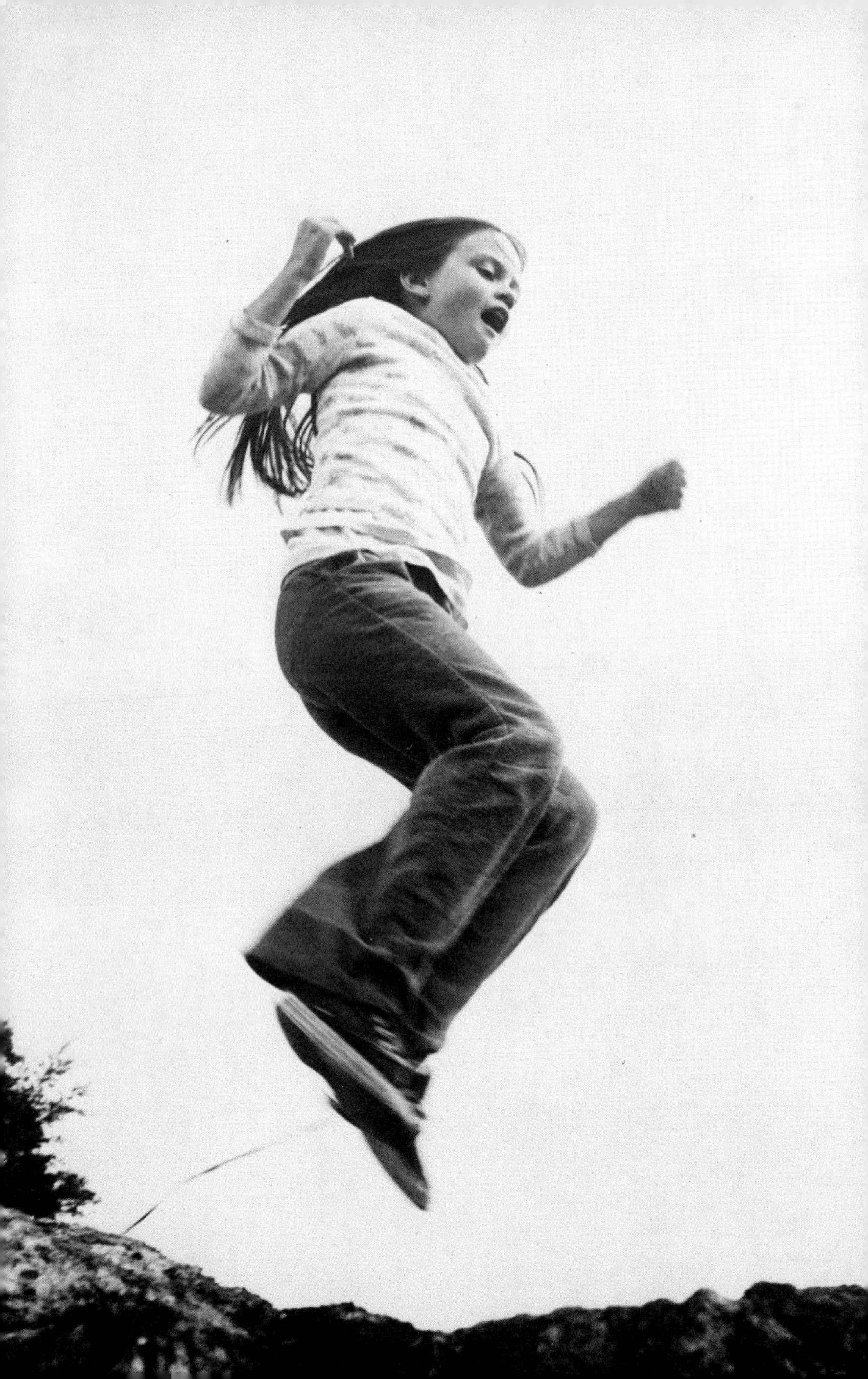

5

Movement and Cognition

This chapter is designed to help the reader better understand the place of movement experiences in the over-all development of the individual. It is very important to be aware of the moving individual as more than simply a body in motion. Each time a person moves, many qualities are brought into play that are not purely physical factors. In other words, this chapter is concerned with some of the more definitive aspects of education through the physical. In order to be able to take a brief, but comprehensive, look at the relationship between cognition and movement, it is necessary and important to discuss some of the subaspects of movement, and also, to see what some of the authorities in the area of cognitive development have said.

Education is based on the premise that the human organism functions as a mind-body entity. In other words, a primary objective of education is to educate the whole man—not his mind alone or his body alone. Many educational theorists support the belief that movement experiences, beginning in infancy, give rise to eventual cognitive development, often referred to as "intelligence." These theorists tell us that movement experiences provide the vital primary means through which children first explore, then relate to, and finally communicate with their environment. Further, the educational theorists propose that the child cannot become an intelligent being if he does not have an opportunity to experience the inherent, natural forms of movement.

Apparently, movement experiences enhance cognitive functioning because movement is the key to the development of perception that comes about through a wide variety of sensorimotor experiences. Sensorimotor experiences help the individual to interpret his environment, and to form

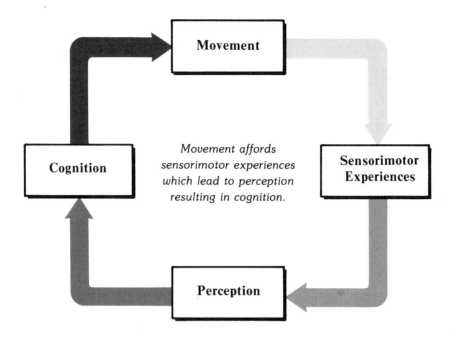

Movement

Cognition

Sensorimotor
Experiences

Perception

*Movement affords
sensorimotor experiences
which lead to perception
resulting in cognition.*

concepts about that environment that lead to the development of cognition. This principle may be illustrated by a simplified theoretical model as shown here:

Movement. Movement is any form of human motion or locomotion. In physical education, we generally speak in terms of "movement behavior," a phrase that is more comprehensive and descriptive than the single word "movement." According to Cratty's definition:

> *Movement behavior refers to overt movements of the skeletal muscle . . .
> movement behavior is observable movement of the body, excluding such
> functions as visceral changes, the conduction of nerve impulses, and circula-
> tion of body fluids. Movement behavior is observable and not simply record-
> able movement, for most internal fluctuations are measurable by various
> devices.* [1]

Sensorimotor experiences. A sensory experience is any information received or monitored by the body's sensory mechanisms, including but not limited to, sight, sound, taste, smell, touch, and kinesthesis. Taking this definition a step further, sensorimotor experiences are the action phase, or the skills that help the individual to replicate, explore, and interpret sensory

1. Bryant J. Cratty, *Movement Behavior and Motor Learning.* (Philadelphia: Lea and Febiger, 1967), p. 9.

experiences. Stallings pointed out that, " . . . most perceptual abilities are the result of integration of sensations from more than one modality."[2]

Perception.   Perceptions help the individual to interpret environmental stimuli. Initially, sensory and sensorimotor experiences may have no special meaning for the infant and growing child, but meaning comes eventually from the developing discriminatory abilities of the individual as he matures. Harrow said that:

> *Perception is the precursor of action; it is the process of becoming aware, attending to, or interpreting stimuli. It involves assembling pertinent cues from various perceptual modalities or stimulus situations . . .*[3]

Cognition.   Cognition is the organization and systematization of perceptions into ideas and bodies of knowledge which the individual uses to form generalizations about his environment. Robb wrote that:

> *Cognitive learning refers to changes in the behavior of a person in the areas of problem solving, concept formation, reasoning, and acquisition of knowledge through memory and/or understanding. Cognitive learning deals with conscious awareness and involves the mental processes associated with thinking.*[4]

PERCEPTION AND THE CHILD

Perceptual awarenesses which come from movement-centered sensorimotor experiences are of particular interest to movement specialists. Perceptual-motor theorists and specialists alike generally agree that perceptual development leads to concept development, and that perceptual competence is the key to cognition. Further, these same individuals point out that the development of perceptual abilities is an action-oriented process, and that action connotes movement:

> *. . . the concept of perceptual-motor development is one which deals with changes or improvements in the child's afferent or sensoriperceptual capacities—changes which are grounded in a steady and continuous im-*

2. Loretta M. Stallings, *Motor Skills: Development and Learning.* (Dubuque, Iowa: Wm. C. Brown Co., 1973), p. 84.
3. Anita J. Harrow, *A Taxonomy of the Psychomotor Domain.* (New York: David McKay Co., Inc., 1972), p. 163.
4. Margaret D. Robb, *The Dynamics of Motor-Sill Acquisition.* (Englewood Cliffs, N.J.: Prentice-Hall, Inc., 1972), p. 10.

provement in the child's capacity to perceive . . . increasingly more complex kinds and quantities of sensory information.[5]

Observer's of young children usually recognize that the child's initial interactions with his environment are almost exclusively motor in nature. It is primarily through these motor experiences that the child begins to gather perceptual information about his world. Increased movement leads to increased perception, which in turn helps the child to develop a set of concepts concerned with the order and meaning of his environment. Arnheim and Petolesi noted that, "Perception cannot be separated from cognition; they must be considered as inseparable, dependent, and reciprocal."[6]

MOVEMENT AND COGNITION—IS THERE A CORRELATION?

There are a number of authorities in the field of educational theory who contend that movement is a key factor in cognitive development. Other respected authorities contend that such a relationship is at best only an assumption, but an assumption with tremendous implications for education. Similarly, researchers have attempted to gain insight into the movement-cognition hypothesis, and their various results often show a conflicting picture. While acceptance of the movement-cognition relationship is not universal by any means, those authorities and researchers who support the theory have made some very strong arguments in its favor. The physical educators, special educators, and psychologists who have studied the theory all seem to agree that much more research is needed before any positive conclusions can be reached. Such research is presently being conducted, and many studies are in the design stage. The data which are currently available represent a rather significant body of knowledge. A representative sample of the literature concerned with the relationship between movement and congition is presented in the sections that follow.

Piaget's Theory

According to Piaget, the development of intelligence follows a very definite and structured six stage course of events. Each of the stages must be experienced by the growing child, and although Piaget gave no landmark

5. Charles B. Corbin, *A Textbook of Motor Development*. (Dubuque, Iowa: Wm. C. Brown Co., 1973), p. 112.
6. Daniel D. Arnheim, and Robert A. Pestolesi. *Developing Motor Behavior in Chidren*. (St. Louis: The C.V. Mosby Co., 1973;, p. 36.

age for the achievement of the sixth stage, he contended that the child completes the first five stages by the beginning of his second year. Piaget's first stage is concerned with the reflexive reactions of the infant; the second with circular motions and reflex adaptations; the third with increased circular motions and actions that are more sustained than previously; while the fourth and fifth stages are marked by further applications of previously learned reactions and a desire to experiment with movements of all types.

In the sixth and final stage, the development of intelligence is marked by innovation and creativity in responses and reactions.[7] Thus, Piaget's theory is based on the hypothesis that intelligence is the end result of what began, in the infant, as a simple reflex. Movement exploration is the connecting and facilitating link between the simple reflex and intelligence. Piaget said that there is " . . . an even greater correlation than there seemed to be between the sensorimotor and the perceptual."[8]

The Montessori Method

Maria Montessori was concerned with child development and its relation to intrinsic motivation, sensory training, and motor experiences. Montessori felt that a primary concern of education was to help the child, through carefully selected movement experiences, to become proficient in walking, balancing, and coordination. The Montessori approach involves presenting the child with demonstrations and a wide variety of behavioral models which the child can observe, compare, and judge and evaluate in ways that are individually relevant and meaningful.

Montessori believed that sensory experiences, which are abundant in movement, enable the child to know his environment and in turn help him to develop his intelligence. She wrote:

> . . . intelligence . . . the sum of those reflex and associative or reproductive activities which enable the mind to construct itself, putting it into relation with the environment.[9]

Newell C. Kephart

Kephart has suggested that, for the child, motor efficiency is a prerequisite for effective exploration of the environment. He said that such movement-

---

7. Jean Piaget, *The Origins of Intelligence in Children*. (New York: International Universities Press, Inc., 1952), p. 348.
8. Ibid. p. x.
9. Maria Montessori, *Spontaneous Activity in Education*. (Cambridge, Mass.: Robert Bentley, Inc., 1964), p. 198.

centered exploration is the basic means through which the child achieves perceptual efficiency. Kephart contended that learning skills are hierarchical in nature, and that advanced learnings are in large part dependent upon the learner's possessing a foundation of fundamental, movement-centered skills. Moreover, he believes that inadequate motor development in the early years serves to inhibit subsequent and more sophisticated learning.

Kephart supported his contention that early and varied movement-oriented skills are important by saying that, " . . . most of the tasks which we set for the child are complex activities combining many basic sensory-motor skills."[10] He suggests that motor experiences and perceptual experiences are interdependent. He asserted that initial school failure may often be traced to perceptual inadequacies, and that perceptual inadequacies tend to stem from inadequate movement-centered experiences.

Rowland and McGuire

These authors suggest that intelligence initially develops as a result of motor activity, and that the intelligence of the young child is governed by the range of motor activity experiences as he develops. Rowland and McGuire contend that the initial perceptions which evolve from these early movement experiences provide the child with the means by which he judges and evaluates his environment.[11]

Barsch and the Movigenic Theory

Barsch believes that movement efficiency and perceptual abilities are very highly related. Barsch is the author of the Movigenic theory, which relates movement efficiency to learning efficiency. Movigenics is a movement-centered curriculum designed to enhance perceptual efficiency. The Movigenic theory, from which the curriculum is derived, involves the study of movement patterns, including their origin and development, and it investigates the relationship between movement and learning. The theory suggests that the individual first learns to move, then moves to learn.[12]

Other Writers

The relationship between perception and cognition has been thoroughly discussed by a number of writers other than those whose theories were

10. Newell C. Kephart, *The Slow Learner in the Classroom.* (Columbus, Ohio: Charles E. Merrill Publishing Co., 1960), p. 33.
11. G.T. Rowland, and J.C. McGuire. *The Mind of Man.* (Englwood Cliffs, N.J.: Prentice-Hall, Inc., 1971).
12. Ray H. Barsch, *Achieving Perceptual-Motor Efficiency.* (Seattle, Wash.: Special Child Publications, 1967).

described in the preceeding paragraphs. For example, Bruner and his colleagues feel that while perception and cognition are definitely related, that this relationship has many psychological overtones. They stressed that:

> ... cognitive growth in all its manifestations occurs as much from the outside in as from the inside out. Much of it consists in a human being's becoming linked with culturally transmitted 'amplifiers' of motoric, sensory, and reflective capacities.[13]

Olson developed a general thesis that was similar in intent to the Montessori Method. According to Olson, there is a strong and direct connection between perception and cognition. He suggested that teachers, rather than presenting a set solution to a problem, should instead demonstrate a variety of alternative solutions allowing the child to evaluate each one, compare them, and discover for himself the most suitable solution. Olson suggested that while words are important, that cognitive development is still possible even in the absence of verbalization and verbal explanations.

> The elaboration of the perceptual world that occurs under the mastery of performatory acts in various cultural media is responsible for the development of what is usually called intelligence.[14]

Kleinman, in a comprehensive article concerned with early childhood movement experiences, concluded that:

> In spite of the fact that many of the principles of learning are not fully understood, sufficient evidence exists to support the contention that there is a relationship between motoric and ideational learning.[15]

THE FINDINGS OF THE RESEARCHERS

A selected survey of some recent research studies that have been concerned with the correlation between movement and cognition shows no distinctly clear-cut consensus. There are, of course, many reasons why similar studies yield differing and often conflicting results. Many of these reasons have to do with the design and conduct of the study itself. Yet it is worthwhile, for our purposes in this chapter, to review some of these

13. Jerome S. Bruner, et al., *Studies in Cognitive Growth.* (New York: John Wiley and Sons, Inc., 1967). p. 1.
14. David R. Olson, *Cognitive Development: The Child's Acquisition of Diagonality.* (New York: Academic Press, 1970), p. 202.
15. Matthew Kleinman, "A Central Role for Physical Education in Early Childhood," New York University *Education Quarterly* 6 (Spring 1975): 23.

studies in order to help the reader draw some personal conclusions, and perhaps be motivated to study this area further, either through personal research or an indepth review of the literature.

Ismail and his colleagues,[16] Lipton,[17] and Schmidt and Johnson,[18] all very strongly supported, on the basis of their research, the hypothesis that a program of intensive movement experiences enhances cognitive development. For example, Ismail and his fellow researchers concluded that:

> ... the evidence points to a positive relationship between some motor aptitude items, especially coordination and blance, and well established measures of intelligence and scholastic ability.[19]

Broadhead's results, with educable mentally retarded children, led him to take a middle-of-the-road position: "For EMRs research has indicated a positive, though low, correlation between measured intelligence and gross motor performance."[20]

At the other end of the spectrum, Chasey and Wyrick[21] were able to conclude that, at least in the early school years, movement experiences do not significantly enhance cognitive learning. In two separate studies, Thomas and Chissom[22] reached similar conclusions, finding that:

> ... while previous research had indicated that the perceptual-motor measures were good concurrent predictors of academic performance, the results of this study indicated that the measures were unsuccessful in predicting performance 1 year later.[23]

THE COMPONENTS OF PERCEPTUAL-MOTOR EFFICIENCY

Among the components of perceptual-motor efficiency that are thought to play a significant role in cognitive development are postural and

16. A.H. Ismail, John Kane and D.R. Kirkendall, "Relationships Among Intellectual and Nonintellectual Variables," *Research Quarterly* 40 (March 1969):82–92.
17. Edward D. Lipton, "A Perceptual-Motor Development Program's Effect on Visual Perception and Reading Readiness of First-Grade Children," *Research Quarterly* 41 (October 1970):402–405.
18. Richard A. Schmidt and Warren R. Johnson, "A Note on Response Strategies in Children With Learning Difficulties," *Research Quarterly* 43 (December 1972):509–513.
19. Ismail, op. cit., p. 91.
20. Geoffrey D. Broadhead, "Gross Motor Performance in Minimally Brain Injured Children," *Journal of Motor Behavior* 4 (June 1972): 109.
21. William C. Chasey and Waneen Wyrick, "Effect of a Gross Motor Developmental Program on Form Perception Skills of Educable Mentally Retarded Children," *Research Quarterly* 41 (October 1970):345–352.
22. Jerry R. Thomas and Brad S. Chissom, "Relationships as Assessed by Canonical Correlation Between Perceptual-Motor and Intellectual Abilities for Pre-School and Early Elementary Age Children," *Journal of Motor Behavior* 4 (March 1972):23–29.
23. Jerry R. Thomas and Brad S. Chissom, "Prediction of First Grade Academic Performance from Kindergarten Perceptual-Motor Data," *Research Quarterly* 45 (May 1974): 152.

locomotor effectiveness; laterality and directionality; auditory perception; visual perception; tactile perception; and kinesthesis. We will discuss each of these components separately so that their contributions to cognitive development can be seen more clearly.

Postural and Locomotor Efficiency

These factors comprise the foundation of perceptual-motor effectiveness, because when posture and locomotion are efficient it becomes much easier to move through and explore the environment. Much of what is to be explored cannot come to the child, and thus the child must physically go to those things it wants to explore and learn about. The child uses locomotion as an effective learning tool. Further, as Hall has expressed it:

> The efficient use of his body helps each child to approach his maximum potential. Such training is essential because the body is a medium for learning, and learning—an outgrowth of experiencing and doing—is blocked when the child cannot move efficiently.[24]

Laterality and Directionality

Laterality is the awareness that the body has both a right and left side. Directionality is the extension of laterality into the external world, and involves concepts related to up and down movements, movements that are toward and away from the body, or movements from side to side or across the midline of the body.

Some perceptual-motor theorists have suggested that the development of laterality and directionality provides the child with his first information about the size and dimensions of his environment. Laterality and directionality are very closely allied with body awareness. On this subject Corbin wrote:

> Body awareness . . . refers to the multidimensional image which the individual has of himself as a 'physical entity' . . . it refers to the awareness, identification and/or evaluation of the proportions, dimensions, positions and movements of the individual's body and/or body parts.[25]

Auditory Perception

Auditory perception is more than hearing alone, since hearing implies only the ability to monitor sound. Auditory perception involves the ability not

24. Sue M. Hall, ed., *Children and Fitness.* (Washington, D.C.: AAHPER, Report of the National Conference on Fitness of Children of Elementary School Age, 1962), p. 15.
25. Corbin, op. cit., p. 140.

only to monitor sound, but to be able to translate what is heard into meaningful information.

Movement not only produces sound, but helps to add a dimension of meaning. Through movement experiences, the child can be given an opportunity to perceive similarities and differences in sounds, so that he can better categorize and systematize sounds into meaningful information. Stallings has delineated many of the components of auditory perception:

> ... tasks include the ability to (A) identify the source of sounds, (B) discriminate among sounds or words, (C) reproduce pitch, rhythm, and melody, (D) select significant from insignificant stimuli, (E) combine speech sounds into words, or (F) understand the meaning of environmental sounds in general.[26]

Auditory spatial awareness can be developed through movement experiences that help the child to determine where others are, or where objects are, in relation to his own body. Movement may take the person toward or away from a sound, to one side or the other of it, or above or below the source of sound. Because movement can take the individual to each of these places in relation to a sound source, movement becomes an important means of using sound to add dimension to space.

Visual Perception

Visual perception involves the ability to interpret and derive meaning from objects that are subject to visual scrutiny. The fact that sight tends to be the most heavily relied on sensory mechanism indicates that the ability to derive meaning from things visually observed is of unparalleled importance. Visual perception and movement are closely allied in a variety of ways. Visual-motor experiences occur when the individual simultaneously sees and manipulates objects in the environment. Since object manipulation is concrete and tangible, manipulation paired with vision adds a further dimension to perception, concept formation, and cognitive development.

Movement experiences aid the child in developing his ability to track objects visually. Examples of visual tracking include following the flight of a batted, thrown, or kicked ball, and reading from left to right across a printed page. Virtually all movement experiences require some degree of tracking ability. Moreover,

> Sounds combined with visual information provide a more precise representation of events in space. Auditory perception supplements visual information about our space world ... auditory perception is not as critical to motor performances as is visual perception.[27]

26. Stallings, op. cit., p. 81.
27. George H. Sage, *Introduction to Motor Behavior.* (Reading, Mass.: Addison-Wesley Publishing Co. 1971), p. 186.

Tactile perception involves the ability to derive meaningful information from objects that are touched or manipulated. Tactile perceptions are among the most concrete means by which the environment is experienced, because these perceptions help the individual to discern whether an object is, for example, rough or smooth, heavy or light in weight, or hard or soft. The opportunity to touch, feel, and manipulate objects in the environment implies a heavy dependence upon movement as a basic means for providing these opportunities. Active, moving individuals can experience more tactile sensations than will less active, more sedentary individuals.

Tactile perception helps to increase manual dexterity because it enables the individual to determine whether or not objects have been grasped effectively. Further, tactile and visual perception often support each other when the individual is engaged in forming concepts about his environment. The combined perceptions which stem from simultaneously seeing and manipulating an object are more informative than the perception that arises from either of these two sensory modalities functioning by itself.

The senses, as receptors of the stimuli that surround us, provide the information for translation and response to express effective behavior. Viewed as an information-processing model, the organism attempts to match output with input ... If the senses are not functionally and operationally sound, the probability of an appropriate response is lessened ... In motor learning and performance, visual, proprioceptive, and tactile receptors play an important role in assisting the individual toward the achievement of his objective. [28]

Because tactile perception is an action affair, its development is facilitated by movement focussing on tactile contacts with the environment. Particularly for young children, movement experiences in physical education should center around providing the widest possible variety of tactile experiences.

Kinesthetic Perception

Kinesthetic perception is the awareness of the position of the body or body parts in space, and in addition to this is the awareness of the body in relation to other objects or individuals in the environment. Kinesthetic perception provides information about motion and the speed of movement, about the direction of motion, and about the velocity and trajectory of a movement when the body is propelled or moved through space.

28. Robert N. Singer, ed., *The Psychomotor Domain: Movement Behaviors.* (Philadelphia: Lea and Febiger, 1972), p. 4.

Kinesthetic perception develops from movement experiences, and physical education has a myriad of movement activities that can be used to heighten kinesthesis. Examples of these activities are stunts and tumbling, balance activities, and many of the track and field events, plus swimming, diving, and the trampoline. Skilled movement depends to a great degree upon kinesthesis. Sage wrote:

Kinesthesis is the discrimination of the positions and movements of body parts based on information other than visual, auditory, or verbal . . . The immediate stimuli arise from changes in length and from tension, compression, and shear forces arising from the effects of gravity, from relative movement of body parts, and from muscular contraction.[29]

SUMMARY

In this chapter we have examined, if only briefly, how certain kinds of movement experiences help to foster perceptual and cognitive development. While much of learning theory is speculation, and we must recognize it as such, we must also be aware as physical educators that we do have an ever-increasing bank of data that helps us to understand how to use movement as a tool for the education of our students—for education through the physical.

Until such time as we have more conclusive facts and information at hand, the authorities in the field and the educational researchers have shown us that it is highly likely that:

- Movement experiences provide a virtual universe of sensory experiences that are needed if the child is going to develop to his full potential.
- Without movement there would be a most significant deficit in these needed sensory experiences because the individual needs guidance and a planned program designed to heighten sensory awareness.
- Without sensory experiences, the kinds of perceptual awarenesses essential to learning, concept formation, and cognition might remain undeveloped, hampering the full growth of the individual.

Movement specialists must address the issues of learning theory with scholarly attitudes. They must search to determine the ways in which such relationships as movement and cognition might exist. They must then convert this knowledge into movement-centered curriculums which will serve each child in the manner most relevant and meaningful to that child.

29. Sage, op. cit., p. 117.

SUGGESTIONS FOR FURTHER READING

Bloom, Benjamin S., Ed., *Taxonomy of Educational Objectives. Handbook I: Cognitive Domain.* New York: David McKay Co., Inc., 1956.

Krathwohl, David R., Benjamin S. Bloom, and Bertram B. Masia. *Taxonomy of Educational Objectives. Handbook II: Affective Domain.* New York: David McKay Co., Inc., 1964.

Singer, Robert N. *Motor Learning and Human Performance.* New York: The Macmillan Co., 1968.

Vodola, Thomas M. *Individualized Physical Education Program for the Handicapped Child.* Englewood Cliffs, N.J.: Prentice-Hall, Inc., 1973.

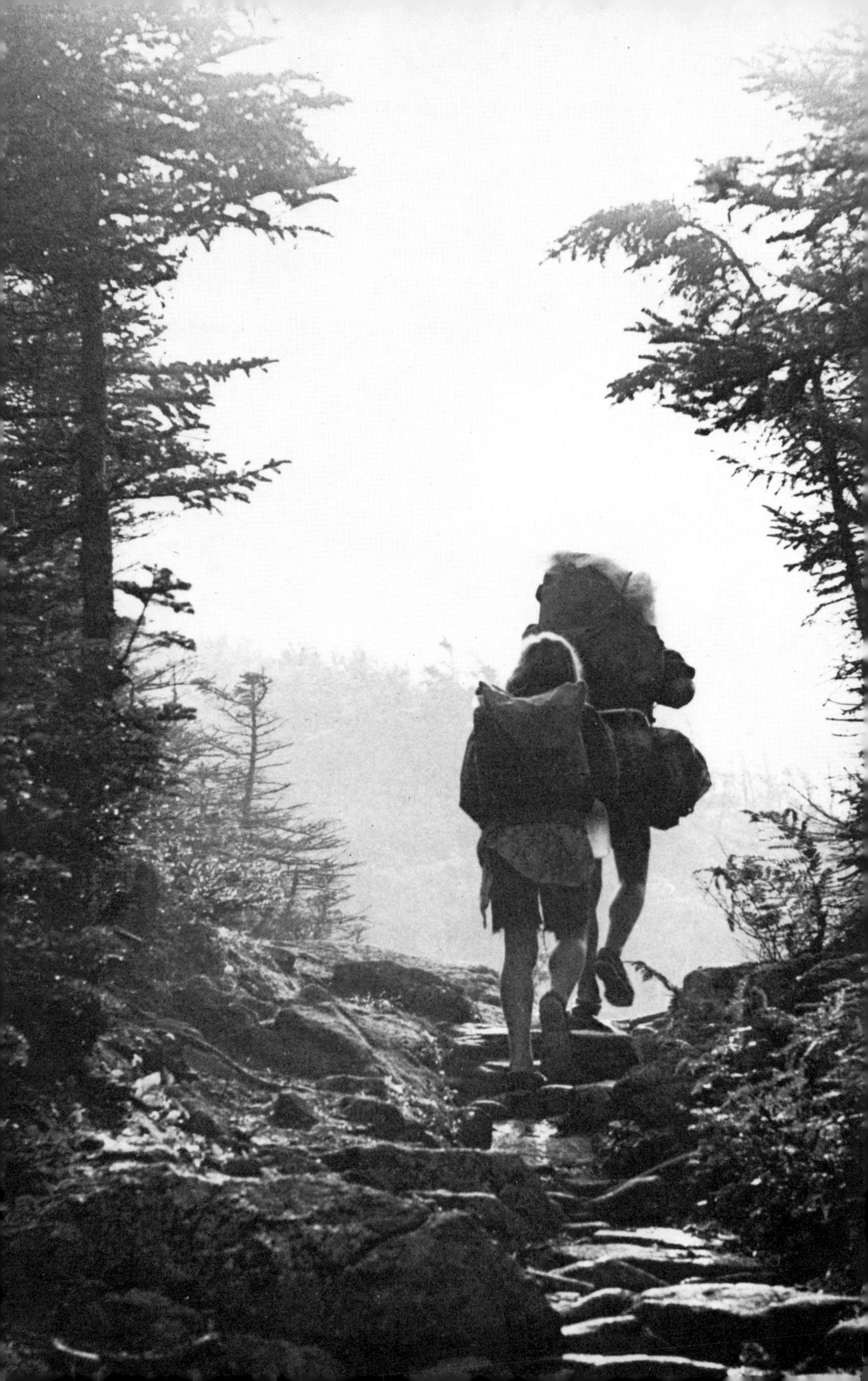

6

Self-actualization through Movement

The life of the individual is generally measured by two terms, quantitative and qualitative. The quantitative aspect of life is the time between birth and death, and thus is measured purely in terms of time. The qualitative measure of life encompasses the variety of experiences the individual encounters in the course of life. While the quantitative and qualitative aspects of life are not necessarily related, the latter usually connotes both variety and richness. In other words, a full, good life. However, as recipients of the benefits of advanced science and technology, we sometimes become lazy about seeking out new experiences, resulting in a life characterized by a chain of repetitive experiences that are narrow in scope. To give the fullest measure of quality to life, the individual must be motivated to seek out experiences that are personally fulfilling and self-actualizing. In this chapter we will investigate some of the ways in which the experiences of life can become richer and more meaningful.

THE HUMANIZING EFFECT OF A MULTIFACETED LIFE

Many activities enhance the quality of life and have a humanizing effect on the individual. Movement experiences are not the least among these activities, because they afford the individual an opportunity to engage in a pursuit that is generally favored by society.

Of late it has become increasingly difficult for man to become aware of his unique existence. He is constantly being categorized, functionalized, labeled, and numbered. He is a passive witness to the demise of his own uniqueness and to the extinction of his own being. Man is handing over his personal identity in exchange for the comfort and security afforded him in the Heideggerian they . . .man's relative aloneness in sport can provide an opportunity for seizing upon the awareness of one's unique existence.[1]

In underdeveloped societies, where life is marked by a continual struggle for subsistence and survival, it is a luxury to be able to seek out experiences that will expand life. In more developed societies, such as ours, the pursuit of new experiences that will enrich life and bring pleasure is a never-questioned phenomenon. While those in underdeveloped societies may need and desire such experiences as much as we do, fulfilling the basic needs of life must always come first if the society is to survive. Once the basic needs have been fulfilled, only then can individuals begin to pursue the experiences of life for the sake of pleasure and self-actualization. Harper said:[2]

> *. . . man must become aware of his unique existence (that he is). Man must realize that he is before he can attempt an understanding of who he is.*

The ascendence from survival-motivated activity to activity for the sake of self-actualization has perhaps best been explained by Abraham Maslow through his "Hierarchy of Needs." Understanding Maslow's needs hierarchy will help to set the framework for understanding how the individual can realize joy and fulfillment. This basic understanding is essential for all educators who believe in the humanistic goals of education. More specifically for the physical educator, this basic understanding will help to clarify the ways in which movement experiences may help to enhance the quality of life. Maslow wrote:

> *Some values are common to all (healthy) mankind, but also some other values will not be common to all mankind, but only to some types of people or to specific individuals.*[3]

MASLOW'S HIERARCHY OF NEEDS

According to Maslow, there are five levels of human needs, and he contends that the lower level needs must be met and satisfied before the individual can find gratification and satisfaction at the higher need levels.

1. William A. Harper, "Man Alone," *Quest* 12 (May 1969): 57.
2. Harper, op. cit., p. 58.
3. Abraham H. Maslow, ed., *New Knowledge in Human Values.* (Chicago: Henry Regnery Co., 1971), p. 119–136.

The five basic needs, in order from lowest to highest, are physiological needs, safety needs, love and belonging, esteem, and self-actualization. Individuals tend to ascend this ladder one rung at a time, beginning with the physiological needs on the lower-most rung, and reaching self-actualization on the upper-most Maslow writes:

It has by now been sufficiently demonstrated that the human being has, as part of his intrinsic construction, not only physiological needs, but also truly psychological ones.[4]

Let us examine each of these needs on Maslow's hierarchy individually.

Rung One: Physiological Needs

The basic human concern at the physiological need level is one of survival, and this need seems to center around securing the various nutritional elements needed for sustaining life. These nutritional elements include, for example, air, water, vitamins, minerals, and various foods. Unless the individual is given, or can secure, these basic nutritional elements, life will be inadequately sustained, and progress up the ladder will be halted. Lower level need fulfillment is dominant over higher level need fulfillment. In other words, if the individual cannot satisfy the needs of a lower level, his progress stops at that stage, and any upward movement is precluded unless or until the lower level needs have been satisfied. In addition to this, the individual will not be motivated to move to a higher level unless lower needs have been satisfied.

Rung Two: Safety Needs

At this level, the basic human concern is that of being free from danger. Maslow said:

Safety is a more prepotent, or stronger, more pressing, earlier appearing, more vital need than love, for instance, and the need for food is usually stronger than either.[5]

In their desire to achieve safety, individuals tend to form groups for mutual security and protection, because they desire a life characterized by predictability and freedom from the unknown. Once the safety needs have

4. Ibid., p. 123.
5. Ibid., p. 123.

been satisfied, the individual proceeds to the next rung on the ladder of needs.

Rung Three: Love and Belonging

On this level, the primary motivators of human behavior are the needs for love, affection, affiliation, and friendship. When the individual has reached this level, the basic physical needs on rungs one and two have been satisfied and are no longer dominant, allowing the individual to concentrate on the fulfillment of psychological needs. At levels one and two, the role of movement is oriented toward survival and safety, and movement is used solely as a tool for the fulfillment of physical needs. At the love and belonging level, which is a psychological level, movement is transformed into a means for enriching life. At this level, individuals begin to seek out interpersonal relationships, they pursue affiliations, and want to become part of a group. Achieving these goals, such as group acceptance, leads to satisfaction and fulfillment.

> Early group acceptance and self-esteem of the child stem almost solely from his appearance and ability to engage actively in play . . . Without active participation within the group, the child . . . may find personal adjustment difficult. [6]

At level three, skilled movement has the potential for becoming a common denominator that draws people together in a spirit of mutual belonging. Team-type movement activities are but one kind of experience that may function as the needed common denominator. Through such activities life becomes enriched because the individual receives satisfaction and fulfillment from group participation. Thus, the psychologically-based need for love and belonging is also fulfilled.

Rung Four: Esteem Needs

Upon fulfillment of the love and belonging need, the individual ascends one more step up the ladder in pursuit of satisfying the need for esteem, or the achievement of status within a group. Along with a desire for status, the individual also wants the other members of the group to recognize him as a self-confident, reputable individual.

> . . . the formation of personal identity takes place by the process of internalization. For example, the internalization of 'one who can walk' is one of the

6. Daniel D. Arnheim, David Auxter, and Walter C. Crowe. *Principles and Methods of Adapted Physical Education.* (St. Louis: The C.V. Mosby Co., 1973), p. 35.

many steps in child development which contributes to a more realistic self-concept and self-esteem. The growing child must, at every step, derive a vitalizing sense of actuality from the awareness that his individual way of mastering experiences is a successful variant of group identity.[7]

There are many ways in which the individual can achieve satisfaction at this needs level, and movement experiences are not the least of these ways. Because good motor skills, and the activities that develop them are themselves held in esteem by most groups, the individual who moves well and can play many games will also be looked upon favorably. If the individual is successful in activities held in high regard by the group to which he belongs, the individual will in turn be held in esteem by that same group. The development of positive self-concepts is enhanced when the individual knows that he is held in esteem by members of his peer group. Further, individuals typically gravitate toward those activities where reinforcement from others serves to at least partially fulfill the need for esteem. This perhaps helps to explain why individuals tend to enjoy doing most those things that they do best.

The fulfillment of esteem needs is particularly important for children and youth, whose feelings about the "self" still remain in the formative, plastic stage. Movement efficiency may become at least part of the means for developing a clearer sense of the "self."

In search for answers about the role of games in the physical education program of an elementary school, we must (1) try continually to gain deeper insight into the nature of games and to analyze the demands of the games on the players; (2) try to give each child ample opportunity to become competent in games play and to enjoy playing at his/her level; (3) give each child a basis for choice that does not reflect constant failure; (4) continue to try to gain insight into the child's point of view.[8]

Upon fulfillment of esteem needs compatible with the individual's desire for status within an affinity group, that individual arrives at the point where he is ready to approach the last rung on the needs hierarchy.

Rung Five: Self-actualization

In terms of the individual and his needs, self-actualization is the most intrinsically satisfying experience. When the individual has reached this stage in his development, all the lower needs levels have been satisfied,

7. Stephen V. Dillon and David D. Franks. "Open Learning Environment: Self-Identity and Coping Ability," *The Educational Forum* 39 (January 1975): 157.
8. Marie Riley, "Games and Humanism," *Journal of Physical Education and Recreation* 46 (February 1975): p. 49.

and the individual can begin to experience the freedom to choose to become the kind of person he wants to become. The self-actualizing person is the architect of his own destiny, and he is better able to achieve excellence in accord with his potential. Humanization of the individual is an outgrowth of self-actualization, which may be realized in part through the development of movement skills. Maslow wrote:

> ... it looks as if there were a single ultimate value for mankind, a far goal toward which all men strive. This is called variously ... self-actualization, self-realization, integration, psychological health, individuation, autonomy, creativity, productivity ... this amounts to realizing the potentialities of the person ... becoming fully human, everything that the person can become.[9]

MASLOW'S HIERARCHY AND MOVEMENT EXPERIENCES

In retracing Maslow's needs hierarchy, we find that movement experiences on the first two rungs, physiological needs and safety needs, are directed solely toward the fulfillment of physical needs rather than toward the needs designed to enrich and expand life. At the lower two stages of need fulfillment, then, the individual generally shows little interest in pursuing psychologically-based fulfillment. If the two lower needs levels are not adequately satisfied, then any significant motivation to pursue the three higher need levels will be lacking. Thus, we may safely assume that until the two lower need levels are satisfied, they remain dominant, and will tend to suppress the achievement of satisfaction at the higher need levels. In this regard, however, we should once again heed the words of Maslow:

> Self-actualization is a relatively achieved 'state of affairs' in a few people. In most people, however, it is rather a hope, a yearning, a drive, a 'something' wished for but not yet achieved ...[10]

Among primitive societies and relatively underdeveloped cultures there is little opportunity to fully ascend the needs ladder. These societies live a life-style almost totally dependent upon the need for survival, and thus are confined almost totally to filling the needs on rungs one and two. On the other hand, individuals living in more advanced societies and more developed cultures have more time and more freedom to pursue experiences that will help them to climb the ladder toward self-actualization. Life in the more advanced and developed cultures is more conducive to the pursuit and eventual achievement of the higher levels of the hierarchy of needs. Movement experiences as a factor in the enrichment of life is

9. Maslow, op. cit., p. 123.
10. Maslow, op. cit., p. 130.

*To give the fullest measure of quality to life, the individual must be
motivated to seek out experiences that are personally fulfilling and
self-actualizing.*

especially pertinent for these latter cultures and the people who live in
them.

The pursuit of an active life-style is one way to enrich and broaden
life, and therefore ascend upward toward the ultimate goal of self-
actualization. When an individual can communicate with others and
relate to them through movement, then he has also achieved the means for
satisfying the needs for love and belonging, for esteem, and for self-
actualization. Movement, and more especially skilled movement, adds

dimension to life by increasing the potential for knowing not only other individuals, but knowing the self as well. To conclude with the words of Maslow is perhaps most appropriate:

> Achieving basic-need gratifications gives us many peak experiences, each of which are absolute delights, perfect in themselves, and needing no more than themselves to validate life.[11]

THE NEED TO PLAY

Movement experiences become enrichment factors for the individual because they seem to be basic, natural ingredients of life. One theory of play that has been called the "recapitulation theory" suggests that man has genetically inherited a need for play experiences. The recapitulation theory suggests further that historically man tends to repeat, or recapitulate, the fundamental activities of his ancestors, and that play is included among these activities.[12]

Play experiences, the overwhelming majority of which are founded on movement, are very likely a part of the natural day-to-day needs of individuals. The recapitulation theory would therefore seem to be especially valid beginning at the love and belonging hierarchical needs level. In spite of the recognized need for play experiences as a part of daily living, it would seem that many adults have forgotten how to play. This is due, at least in part, to our technology-based culture. The individual who does not play, significantly narrows the range of experiences that will help him to enrich his life. It seems ironic that this should be the case when our modern world offers so many opportunities, in spite of and because of technology, to engage in activities that will help to enrich life. Bates comments on this paradox and irony:

> We now have, at least in the countries with 'advanced' economies, an abundance of goods and services for everyone . . . We have a wide variety of machines to replace physical labor, giving leisure time to all . . . Yet our time has also been called the 'age of anxiety.' We have goods and services, but we don't quite know what to do with them. We have leisure, but we are not sure how to use it for the greatest satisfactions . . . Utopia is here—and we are afraid . . . The problem of our age then, is to gain the wisdom we need to use our growing power intelligently.[13]

---

11. Maslow, op. cit., p. 124.
12. Franklin Parker, "Sport, Play, and Physical Education in Cultural Perspective," *Journal of Health, Physical Education, and Recreation* 36 (April 1965): 80.
13. Marston Bates, *Man in Nature.* (Englewood Cliffs, New Jersey: Prentice-Hall Inc., 1964), p. 107.

Bates' disarmingly accurate observation provides a sad commentary on the ways in which we have failed to adjust to our world. It would seem that we have failed to come to grips with life, and in so doing have cheated ourselves of many opportunities to enrich our lives and live them to the fullest.

PROBLEMS AND REDIRECTIONS IN PHYSICAL EDUCATION

The fact that movement experiences have not been accepted more universally as enriching experiences may be an indictment of physical education and physical educators. It is the movement professionals who help society-at-large to draw conclusions about the relevance of movement experiences to modern life. Although we, as a culture, appear to be highly interested in skilled movement, we seem to be living in the age of the spectator rather than the age of the participant. Perhaps physical education has failed to get across the message that movement is an essential part of life, that it enriches and enhances life, and that it has direct carry-over value to the areas of physical well-being, recreational and leisure-time pursuits. Gerber says:

> Contemporary physical educators are searching for new meanings and purposes consistent with our new times. For us the contribution of non-physical educators concerned with the growth of education in general provide insights that are fundamental to the evolution of physical education.[14]

In order for us to justifiably claim that movement enriches all of life, there must be come redirection of professional efforts. In recent years, one welcome redirection has been the emphasis on lifetime activities, those movement activities in which the person can engage throughout life. These activities include, for example, tennis, golf, swimming, bowling, horseback riding, bicycling, skiing, and jogging. One characteristic of these and other lifetime activities is that the individual may set participation limits based on his own needs and capabilities. Also, a pleasurable and satisfying experience is not precluded by the necessity of enlisting large numbers of people to form teams. The lifetime activities tend to be participated in on an individual basis, or in company with one or two other individuals as desired.

The enrichment of life through participation in lifetime activities is one means of circumventing the dilemma to which Bates has alluded.

14. Ellen W. Gerber, "Learning and Play: Insights of Educational Protagonists," *Quest* 11 (December 1968):49.

Lifetime activities continue to enrich life throughout the years because they afford the individual a wide variety of opportunities for joyful, self-actualizing experiences. Moreover, they are truly re-creative, and promote associations with others which help stimulate the humanizing process.

Physical Play as a Diversion from Routine

Play, as an enriching life force, offers stimulating diversion from tedium and routinization of life. Implicit in the pursuit of diversion is the opportunity to experience a psychological release from those parts of life which are devoid of rewarding experiences and personal satisfaction; those experiences which are, in effect, dehumanizing.

For many individuals, life is not only tedious, but sedentary as well, This state is often referred to as "getting into a rut," and is the antithesis of a full, rich life. Perhaps even more significantly, inactivity may prove damaging to both the mental and the physical health of the individual. It is a biological fact of life that the human body depends on activity of a physical nature for continued physical well-being. Tedium often, on the other hand, results in tension, and the build-up of tension in the absence of socially acceptable means of release, can be hazardous to continued mental health.

> . . .exercise is a basic need of life. This need is deeply imbedded in man's biologic nature as well as his attitudes and psychologic urges by the countless ages during which the evolutionary processes operated to make him as active moving being . . . man is stuck with his heritage both from the standpoint of his heredity and his environment. He can change neither-only his mode of living in that environment.[15]

Dr. William C. Menninger, head of the world famous Menninger Clinic, has articulated the value of movement experiences, particularly with regard to adults, as relievers of psychological stress and tension. According to Menninger, many people fail to realize that play experiences have values other than fun. He suggests that the important values of play experiences lie in the diversion from routine and release from emotional stress. Menninger says that fun is only a relatively incidental outcome of the play experience, and that individuals with good mental health tend to supplement their daily routine with voluntary, enjoyable activities. Such individuals, though often busily engaged in other pursuits, make time for play. Menninger believes that the satisfaction which results from these

15. Harold M. Barrow, *Man and His Movement: Principles of His Physical Education.* (Philadelphia: Lea and Febiger, 1973), p. 130.

voluntary play experiences fulfills deep-seated psychological demands which transcend the superficiality of fun for the sake of fun.[16]

Among the problems of individuals caught up in a tedious and sedentary life is the fact that many of these individuals either do not know how, or have forgotten how, to play, and that they become passive spectators who play vicariously or not at all. The recent phenomenal rise in numbers of spectators attending sporting events appears to indicate a rather definite trend. Menninger believes that the individual with a healthy personality shuns play that is vicarious or nonpurposeful; rather, he tends to take his play seriously. Menninger asserts that there is evidence which suggests that an inability or unwillingness to play is evidence of insecurity and a personality disorder.[17] Moreover, Ulrich has written that:

> With regard to the student's social desires, research indicates that those individuals who move with freedom and security tend to be adjusted individuals in other aspects of their being.[18]

Physical Well-being Helps to Enrich Life

Continued participation in movement experiences throughout life helps to enrich life by indirect means, as we have seen. Also, participation through the adult years, after formal school experiences in physical education have ended, helps the individual to maintain a body that is physically capable of varied experiences. However, the achievements of our technological age tend to weaken the individual's motivation to participate in physical activity as an on-going facet of life.

Contemporary society, blessed with unprecedented scientific and technological breakthroughs, basks in comfort, luxury, and laziness, and each of these connotes a passive, inactive life-style. Contemporary society runs the risk of becoming hypnotized by passivity in much the same way a child becomes obsessed with a new toy. Technology, however, encroaches on life in very subtle ways. Because man is caught up by the unprecedented, rapid adoption of passivity as a way of life he often fails to see far enough ahead to realize the consequences.

An organism will be incomplete if it attempts to adapt to a life-style for which it was not desiged or intended. Man is designed for movement, and he will not be able to adapt comfortably or fully to a life of ease, no matter how attractive that idea may seem. While a life-style of ease is immediately satisfying, in the long run the individual may be betrayed both physically and mentally. The diseases and disorders associated with what

16. William C. Menninger, "Recreation and Mental Health," *Recreation* (November, 1948):342–343.

17. Ibid.

18 .Celeste Ulrich, "The Tomorrow Mind," *JOHPER* 35 (October 1964): 83.

some falsely believe to be "the good life" are increasing, and this increase seems to be in direct proportion to man's growing obsession with spectatorism. The "good life" is, in this connotation, a false prophet, luring man into sacrificing a rich and varied existence for a life of ease now, but disenchantment later.

Daily Living and Its Effect on Movement

The life-style and personality of the individual is often reflected as the individual participates in movement experiences. The intensely aggressive and competitive individual tends to be that way both within and outside of movement activities. For those who compete in this intense manner in play, there may be little real diversion from daily experiences in life, which for the same individual may be equally as intense. Perhaps such individuals have never learned to relax, or more specifically, they have never been taught or learned how to use movement as a form of diversion and relaxation. On this general topic Martens writes:

Perhaps sport or physical activity may help in controlling aggression but it is not a catharsis, nor does it provide relief for instinctively generated tensions or excess energy.[19]

Perhaps more individuals would pursue movement experiences as diversions from daily routine, and hence use these experiences as recreative experiences if they understood the concept of recreation and the use of movement experiences as a tool for recreation. Recreation, or "re-creation," meaning "to make new again," can occur only if the experience is a real alternative to tedium and routine. Truly recreative experiences do not reflect aggression, competition, or tension; rather, they are alternative experiences that help to ameliorate tension and enrich the life of the individual.

It is unfortunate that the rigors and tensions of daily living are not just going to get up and disappear. On the contrary, the tensions of life seem to be increasing and steadily gaining momentum. This has been brought about by at least two major causes: (1) although science and technology have brought about some very positive and far-reaching achievements, they have also created the tools for and brought about a life-style that breeds aggression, competition, and tension; (2) people have left rural and semi-rural environments and moved to cities and large metropolitan areas in search of a better, easier life. City living in itself,

---

19. Rainer Martens, *Social Psychology and Physical Activity.* (New York: Harper & Row, 1975), p. 125.

where masses of people may have little room to breathe and less to recreate, tends to foster the development of pressure and tension.

While science and technology have helped to increase human productivity, the need to produce even more, and to produce faster, nurtures the development of aggressive and competitive behavior. In what is probably a related occurance, there is an increase in the number of people with mental and physical disorders caused by the unrelenting emotional stresses of daily life. The facility with which the individual can successfully cope with such stresses may depend largely upon his personal repertoire of alternative, recreative, noncompetitive experiences. These experiences can provide the critical means by which the individual can relax, recreate, and achieve personal fulfillment and satisfaction. The building blocks for such experiences can be laid down in physical education through programs that stress the recreative movement experiences that have lifetime carry-over value.

Alternatives

Where do we go from here with regard to the place of movement experiences as essential factors in achieving a full and satisfying life? First, physical education must remain firmly committed to the principle of providing those movement experiences that will enrich and enhance life. We must then identify those movement experiences that help to build feelings of self-worth, adequacy, personal fulfillment, satisfaction and pleasure in and for the individual. We must also seek to determine the specific ways in which we can maximize the desired effect of each activity on the individual involved. Only then will movement experiences become facilitators of an enriched life; and only then will movement experiences become efficient and effective tools of humanization.

Just as no two pupils are alike, so are no two paths to personal enrichment and fulfillment alike. Each individual has his own unique characteristics and potentials, and each will seek, with varying degrees of success, to find fulfillment in his own unique and very personal way. While the paths to self-actualization are diverse, the goals are universal and humanistically oriented.

Cratty has called movement, " ... the important expressive aspect of the human personality ..."[20] For those who view education from a humanistic perspective, there remains the task of discovering how to best guide students through the vast array of potentially satisfying learning experiences. It must be remembered, though, that because of individual

20. Bryant J. Cratty, Movement, Perception and Thought. (Palo Alto, Calif.: Peek Publications, 1970), p. 2.

differences, even the most potentially satisfying experience may not be inherently or automatically the best experience for each individual.

> ... *motivation, is primarily a result of hereditary endowment, and while the developmental pattern is similar for the whole species, each child, because of his unique hereditary endowment, will follow this pattern at his own rate. This explains why all children are not ready for all the same experiences at the same time.*[21]

Any given experience that might be satisfying for one individual might have an opposite and stressful effect on another. Whether or not a given experience will be pleasurable and satisfying is determined largely by how the individual relates to and personally identifies with the experience.

Educators, and physical educators especially, who subscribe to the goals of a humanistic education will make a strong attempt to identify the various ways in which different experiences affect different individuals. For only in this way can we identify the divergent roads by which a full life can be achieved. Although the task may seem monumental, any effort that best serves the needs and interests of students is an effort worthy of pursuit.

SUMMARY

Our discussion in this chapter was concerned with the ways in which the life of the individual could be enriched by participation in movement activities as an on-going life-style. We have pointed out that once formal schooling, and therefore a formal physical education program, has ended, the individual must continue to seek out movement experiences if life is to be lived enjoyably and in a satisfying manner.

The problems encountered by modern man living a high-paced life in a high-paced world have been cited, and we have attempted to show how the individual can use movement as a tool for coping with the tensions and pressures of modern life. Further, Maslow's steps to self-actualization, which are in reality a blueprint for living, have been summarized and discussed. We have also noted the increase in spectatorism and its relationship to a decrease in spontaneous play and recreation. To draw the discussion together, it is worthwhile to note this commentary on play by Kretchmar and Harper:

> It was once asked what would happen to play if it were shown to have absolutely no beneficial results. Would play terminate? Once its useful ends were negated would its captivating effect on man likewise end? It is con-

21. Charles B. Corbin, ed., *A Textbook of Motor Development.* (Dubuque, Iowa: Wm. C. Brown Co. Publishers, 1973), p. 8.

tended that play would not cease. It would, in fact, continue as before, perhaps with even more success because of its less artificial place in man's life.[22]

SUGGESTIONS FOR FURTHER READING

Maslow, Abraham. *Motivation and Personality*. New York: Haper & Row, 1970.
"Quest for Tomorrow." *Quest* January 1974.
Sharkey, Brian J. *Physiology and Physical Activity*. New York: Harper & Row, 1975.
"The Language of Movement." *Quest* January 1975.

22. R. Scott Kretchmar and William A. Harper. "Why Does Man Play?" *JOHPER* 40 (March 1969): p. 58.

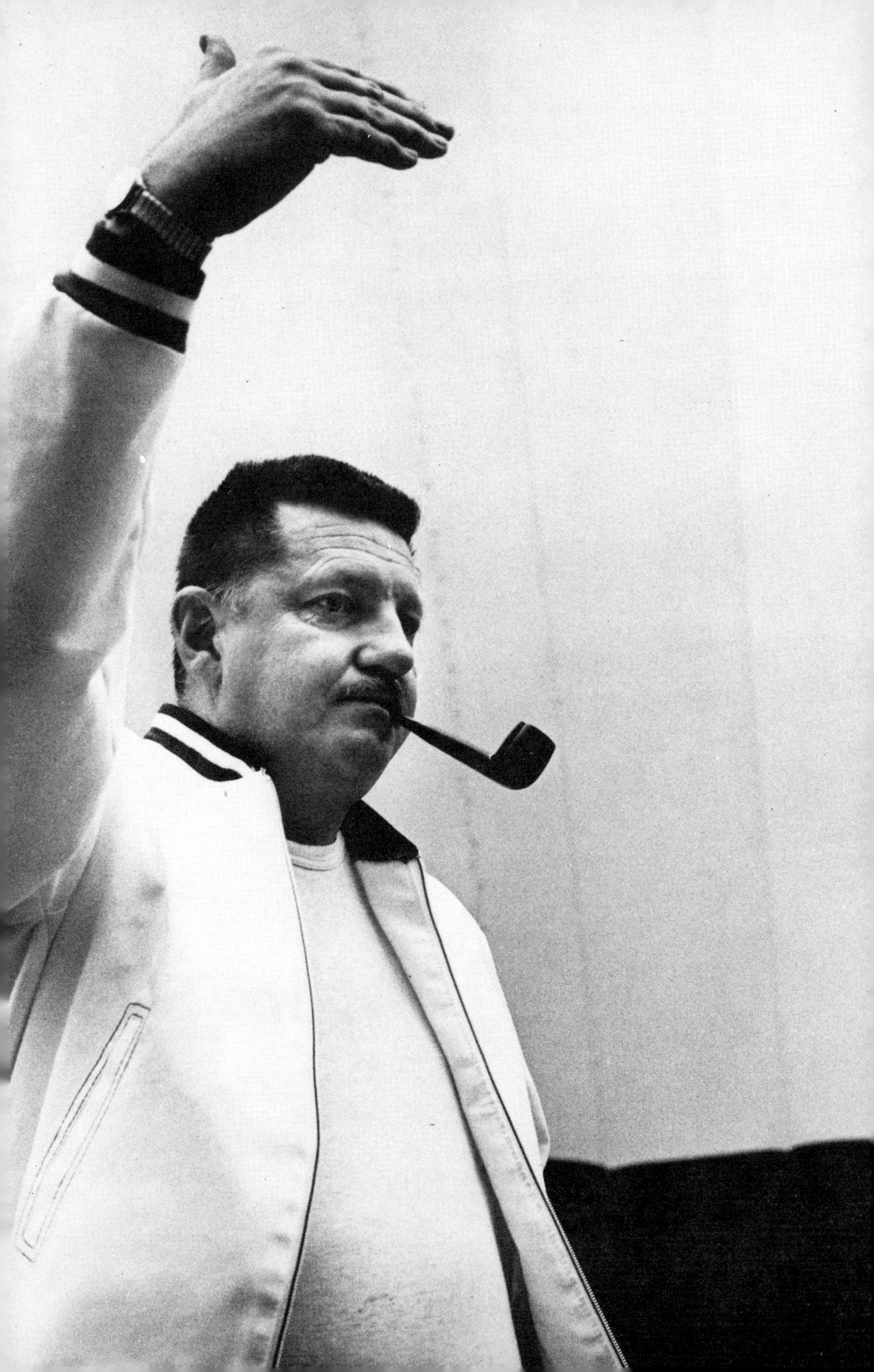

7

Stereotyping the Physical Educator

The term *stereotype* refers to groups or persons who are seen in the same context by the rest of society, a context that is often derogatory. Members of stereotyped groups seem to have no individuality—instead they seem to have adopted a common group identity. Anyone who is truly an individual but who is even peripherally associated with a group that has been stereotyped tends to be stereotyped also, in spite of the fact that the stereotype may be totally wrong as applied to that individual. According to the dictionary definition, individuals who are stereotypes are " . . . lacking originality or individuality."[1] Individuals who are stereotyped are usually characterized as having been cast out of the same mold, and the adage that "once you've seen one, you've seen them all" is generally applied.

Stereotypes, much like caricatures, tend to be exaggerations of reality. Individuals who are victims of stereotyping are frequently defensive, and sometimes develop attitudes and behavior patterns that only help to perpetuate the stereotype. While not all stereotypes are untrue or even undesirable, many are born out of ignorance and prejudice. In the latter case, the individuals who have been stereotyped often suffer from a lack of self-esteem and self-worth, and they suffer further because a derogatory stereotype sometimes makes the individual socially unacceptable.

In this chapter we will discuss some of the stereotypes that have grown up around physical education and physical educators, and will

1. *Webster's New Collegiate Dictionary.* (Springfield, Mass.: G. & C. Merriam Co., 1953), p. 831.

attempt to come to some determination of how the poor stereotypes can be ameliorated.

EXAMPLES OF STEREOTYPES IN PHYSICAL EDUCATION AND SPORT

Some of the stereotypes that have grown up around physical education and sport are far from derogatory, but they may be misleading, since we have said that stereotypes tend to lump people together into a class. Thus, gymnasts and dancers are often stereotyped as graceful people who tend to be rather artistic, creative, and innovative. Yet not all individuals who dance or enjoy attempting the various gymnastic skills are graceful or artistic or creative or innovative. Some dancers and some gymnasts are not particularly proficient in movement, yet the pleasure they derive from what they do makes up for any deficiencies they may have. Yet, when we hear that a certain individual dances or is a gymnast, we also immediately place upon them the stereotype commonly associated with that activity.

Other stereotypes concerned with physical education and sport are not only misleading, but may be negative and inhumane as well. For example, football players are often stereotyped as being "dumb," hockey players as undereducated, and it is sometimes said that baseball catchers "wear the tools of ignorance." Male dancers are frequently said to be less than masculine, and some people contend that female athletes lack femininity. Yet we know that in order to play football well the player needs to be highly efficient both mentally and physically; that many hockey players not coincidentally are college graduates, and some have even completed graduate school; and that the baseball catcher is really the architect of each game. Also, the strenuous and demanding athletic aspects of dance are just now beginning to be recognized, and the realization is only now coming about that women athletes approach sport from a feminine viewpoint.

The preceeding are but a few examples of stereotyping in physical education and sport. Most stereotypes have an adverse effect upon individuals and sometimes turn people away from physical activity because they fear they will be harmed by an adverse stereotype. This has served physical education and sport poorly, because a majority of the stereotypes are incorrect and unearned.

PHYSICAL EDUCATORS AND THE STEREOTYPE

In some quarters, physical educators of either sex are referred to as "jocks," a stereotype connoting crude and dumb. Specifically, as applied to female physical educators, the term "jock" has also been used to infer a lack of femininity. In fact, the jock stereotype is such a common one that physical education undergraduates and physical educators as well are sometimes heard to use the term in reference to themselves. This is a defensive reaction, for how can a derogatory remark be a personal insult if you apply it to yourself before someone else can? Such reactions and attitudes only help to perpetuate and nurture negative stereotypes and self-images.

The stereotyping of physical educators that comes from society at large has caused some physical educators to develop feelings of inferiority about their educational speciality. The intensity of much of the stereotyping has resulted in a self-fulfilling prophecy in that as physical educators, many of us really believe that our stereotype is accurate. We have come to believe that we are indeed engaged in teaching an inferior subject in comparison to the rest of the school curriculum.

Unfortunately, the negative stereotypes concerned with physical education and physical educators are not going to go away simply through wishful thinking. Rather than hoping for a miracle cure, we need to develop ways of positive thinking that will prevent further stereotyping and dilute the existing stereotypes. Before talking in terms of what can be done though, let us investigate the reasons why the stereotypes concerned with physical education and physical educators have evolved in the first place.

Stereotypes and Credibility Gaps

In some respects, physical educators may be unwittingly nurturing their own negative stereotypes by failing to practice what they preach. Physical educators adhere to the axiom that lifelong participation in movement experiences is not only desirable but necessary as a step toward personal fulfillment. Physical educators are often heard to suggest that participation in movement experiences helps the individual to become more well-rounded. The credibility gap occurs when we realize that many physical educators are not themselves well-rounded individuals.

Many of us do not ourselves seek experiences that are concerned with anything in the daily newspapers beyond the sports sections. Many of us watch television only when the telecast has to do with athletics, and read only those books and magazines that have something to do with sports. Many physical educators seem to live rather narrow lives that are bounded by the gym, playing fields, and locker room, and we cannot, in view of such an existence, hold our own in social conversations that go beyond the world of sport. Thus, what we propose for others we frequently fail to do ourselves. Where we suggest that movement experiences are essential for a full life, we tend to forget that for us, education through the physical connotes more than a life centered almost entirely around movement.

Physical educators, like their clients, must also try to become well-rounded individuals. Physical educators must seek out nonmovement pursuits. Any less reciprocal commitment by physical educators is hypocritical, and tends to widen the credibility gap while reinforcing the stereotype.

It is not really so difficult to understand how and why some physical educators tend to limit themselves to the world of movement, and seem to forget that there are other interests and other experiences to be investigated and enjoyed. For some physical educators, the world of movement tends to be almost totally engrossing, and it becomes all they need or desire in the way of self-actualization. For such individuals, the usually polarized concepts of work and play seem to blend together and become almost indistinguishable. Thus, by their own doing, these individuals present themselves as being out-of-step, aloof, and narrow in their interests. Is it any wonder then why individuals like this are sometimes stereotyped as being non- or anti-intellectual? While they may indeed be highly intelligent, they set themselves as a class apart, and unwittingly give credence to a stereotype.

If the foregoing is in fact a partial yet plausible explanation for the stereotyping of physical educators as "jocks" with limited intellectual interests, what then can we do about this image, and in what vein should we respond to the detractors of the field and its specialists?

Criticism and the Defensive Reaction

In the face of criticism, whether earned or incorrectly applied, many people tend to go on the defensive, blaming others, the circumstances, or by implying that they cannot control incidents or the conditions that have justified the criticism. Sometimes, physical educators go on the defensive by failing to respond at all, and this only perpetuates the problem and the stereotype. We have all witnessed the physical educator who associates only with other physical educators, or who makes it a policy never to stray far from the gym or playing field into other parts of the school building. These are defense mechanisms by which criticism may be avoided, but they are also reactions which do nothing to correct a stereotype.

Also, many physical educators feel that they must apoligize for the fact that education of the physical is one of the goals of physical education. In developing defensive replies to criticisms of this goal, physical educators themselves fail to take into account the activity needs of the human body. As with any complex and highly sophisticated machine, the human body functions best when it is well cared for and correctly used.

There is little need, nor is there room, in physical education for self-deprecating and defensive reactions to criticisms coming from outside physical education. The critics and criticisms of physical education as a curricular subject have been around for a long time. Criticism is good and necessary in many ways because it helps to keep people on their toes and involved. Without properly placed criticism there would be no change and no progress because we would all become very complacent and locked into the status quo. That would inevitably lead to a very dull world populated by very dull people.

Where criticism is misplaced, however, any field needs people who can respond without resorting to dangerous and self-defeating defensive reactions. In physical education we need physical educators who are proud of what they do, and who can articulate why they do it. We need physical educators who can verbalize the necessity for meaningful movement and physical activity in the life of the individual.

Physical educators who are self-confident and take pride in their educational speciality, and who can articulate both the historical and modern relevance of movement will do much to alleviate external criticism of the field. By adequately responding to the issues, physical educators can face the challenge rather than attempt to rationalize it away, or hide from it, and they can help physical education to take another step toward achieving that much sought-after professional status.

The Need to Be Articulate

We have suggested that physical educators need to develop the ability to speak, and speak well. There are two major reasons why movement specialists need to be able to articulate and verbalize about their field. This need may be greater for movement specialists than it is for people in nonmovement related specialities in education.

For some reason, many people who are outside of physical education tend to stereotype physical educators as being incapable of meaningful verbal communication and expression. This stereotype is seemingly not ever applied to other educators whose fields are looked on as more academic and, by association, more intellectual than is physical education. Very possibly, the subject areas other than physical education are stereotyped as being refined and scholarly while physical education is the antithesis of this. Thus, when people in physical education fail to communicate articulately, for any reason, the stereotype is reinforced. Surprisingly enough, when a physical educator displays ease and proficiency in verbal communications, those who have stereotyped the field seem to register shock and surprise that a physical educator could be so articulate! This upgrading of our public image presents a tremendous challenge to the field.

Secondly, movement specialists are frequently called upon to speak in public, for example at such diverse gatherings as school board meetings, at PTA meetings, and sometimes as guests on local radio and television shows. The ability to speak easily and correctly, in other words, to be articulate, goes a very long way toward improving the elusive public image of physical educators and physical education.

The Sedentary Physical Educator

It is indeed hypocritical for physical educators to attempt to educate about the lifetime benefits of physical activity if they themselves are sedentary, or overweight, or obviously poorly conditioned. Unfortunately, the critical public eye seems to focus on those physical educators who portray an image directly opposite to what the public expects and deserves to see. Certainly, the majority of physical educators are physically attractive, take good care of their bodies, and balance the demands of their work with adequate amounts of rest, exercise, and recreation. But consider for a moment the kind of image presented by those few physical educators who are, because of overindulgence and self-neglect, sedentary and very probably obese. Such individuals provide at least some of the raw material for drawing adverse stereotypes, and they help in no small way to further damage the image of physical education.

Because physical education is not yet a profession, there is little of a tangible nature except for peer pressure that can be done to remove the incompetent, uncaring individual from the field. Among doctors, who are professionals, the American Medical Association serves as a watchdog agency, as does the American Bar Association for lawyers. There is no such organization to which educators can turn for guidance and assistance. We must, instead, attempt to educate from within so that we impress on all physical educators and prospective physical educators the need to live personal lives that are in line with the stated objectives of physical education. We must educate that to do less is harmful to our self-image as physical educators, and is moreover a mockery of the field.

The Parade of the Animals

Physical education and athletics are often considered by the public to be one and the same, particularly in cases where a physical educator is also actively engaged in coaching some varsity sport. In recent years, the practice of assigning animal nicknames to teams and players on those teams has become more and more prevalent. While it is undisputed that the names of certain animals connote strength and virility, such as tiger and bear, it is unfortunate that associated terms like "crusher" and "killer" are also commonly appended to players. To earn such a title is often an honor, and is frequently an honor bestowed on only the best and most aggressive players.

There seems to be widespread use of such supposedly motivating phrases as "Kill 'em, tigers!" throughout the world of sport. The use and acceptance of such phraseology is unfortunate, and even more appalling because such usage sometimes filters down to the physical education class level. This does not help to dignify physical education or to improve the image of physical educators who have adopted the use of such language with their students. In fact, the use of this kind of terminology is offensive to much of the public, and does little to enhance the credibility of the humanistic aspect of physical education. Physical education and physical educators are probably less responsible for the phenomenon of the animal image than is athletics, and professional athletics in particular. But we must realize that physical education is nonetheless affected through guilt by association.

The Machismo Ethic

The word "machismo", implying strength, assertiveness, and masculinity, is of Spanish origin. In Spain and in many other countries the male is expected to be aggressive and domineering. If he is not so inclined, his masculinity is suspect, and he is said to lack machismo. This term has recently come into prominence in sport and an athlete is said to have machismo if he is virile, courageous, and aggressive, and most especially if he believes in playing to win at any personal cost. In the machismo ethic, any behavior not specifically descriptive of what is expected of the male is relegated to females. Thus, the machismo frame of reference is very definitely a stereotype, and one that ends to separate acceptable masculine behavior from acceptable feminine behavior. There is very little allowance made for the shadings and nuances of behavior that cross over the strictly delineated male-female lines. A male dancer is as unacceptable in the machismo ethic as is the female shot putter. Neither male dancers nor female athletes can achieve machismo in the purest definition of that term.

The desire for machismo among males creates a powerful motivation for participation in physical education and sports. These areas become a naturally fertile ground for those in pursuit of machismo because courage, prowess, physical skill, and aggressiveness are encouraged and rewarded. Many males are drawn to physical education and sport for no other reason than that through them, a highly desirable male stereotype, or machismo, can be achieved.

Girls and women have never been encouraged to become actively engaged in physical education and sport in machismo-conscious cultures. Even in cultures that have not actively pursued the machismo ethic, girls and women have not really been encouraged to be more than semi-active participants, and they have been guided into physical activities in accordance with arbitrarily designated and stereotyped sex roles. In effect, the machismo ethic has tended to stereotype as "masculinized" those women who choose to defy their assigned roles in physical education and sports. The machismo ethic has manifested itself in sex role dilemmas for both males and females alike.

The humanistic aim of physical education is the direct opposite of the objectives of machismo. Humanism demands that each individual have full opportunity to pursue those activities that are of interest so that each individual will have full opportunity to achieve his or her own unique potential. We must, as a humanistic society, attempt to reject the machismo ethic so that individuals will not be locked into stereotyped roles which they may neither desire nor be comfortable with. This is not a problem of physical education and sport alone, but rather one which has an effect on large segments of society.

NEW NAME-NEW IMAGE?

Some physical educators have contended that much of physical education's problems with a stereotyped image rests in the title "physical education." They feel that the word "physical" has a somewhat less than respectable ring when applied to an academic field. They also suggest that individuals outside of physical education have drawn the implication that "physical" education is not quite so worthy of human pursuit as are subjects that are primarily intellectual, such as English or mathematics. There are some individuals both within and outside of the field of physical education who advocate a change of name. They feel that the phrase "physical" education inadvertantly implies *education of the physical* only while disregarding the very important concept of *education through the physical*. They further suggest that the title "physical education" unwittingly draws attention away from the "whole man concept," and instead serves to distort and misrepresent the real nature of physical education.

Currently, the advocates of a new name for physical education are having some influence in effecting change. Some college and university physical education departments have either retitled themselves or are seriously contemplating doing so. Among the new names currently in favor are: sport science, kinesiology, and alternatively, either biokinetics or human kinetics. These names, and others of a similar nature are thought by many people to be more accurate and to describe the field better than does the name "physical education."

Sport Science

Because the domain of movement draws upon all of the major categories of science, such as physical science, the biological sciences and the social sciences, some leaders in physical education feel that the field should retitle itself "sport science." The respective bodies of knowledge of each of the sciences relate directly to physical education, and in fact, physical education draws directly from these sciences in preparing future teachers. But is that all? Prior to the time the name of "sport science" was proposed, Henry wrote:

There is indeed a scholarly field of knowledge basic to physical education. It is constituted of certain portions of such diverse fields as anatomy, physics and physiology, cultural anthropology, history and sociology, as well as psychology. The focus of attention is on the study of man as an individual . . .[2]

Kinesiology

There are those who advocate calling physical education "kinesiology," since kinesiology has its roots in two Greek words which combined mean "the study of movement." The proponents of kinesiology feel that movement study, in its broadest context, implies not only the physical aspects of movement, but rather all aspects of movement as each relates to the entire spectrum of human movement. Yet on the surface, the single word kinesiology appears to be limited in descriptive scope, where depth and breadth are the needs. Meyers has warned that:

Unless physical educators apply the concepts of the related fields of anatomy, physiology, and kinesiology, they are no more than lay teachers, not truly 'professional.'[3]

Biokinetics or Human Kinetics

The term "bio," meaning "life," and the term "kinetics," meaning "movement," appeal to some individuals as an alternative name for physical education. Advocates of biokinetics feel that this choice is broader and less limiting than is "physical" education, and that biokinetics implies a multidimensional approach. Those who prefer the title human kinetics say that this title speaks more expressly in terms of the study of human movement and all of its ramifications. But as Ariel has written:

Historically, little was known about the physical components of human movement . . . We continue teaching many activities without scientific evidence as to their effectiveness for meeting biological objectives . . .[4]

WHAT'S IN A NAME?

The proposed new names for physical education as described in the preceding sections are but a limited sample of the efforts to change the

2. Franklin M. Henry, "The Discipline of Physical Education," *JOHPER* 37: September 1964.
3. Edward J. Meyers, "Exercise Physiology in Secondary Schools: A Three Dimensional Approach," *JOHPER* 46 (January 1975): 30.
4. Ariel, Gideon B. "Physical Education: 2001?" *Quest* XXI: 49–52, January 1974. p. 50.

title of the field to one that will be more appropriate and more acceptable. The desired outcome of a change of name is a more accurate portrayal of physical education's efforts to study, serve, and fulfill human needs as they relate to movement.

The Argument for Change

Part of the name-change efforts stem from an attempt by some physical educators to upgrade the field and present an improved image to the public. Also, since physical education has the humanistic goal of fulfilling human potential through movement, supporters of a new name feel that "physical education" is simply not dignified enough or expressive enough. The physical is certainly involved when human potential is fulfilled through movement, but of equal significance are certain of the non-physical outcomes. Physical education, as noted previously, also has developmental objectives that relate to the mental and social aspects of life, in other words, education through the physical.

If a change of name can effectively enlighten the public's perception of the complete mission of physical education, then a name change will be of benefit. Physical education will grow in stature if a name change will enhance its image and dignity in the public eye. If the public is caused to hold physical education in higher esteem through a change of name, then inaccurate and limiting stereotypes might be replaced by new levels of understanding and appreciation. Thus, as the image of physical education grows, so too will grow the image and esteem accorded physical educators.

The Argument against a Name Change

The proponents of the status quo see honor rather than limitations in the name "physical education." They contend that as physical beings, no other subject in formal education serves people as meaningfully as does physical education. They assert that because we live largely sedentary lives that we are in dire need of physical activity, and that a field engaged in providing these activities—physical education—is already appropriately named. They go on to note that the title "physical" education is not limiting, but instead directly implies the mission of the field and affords the desired and proper image.

Further, and perhaps more importantly, those who would prefer the field to continue to adhere to the name "physical education" feel that there is nothing at all to be gained by a mere change of name. These individuals contend that it is not the name, but the service rendered that is of primary importance. They feel very strongly that the current agitation for a change of name is nothing more than a defensive reaction to public criticism and stereotyping. What is needed, they contend, is a concerted and positive effort to improve the quality of what we do and how we do it.

In support of this very important point concerning the provision of a quality physical education Jewett and her colleagues wrote:

> The current status of physical education teaching calls for significant educational change. One of the prerequisites to such change is the development and utilization of a conceptual framework relevant to today's and tomorrow's curricular decisions.[5]

We must bear in mind that, no matter what it is eventually called, physical education will still tend to be negatively stereotyped unless it finds a way to satisfy the demands and expectations of its critics. Efforts to change the name of the field must be founded on the valid premise of better service to humanity. Just as there are no short cuts to quality, there is no short cut to acquiring dignity, esteem, an acceptable image, and professional status.

SUMMARY

In this chapter we have looked at some of the stereotypes that surround physical education, physical educators, and the associated world of sport. We have defined and described the common stereotypes and have attempted to show their effect on physical education's public image. We have shown how physical educators, by their own actions, sometimes help to perpetuate negative stereotypes. We have also talked about some common cultural beliefs that lead to stereotyping.

Also, we have tried to pin point the actions that might be taken to dilute and eventually eradicate the negative stereotypes concerned with physical education. We have reached the conclusion that change must come from within, and that stereotypes will be replaced by an acceptable image only when we have finally determined how to improve the quality of our programs and our methods of presenting them to the public.

SUGGESTIONS FOR FURTHER READING

Longo, Paul, "Opening the Door to the Open Classroom." Kappa Delta Pi *Record,* 11, April 1975:98–99; 117.

5. Ann L. Jewett, Sue Jones, Sheryl M. Luneke, and Sarah M. Robinson, "Educational Change Through a Taxonomy for Writing Physical Education Objectives," *Quest* XV (January 1971): 32.

Jewett, Ann E. "Who Knows What Tomorrow May Bring?" *Quest* 21, January 1974:68–72.

McGlynn, George H., ed., *Issues in Physical Education and Sports*. Palo Alto, Calif.: National Press Books, 1974.

Sage, George H., ed., *Sport and American Society*. Reading, Mass: Addison-Wesley Publishing Co., 1970.

Siedentop, Daryl. "On Tilting at Windmills While Rome Burns." *Quest* 18, June 1972:94–97.

Vanderzwaag, Harold J. *Toward a Philosophy of Sport*. Reading, Mass: Addison-Wesley Publishing Co. 1972.

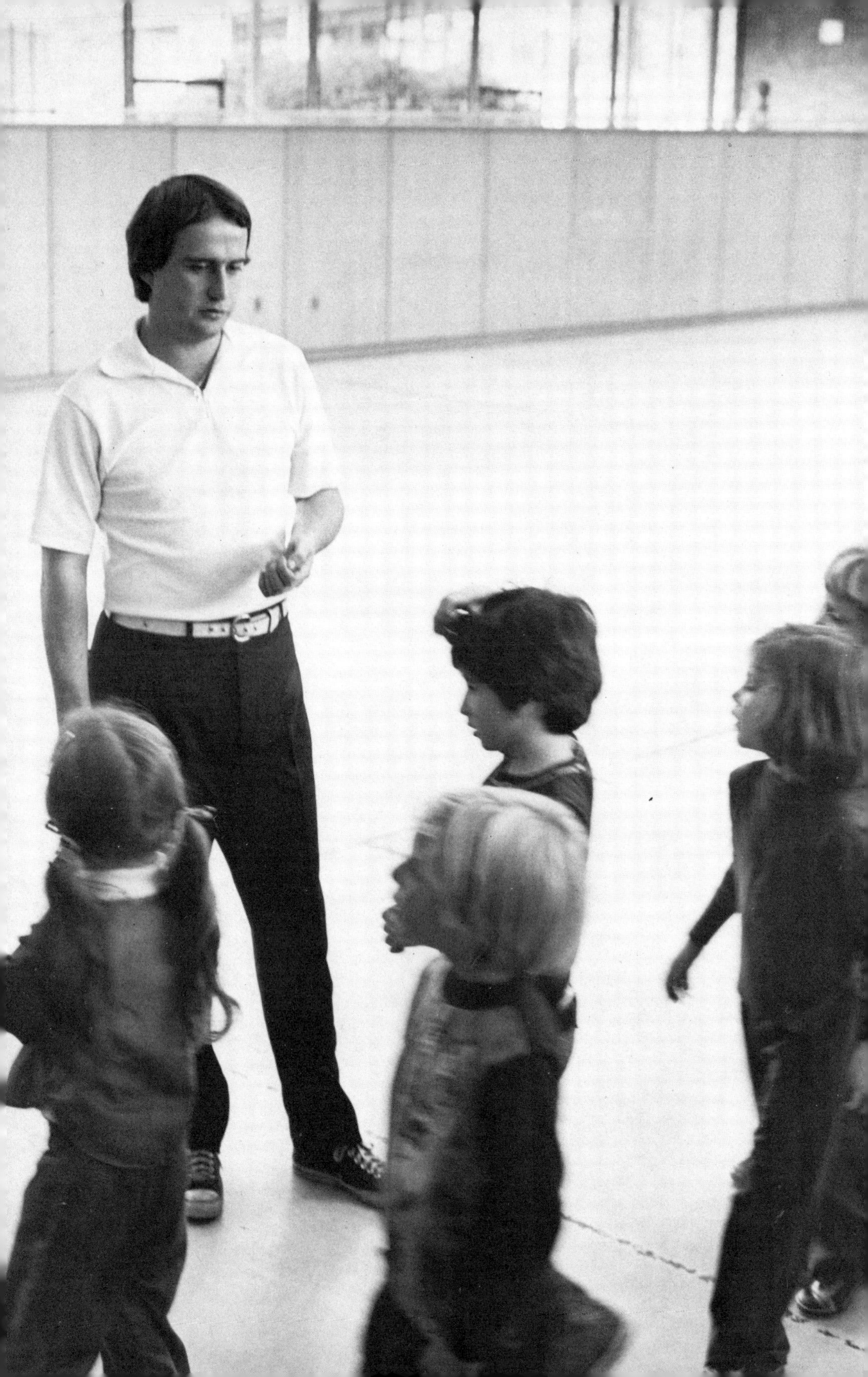

8

How Should We Be Led?

Does a new kind of physical education need a new kind of leader? If physical education is to fully adopt a humanistic approach, can the field make rapid progress under the kind of leaders we now have? What changes in leadership, or what modifications in leadership, does physical education require if it is to meet the challenges of this century and the fast approaching twenty-first century? This chapter presents fourteen questions formulated to provide some answers to the problems of leadership. They are specifically addressed to the challenge of providing a humanistic physical education. The discussions that accompany each of the questions are designed to serve as a frame of reference for the reader. These discussions are purposely not definitive, because it is hoped that the reader will be motivated to seek answers to each one on a broader, freer-ranging, and more personal basis.

1. WHY SHOULD PHYSICAL EDUCATION SEEK A NEW KIND OF LEADER?

The world in which we live is in a state of constant change. With very few cultural exceptions, technological advances are changing our world more rapidly today than ever before in history. For those individual who will live most of their lifetimes in the twenty-first century, change will be a way of life and a constant force in the life-style of the people. While identifying changes as a constant may seem paradoxical at first glance, even in our twentieth-century society new ideas and value systems seem, almost daily, to be adopted in place of the old. Many of the facts in which we firmly believed yesterday are rendered obsolete for today on the basis of new evidence, and, we are rather accustomed now to acknowledging that today's truth may be tomorrow's fiction.

Within any society, progress comes about through modifications of old facts, ideas, values, and needs, and/or the development of new ones. A society that is constantly and rapidly changing does need, however, to retain some of the old ways if for no other reason than the sake of security. Educational systems, while not themselves impervious to change—nor should they be—can provide some of the security needs of a society. Therefore, education must constantly strive to define and redefine its leadership models. Education, and physical education, need the kinds of leaders that will address themselves to current and future problems, issues, challenges, and needs. Sage has observed that:

> Leadership is the process of influencing the activities of an organized group toward goal setting and goal achievement.[1]

A new leadership model needs to be in touch with the needs of tomorrow, and one of these critical needs will be a humanistic frame of reference. Humanism will help to serve as an antidote to what probably will be highly impersonal future societies. Physical education needs a new leadership model because the current state of the field has already manifested itself as a challenge to "catch up" with the rest of education. If physical education continues to lag in supplying a new leadership model, it will find no time to do so in a faster moving future.

2. WHEN IS A NEW LEADERSHIP MODEL NEEDED?

It is probably correct to assume that a viable educational field is always alert to new leadership models who are closely attuned to the social and cultural climate they live in. Sometimes, when a new leader emerges, the experience is a traumatic one for all of those accustomed to another style. An old style, or old leadership model, is frequently defended vociferously because startling and sudden change is often the disguised accusatory finger of complacency and stagnation. Newness and change typically tend to threaten not only the status quo, but also those who are most comfortable with things the way they are.

New leadership models must be actively sought so that change *will* be brought about. Otherwise, a field will find itself in poor position to act

---

1. George H. Sage, "The Coach as Management: Organizational Leadership in American Sport," *Quest* 19 (January 1973):35.

and to become more meaningful. It is a little like varsity athletics—the athletes go into a contest with a game plan, and then alter and modify that plan in order to make the game run more smoothly. And like that team, the educational field that only too late recognizes that sociocultural changes have taken place, finds itself playing a catch-up game.

The search for new leadership models, then, should be an ongoing process because society itself is continuously evolving and changing. However, this is not meant to imply that there should be a preoccupation or obsession with change, because change for the sake of change is as bad, or worse, than no change at all. Bronson has warned that:

> Considered as a formal institution, the educational system does not significantly nourish the society which supports it. It leaves too many people careless of or callous to the interconnectedness of things and to the interrelatedness of people.[2]

Change is a reality, and physical education will be in a position to serve society more dynamically if it continues to seek out, and listen to the ideas of, new leadership models.

3. MUST TRADITIONAL LEADERSHIP MODELS BE CAST ASIDE COMPLETELY?

Those individuals who are highly resistant to change tend to defend traditionalism by attacking change. They contend that much of what is new is not long lasting, and that sometimes the desire to make changes is based on nothing more than attempting to keep up with current fads. For these individuals, tradition is to be defended and perpetuated because it is based on what they feel to be sound ideas, a sound value system, and because it has demonstrated longevity. The defenders of the traditional suggest that the quest for the new, either inadvertantly or by design, eradicates the old ways, and with them much that is good and useful. These individuals say that change is the antithesis of order and continuity, and that an affinity for change only succeeds in perpetuating faddism.

Tradition is not necessarily cast aside when a new leadership model comes forward. However, a new leader may not hold tradition to be sacred, but instead will attempt to retain the good aspects while casting aside the aspects that are no longer functional or meaningful. A new leader must question both old and new while being subservient to neither. Longo said that:

2. David B. Bronson, "Thinking and Teaching," *The Educational Forum* 39 (March 1975): 349.

No change in organizational structure can be effected which represents only gains without losses . . . if a new approach is to be attempted, educators need to assess carefully what risks and disabilities they are willing to assume . . .[3]

New leadership does not wantonly dismiss traditional models and values. Rather, it demands justification of continuing relevance, since the value of traditional systems rests on their service to people. If human well-being is served, the model or value system which supplies the needed service should not be questioned on the basis of age alone.

4. IS HUMANISM COMPATIBLE WITH A NEW LEADERSHIP MODEL FOR PHYSICAL EDUCATION?

Humanism is concerned with human interests, ideals, aspirations, fulfillment, joy, and self-actualization. The concern of humanism is first and foremost people, and with those experiences that will help people to lead fuller, more satisfying lives. In physical education, movement is a tool through which humanistic goals are approached, and the basic movement concern of the humanistic physical educator is that of using movement as a means for human fulfillment. Grabo has observed that:

Learning to create and perceive relationships among the humanistic experiences of the human race from its beginnings on, is no less significant an activity for the teacher than for the young student.[4]

The humanistic frame of reference is not a concern for the individual's well-being alone, but a concern for the individual as a part of a larger sociocultural group with which the individual must interact. Humanism manifests itself as an abiding concern for the well-being of all individuals. Because physical education has service to people as a central mission, it is highly related to, and compatible with, the objectives of humanism. Thus, the humanistic leadership model in physical education is most viable and easily justifiable.

5. WHAT PITFALLS ARE THERE IN HUMANISM?

The humanistic physical educator has as a primary objective the personal fulfillment of students both as individuals and as group members. A

3. Paul Longo, "Opening the Door to the Open Classroom," Kappa Delta Pi *Record,* 11 (April 1975): 98.
4. Carrol Grabo, "Teacher Education and Integrating the Humanities," *The Educational Forum* 39 (November 1974): 17.

humanistic physical educator tends to use a frame of reference that is humanizing rather than one that leans toward winning, aggression, and competition. Where a traditional leadership model might be preoccupied with students' hair styles and the state of their gym suits, the humanistic leadership model sets different criteria for acceptability. The humanistic physical educator sets standards that are derived out of a concern for people rather than from personal arbitrary and subjective biases. The humanist's standards are created and maintained to best serve the needs of students. This seemingly loose method of setting standards has been highly criticized by the traditionalist faction within physical education. Hoffman has cautioned that:

> In generating rationales for the newer systems of teaching, many enthusiasts seem to have assumed that the older, more established, traditional method of teaching physical education lacks any kind of logical or empirical support.[5]

A pitfall, then, which faces the humanist physical educator is one of confrontation with a long and unquestioned traditional approach. For many decades, physical education has firmly believed in the merits of each student receiving a physical education that was in accord with his own unique potential. This is also very much a part of humanism, yet humanism seems to be considered a "new frontier." The "traditional" and the "new" must collaborate and combine in order to avoid a needless confrontation.

6. WHY IS HUMANISTIC PHYSICAL EDUCATION JUST NOW BEGINNING TO EMERGE?

New social trends emerge out of dissatisfaction or disenchantment with old ways. Our current life-style has been characterized as an impersonal one, and the recent resurgence of humanism seems to be an attempt to place human relationships back on a more personal level. Yee asked:

> What do the most modern classrooms, gymnasiums, curriculum designs, and textbooks matter without a competent and understanding teacher working with the needs and potentials of the learner?[6]

In order to view the resurgence of humanism in its proper perspective, it is perhaps worthwhile to retrace briefly the vast sociocultural changes that have come about in the twentieth century. This century has been marked by a trend toward city living, because people have found that

---

5. Shirl James Hoffman, "Traditional Methodology: Prospects for Change," Quest 15 (January 1971): 51.
6. Albert Yee, "Becoming a Teacher in America." Quest 18 (June 1972): 67.

it is within the cities where the highest-paying jobs may be obtained. It is within the cities that museums, theaters, and large stores have been built, and many people are highly desirous of living in closer proximity to these advantages. Many individuals who left rural life for the cities experienced a kind of cultural shock. While rural life was perhaps unsatisfactory to many because it did not provide all of the material comforts, urban life with its impersonal, fast pace, and even its material advantages, was a rude and harsh experience. The rebirth of humanism seems to be an attempt to go backward in time to a simpler, more personalized kind of life.

It is not unnatural that humanism should emerge in physical education programs at this time. Physical education experiences traditionally have been socially-oriented, and person-centered. Humanistic physical education is just now beginning to be recognized because it is very much in line with current goals being sought by a society that has become disenchanted with a lack of humanism in much of daily life.

7. WHERE DOES THE HUMANISTIC STYLE OF PHYSICAL EDUCATION FIND RELEVANCY?

Physical education is not self-serving, nor is it an end in itself. Physical education exists to serve people through movement experiences. Movement is but one step toward self-actualization, and movement is brought to each individual by the physical educator. According to Lawson:

> With reference to . . . this future society, the need exists for skilled performers who understand the hows, whys, and wherefores of both human behavior in a sociocultural context and the ideosyncratic behaviors manifested in the forms under their management.[7]

Because physical education is a humanistic, people-centered academic field, the physical educator who provides a humanistic program is highly relevant, and gives the program its relevancy. Indeed, humanistic programs could not succeed without leadership whose goals and ideals were anything but humanistic.

8. WHAT IS THE PROGRAM EMPHASIS IN HUMANISTIC PHYSICAL EDUCATION?

The program emphasis within humanistic physical education is multifaceted. Humanism focusses upon individual fulfillment and group interac-

7. Hal A. Lawson, "Physical Education and Sport: Alternatives for the Future," *Quest* 21 (January 1974): 28.

tions. Also, physical education is dedicated to the development and maintenance of health, vitality, and physical well-being. Emphasis upon motor skills is also important, because motor skills are the building blocks of all satisfying movement. Therefore, the program emphasis in humanistic physical education is on doing things differently rather than on doing different things. As Grabo has pointed out, some of the characteristics a teacher needs in order to be truly humanistic are:

> A desire to synthesize by seeking similarities, formulating generalizations, drawing parallels . . . a profound interest in the whole student . . . A tendency toward egalitarianism and nonauthoritarian classroom management . . . A fascination with seeing things from as many vantage points as possible . . . An inclination to seek relationships between seemingly disparate forms of experience . . . [8]

9. WHAT IS THE RELATIONSHIP BETWEEN PHYSICAL EDUCATION AND ATHLETICS UNDER HUMANISM?

Humanism should not be a source of conflict between physical education programs and athletic programs. Both programs see as a goal the acquisition of motor skills, the enhancement of physical well-being, and the implementation of the socialization process. There are, of course, obvious differences between physical education and athletics, but the differences are those of degree rather than kind. Where athletics are designed for individuals who are highly proficient and highly skilled in movement, physical education is designed to serve all individuals no matter what their level of competency.

The interrelatedness of physical education and athletics is perhaps best illustrated by using a series of three concentric circles. The core is the physical education program where all students receive instruction in a wide variety of movement experiences. This area is the largest since it indicates participation by all students.

The middle ring is the intramural and club program, where students may, of their own choosing, select movement experiences to pursue in greater depth. This ring occupies less space than does the physical education program section because many, but certainly not all, students choose to participate in intramurals or club-level sports.

Interscholastic, or varsity, athletics occupy the outermost ring. This is given the smallest area because relatively few students possess either the motivation or the motor skill aptitude for participation on this highly refined and demanding skill level. Physical education and athletics are equals in the humanistic frame of reference, and neither is more or less

8. Carrol Grabo, op. cit., p. 20.

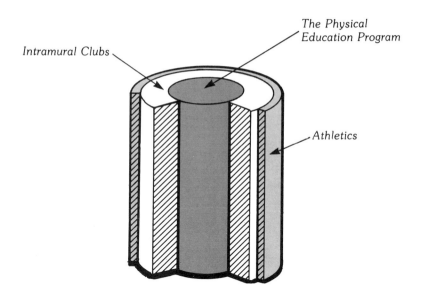

Intramural Clubs

The Physical
Education Program

Athletics

FIGURE 8–1.   The interrelationship of physical education and athletics.

important than the other. Rather, each assumes its own importance based
upon the needs of each student within the program.

**10. IN WHAT WAYS IS THE HUMANISTIC LEADERSHIP MODEL
BETTER ATTUNED TO THE NEEDS AND ASPIRATIONS OF PEOPLE
LIVING IN A TECHNOLOGICAL SOCIETY?**

For most of humanity, the twenty-first century is nothing more than an
unknown, and it seems to many that it will be even more technology-
oriented and impersonal than this century. The humanistic physical
educator is not concerned with mere existence or coping, but rather with
the quality of life itself. Movement is a common denominator among the
world's peoples, and nations and individuals can communicate through
the language of movement. Because movement is so very valuable and
vital as a communicative/expressive mode, then it follows that the
humanistic leadership model will perhaps be better attuned than we are at
present to the needs and aspirations of our students. And our students will
most certainly live well into the twenty-first century. Galloway wrote that:

> Nonverbal language is the language of values and realities that is transmitted
> on silent terms. It is the unspoken culture, understood by all of its inhabitants,
> and learned by the give-and-take of human relationships. [9]

9. Charles M. Galloway, "Teaching is More Than Words," Quest 15 (January 1971): 71.

11. WHERE DOES DISCIPLINE FIT WITHIN THE HUMANISTIC PERSPECTIVE?

Human behavior is so very variable that discipline becomes a most difficult issue to discuss satisfactorily and comprehensively. While two students· may exhibit similar disruptive behaviors, the causes may be very different. The causes of disruptive behavior include, but are by no means limited to, boredom, lack of a challenge or too difficult a challenge, and emotional or health problems. In attempting to resolve disciplinary problems, there is a tendency to treat the symptoms rather than the cause. While this is not totally ineffective or inappropriate, it is only a temporary resolution that serves the student poorly over extended periods of time. It has been widely suggested that the most effective means of behavior modification is to emphasize the problem individual's attributes whenever possible. This is called positive reinforcement.

Positive reinforcement may take many forms, including for example, praise, recognition, attention, or a tangible reward. At the opposite end of the spectrum, a technique called aversion control has sometimes been used. Aversion control involves punishment, and is a form of negative reinforcement. While aversion control is the simpler and faster technique, it is not in keeping with humanism's goals, and has not proven to be an effective means of long-term behavior modification.

The problems of discipline are most certainly serious concerns for the humanistic physical educator. The humanistic physical educator typically attempts to seek out the causes of deviant student behavior rather than resorting to expedient or negative measures that temporarily affect only the symptoms of such behavior.

> . . . we sometimes fail to understand both the meaning of student response and the connection between the meaning of our own behavior for the student and his subsequent reaction.[10]

In reality, then, perhaps the only true discipline is self-discipline; the behavior that is self-imposed through intrinsic motivation. Self-discipline stems from firm beliefs and convictions. The physical educator who is dedicated to the ideals of humanism will use himself as an example for students. Self discipline can be contagious providing students think of their physical educator as an individual worthy of emulation.

12. CAN THE NEW LEADERSHIP MODEL DEVELOP GOOD RAPPORT WITH STUDENTS WITHOUT BECOMING OVERLY PERMISSIVE?

The capacity to develop rapport with students is a most valuable asset for any teacher. Rapport implies a comfortable relationship in which students

10. Galloway, op. cit., p. 68.

and teachers respect each other and their differing goals and values. A teacher who develops good rapport with students has not won some kind of popularity contest, but has instead developed an empathy with, and understanding of students so that there is a common meeting ground for communication.

Rapport and permissiveness are two very different phenomena. Permissiveness has no valid educational purpose because where permissiveness has crept into the educational environment, the teacher will have lost the respect of students, and education will not take place. By encouraging a permissive atmosphere, the educator sacrifices the opportunity to become a credible behavior model for students. While rapport and humanism are eminently compatible, permissiveness really has no place in any educational setting. Maslow has warned that:

> We already know that the main prerequisite of healthy growth is gratification of the basic needs, especially in early life . . . But we have also learned that unbridled indulgence and gratification has its own dangerous consequences . . .[11]

Rapport helps us to understand the nature of the student, and serves as an invaluable frame of reference. Rapport implies guidance, understanding, and a humanistic concern for students.

13. MUST A HUMANISTIC PHYSICAL EDUCATOR BE NONCOMPETITIVE IN ORIENTATION?

Many individuals have conceptualized humanism as the antithesis of competition because humanism emphasizes the uniqueness of the individual. Moreover, there is a common misconception that humanists want everyone to be a winner, and that activities which tend to create losers as well as winners must be avoided. There is nothing in humanism that suggests that competition is undesirable. In fact, it is recognized that a desire to win often precipitates the achievement of a high level of performance. Rather than being concerned with winning per se, the humanist is interested in individual achievement and performance. Competition has a place in humanism because it is recognized that competition often serves as a stimulus to maximum performance.

Humanists accept winning as a tangible mark of a top-level performance. However, humanists are highly resistant to the goal of winning at any cost. Humanists contend that losing can have its advantages also, for there are lessons to be learned from failure as well as from success. The humanist views competitiveness as a means to an end, where competi-

11. Abraham Maslow, ed., New Knowledge in Human Values. (Chicago: Henry Regnery Co., 1971), p. 133.

The capacity to develop rapport with students is a most valuable asset for any teacher.

tion serves as a motivational factor for increased performance and in turn, satisfaction and self-actualization for the performer. As Ingham and Loy tell us:

> . . . a game develops form through synthesis and habitualization. The form is institutionalized through the creation of a frame of values which serves to legitimate the form so that it becomes a taken-for-granted part of the sociocultural milieu.[12]

14. WILL TODAY'S EMERGING LEADERSHIP MODELS BECOME PASSÉ TOMORROW?

What was new and innovative yesterday is common practice today, and in some cases, tomorrow's obsolete irrelevance. The world is attuned and

12. Alan G. Ingham and John W. Loy, Jr., "The Social System of Sport: A Humanistic Perspective," *Quest* 19 (January 1973): 5.

destined to change, and any individual who works with people must be flexible enough to adapt to those changes that will serve people better. Certainly much of what seems new today will gradually pass into obsolescence. This is not a cause for concern unless the innovations that have been substituted are invalid. Change for the sake of change alone is always a questionable practice.

There is nothing sacred about innovation, new methodologies, or new leadership models. If a new idea, method, or technique can be shown to bring about meaningful change, then relevance and validity can be assumed. It is useless to resist the new simply because it is new. Feingold tells us that:

> Given the hard demands of accountability, it no longer will be possible to assume either that the teacher produced the desired learning or that he knows in terms of consequent student behaviors what changes he desires. In effect, since it will no longer be possible to assume the consequences of teacher behavior, it will be necessary to demonstrate resultant learning through the use of appropriate measurement and evaluation.[13]

Meaningful change is but one of the ways in which leadership maintains its relevancy and usefulness.

SUMMARY

The concern of this chapter has been an attempt to establish the role of leadership within humanistic physical education. We began by trying to determine whether or not a new kind of leader is actually needed, and went on to discuss some of the dimensions any leadership role must assume. We have considered the relationship between leadership models, humanism, and such factors as discipline, competition, athletics, and student-teacher rapport.

This chapter was not intended to be a conclusive and finite discussion and resolution of any of the fourteen points that were highlighted. Instead, the brief discussions were designed to stimulate the reader to delve further into the questions raised using the answers provided as a springboard for class discussions, personal resolution, and perhaps the development of other, more probing questions.

13. Ronald S. Feingold, "The Evaluation of Teacher Education Programs in Physical Education," *Quest* 18 (June 1972):33.

SUGGESTIONS FOR FURTHER READING

Berlin, Pearl. "Prolegomena to the Study of Personality by Physical Educators." *Quest* 13 (January 1970):54–62.

Crockenberg, Vincent. "Poor Teachers Are Made Not Born." *The Educational Forum* 39 (January 1975):189–198.

Jewett, Ann E. and Marie R. Mullan. "A Conceptual Model for Teacher Education." *Quest* 18 (June 1972):76–87.

Siedentop, Daryl. "Behavior Analysis and Teacher Training." *Quest* 18 (June 1972):26–32.

Siedentop, Daryl. "On Tilting at Windmills While Rome Burns." *Quest* 18 (June 1972):94–97.

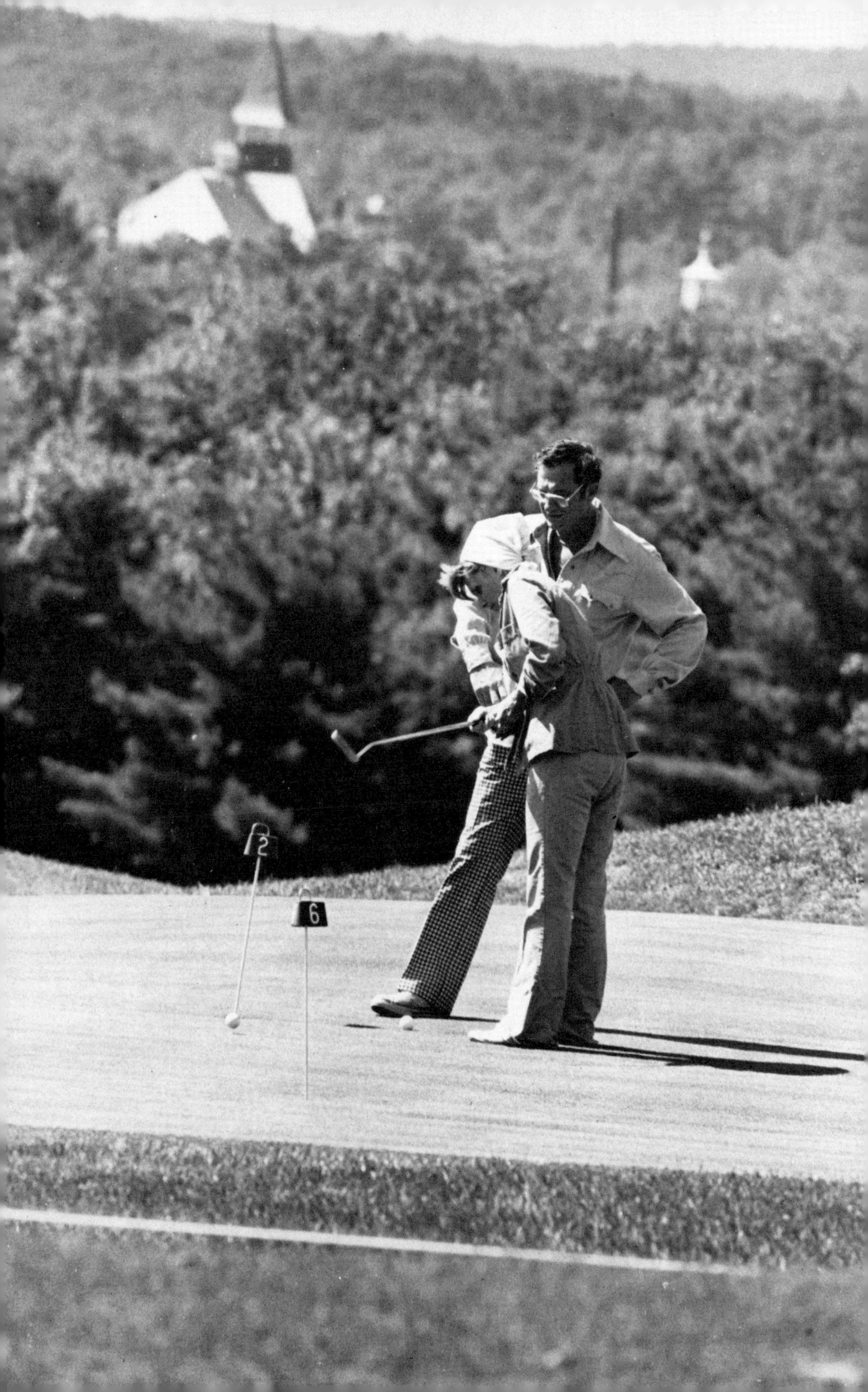
2
6

9

Many Things Under the Sun

Physical educators are producers of a product that is integral to the life of all individuals. The need for physical activity has been with us since the beginning of life on earth. Primitive man was able to survive primarily because he was continually active, and continually engaging in what we now commonly label "human movement." Modern man needs physical activity in order to be able to survive in modern society, for as Van Dalen and Bennett have written:

> From the age of the caveman, the way man has viewed and used his body and mind has had an impact on society.[1]

Further, the same authors have said:

> The joy derived from body movement, social contacts, and from observing skilled performers and well-developed physiques must have been as satisfying to early man as it is to modern man.[2]

Satisfaction gained by the individual from experiences in human movement, the socialization inherent in sharing movement experiences with others, whether as a performer or as a knowledgeable spectator, and

1. Deobold B. Van Dalen and Bruce L. Bennett, *A World History of Physical Education*. (Englewood Cliffs, N.J.: Prentice-Hall, Inc., 1971), p. 3.
2. Ibid., p. 5.

the variety of personal and social benefits to be derived from movement experiences are all, and should be, aspects of the humanistic perspective of today's physical education. As we move further into the age of accountability in education, physical educators must take a comprehensive survey of themselves and their profession. Physical educators must ask, "In what ways can we, through physical education, help the individual to come to a full realization of himself?" To the extent that physical educators can determine a satisfactory answer, they will be better able to state that physical education has indeed begun to zero-in on the humanistic perspective. It is only then that one time-honored goal of physical education, that of helping individuals to become "physically educated," will be fully understood so that this goal can be realistically attained.

> The emergence of a physical education in accord with the direction of third force psychology, humanistic in orientation and design, would be characterized by a thrust toward the ultimate goal of educational experiences, the human goal, the 'self-actualization' of humanness and human fulfillment in the here and now.[3]

Physical educators have as a common goal progress toward a total understanding of the role of movement in helping human beings achieve their potential. Physical education is a multifaceted profession, and each facet in its own unique way attempts to assist each individual to reach not only his own goals in relation to movement, but to make that experience an enjoyable one as well. The remainder of this chapter helps to introduce the reader to the variety of educational levels on which physical educators may serve. Also, specific areas of expertise within physical education which should be understood by all physical educators are defined and explained.

LEVELS OF TEACHING

As the undergraduate major in physical education formulates career goals, he must seriously consider the educational level for which he will prepare. An individual who is thoroughly competent to teach physical education in a high school will not automatically be just as competent to teach physical education to elementary school-age children. The following illustrate some of the varied aspects of teaching competency required by the different educational levels.

3. Stratton Caldwell, "Toward a Humanistic Physical Education." *JOHPER* 43 (1972):31–32.

At one time, much of preschool education and development was largely left to chance. More recently, and with increasing interest, educators have begun to look more closely at the educational needs of the child of preschool age. Preschool education has begun to focus on helping the very young child to build a firm foundation upon which later educational experiences can be fashioned. There is substantial evidence that seems to indicate that children begin to learn even before birth.[4] In view of the vast quantity of learning that occurs from birth through the age when a child traditionally enters kindergarten, it seems logical that educators should pay commensurate attention to the quality and significance of the child's preschool learning experiences.

Preschool learning experiences should be of particular interest to physical educators. Much of the child's initial learning experiences and communication with the environment come about through movement. If we accept the premise that movement is the means for the earliest learning experiences then we may also accept the corollary that the more opportunity a child has to engage in physical activity during his earliest years, then the firmer will be the foundation upon which he will build later movement experiences. This seems to support the premise that children first learn to move, and then move to learn. This has profound implications for the role of physical education in the preschool years.

The preschool child's first experiences as a social being come about largely through movement. Preschool children typically first play by themselves. As they continue to develop, they usually continue to play independently, but within a group setting. Finally, the preschool child begins to seek play companions. This final stage of development is often characterized by unorganized play.[5] The social experiences gained through play are essential if the child is to be successful in later learning experiences. Subsequent learning occurs in the more formal setting of the classroom, which has a group context and a social orientation. Since movement is the primary means by which the preschool child encounters the socialization process, physical education then becomes an important force in the implementation of this process.

In the preschool years it is essential that physical education assist the child in the development of basic motor skills. The basic, or fundamental, motor skills are those skills upon which human movement is based. These skills include:

4. Charles B. Corbin, W. Hottinger, "Babyhood: Pre and Post Natal Periods," in *A Textbook of Motor Development*. (Dubuque, Iowa: Wm. C. Brown Co., 1973), p. 10.
5. Daniel D. Arnheim and Robert A. Postolesi, *Developing Motor Behavior in Children*. (St. Louis: The C.V. Mosby Co., 1973), p. 26.

walking	sliding	pulling	stooping
running	galloping	crawling	bending
hopping	throwing	creeping	stretching
leaping	catching	rolling	twisting[6]
jumping	lifting	climbing	
skipping	pushing	swaying	

While these skills are used inherently as children play in an unguided manner, preschool experiences in supervised play offered through the means of physical education can help to assure that all children will have an opportunity to experience these skills in all their varieties.

While comprehensive preschool physical education programs are not yet to be found in abundance, the impact of such programs is beginning to be felt in school systems that have introduced such experiences for the young child.

Primary

The primary grades serve children from the ages of about five through eight who are in kindergarten through third grade. Movement experiences are essential for these children. Providing movement experiences through formal physical education helps to assure that these children are receiving sufficient physical activity for proper growth and development. Primary level physical education should focus on the refinement of the basic motor skills engaged in during the preschool years. Perfection of these fundamental skills will serve as the building blocks for successful, joyful participation in physical activity throughout life.

The emphasis on the primary level should be upon the socialization process. During the early primary years the teacher cannot expect significant amounts of cooperative group participation. However, by the end of the primary level experience, children should be ready for subsequent and significant group experiences. Because the physical education experience is largely a social experience by the nature of the activities included, the socialization process should come about quite naturally.

In the early primary years, children are engaged in the very important process of learning about themselves. They begin to develop lasting attitudes about formal education and about learning in general. During these years, it is most important that the formal learning experiences offered by the school be positive experiences. Physical education can contribute immeasurably to this experience by providing enjoyable and positive movement experiences. The primary-age child relates readily to movement. Thus, movement may be used as an effective tool through

6. Anita J. Harrow, *A Taxonomy of the Psychomotor Domain*. (New York: David McKay Co., Inc., 1972), p. 52–53.

Motor learning experts try to determine whether or not time-honored teaching procedures and methods are in fact the best ways to teach and learn.

which the young child may derive fulfillment and satisfaction from educational experiences.

Upper Elementary

The upper elementary school-age child is generally from nine to twelve years of age, and is in grades four through six. During these years the child is in the transition period between childhood and adolescence, and sex differences begin to emerge. The sex roles society typically begins to assign during these years tend to stereotype the movement experiences that will be provided for boys and girls. Many of the movement experiences that are limited to one sex or the other exclusively have been traditionally and arbitrarily assigned. This kind of stereotyping and compartmentalizing tends to persist no matter how outdated or irrelevant it is. If physical education is to succeed in emphasizing the humanistic perspective in movement, then continued sex role assignment of movement experiences must be eliminated from the program.

The upper elementary school level is traditionally the focus of separation of programs in physical education by sex roles. Therefore, physical education must go about the task of assuring that all children have the opportunity to sample all of the varieties of human movement available. In this way, the humanistic goal of physical education will move closer toward fulfillment and realization. During the upper elementary school years, as the children move closer into adolescence, they begin to take a noticeably greater interest in their bodies. As physical changes become more obvious, children begin to develop a highly sensitive concept of self-awareness and self-image.

> Physique is one of the most important factors in the total development of personality. It is primarily through exploring and discovering the functions of the body that a child conceptualizes himself as a distinct person. It has been described as the way in which one pictures his body as a system of ideas and feelings that the individual has about his physical structure.[7]

During this period of great physical change, the upper elementary school physical education teacher can be of great assistance in helping young people find identity through movement. Identity begins with the development of a satisfying self-concept that aids in the establishment of positive attitudes about the self. Under the watchful guidance of physical educators, children can be offered a wide variety of movement experiences that will enhance their developing identities and self-images. The importance of possessing a strong, positive identity balanced by a strong and positive self-image is not to be denied in view of evidence that suggests that one must first feel good about one's self before one can begin to feel good about others.

During the upper elementary school developmental period, young people begin to develop and refine many of the motor skills which they will continue to use throughout their lives. At this stage in the educational process, it is most critical that these young people have ample opportunity to develop these skills so that movement activities will become an important and permanent part of their life-style. These are intensely important years for these young people, who deserve the best physical education can offer them in the way of movement experiences.

7. Daniel D. Arnheim, David Auxter, and Water C. Crowe. *Principles and Methods of Adapted Physical Education.* (St. Louis: The C.V. Mosby Co., 1973), p. 35.

The middle school grades include grades seven through nine, and the children are approximately ages thirteen to fifteen. These years encompass a period in the lives of young people that are marked by rapid physical growth, the pressures of puberty, sex-role differentiations, and peer group pressures. Children of this age are on the threshold of young adulthood, and this phenomenon, in itself, creates many pressures and conflicts. Physical education can help to provide valuable opportunities for easing this frequently difficult transition into adulthood.

For many youngsters, the physical educator serves as an adult-role model whom they attempt to emulate. Because physical educators are so often in this unique position, they frequently become the primary adult in whom the youngster confides and with whom the youngster most closely identifies. Thus, the physical education program itself becomes the means through which the youngster develops the skills, attributes and behaviors which will be important to him in the adult world.

Teaching physical education to middle school-age children can be both challenging and rewarding. The challenge comes from the attempt to influence positively the lives of young people who are in a formative period, and in the period of turmoil between childhood and adulthood. The reward comes from the knowledge that the physical educator has provided the kind of program most needed by these youngsters, and one that has helped them to make the transition more easily and with greater confidence.

Secondary

The secondary or high school years usually include boys and girls from the ages of sixteen through eighteen who are in grades ten through twelve. This is the age of young adulthood, and often the most fulfilling years spent in school. Strong and sometimes permanent lifetime bonds and friendships are formed during this period. These young adults are at an age when physical prowess and motor skill performances reach peak levels. Secondary school-age young people tend to perceive physical prowess, physical attractiveness, and skilled motor performance as being extremely important attributes.[8] Physical education can emerge as an important and very meaningful curricular experience.

Among probable causes for concern among secondary level physical educators is the fact that physical fitness and motor performance levels begin to decline among young people in general following their graduation from secondary school.[9] When one accepts the premise that the only true

8. Charles A. Bucher, *Foundations of Physical Education.* (St. Louis: The C.V. Mosby Co., 1972), p. 421.
9. Ibid., p. 420.

education is that which becomes fully and permanently integrated into the life-style of the individual, then perhaps it is wise to ask whether or not the secondary school physical education experience truly physically educates the young adult. It has been suggested that physical educators on the secondary level should put more emphasis on the "why" of human movement experiences. Perhaps if students fully understood the significance of continued physical activity they would pursue an active course throughout their lives, and come to regard such activity as an investment in the future.

Lifetime Sports

Complementing an increasing concern for continued activity participation beyond secondary school years has been a surge in lifetime sports instruction. Lifetime sports by definition are those movement activities in which the person can participate literally throughout life. Common to all lifetime sports is that the intensity of these activities can be readily geared by the participant to his own unique activity needs. Golf, skiing, tennis, dance, swimming, bowling, archery, and jogging are but a few selected examples of lifetime activities that are gaining increasing recognition in contemporary secondary school physical education programs.

This new emphasis on the lifetime sports is not meant to dilute traditional program emphases, but is rather recognition of the fact that the postschool-age individual is more likely to seek out nonteam oriented activities as recreational pursuits.

With an increased life span, shorter work week, and early retirement becoming realities of modern life, it would seem entirely appropriate for the contemporary secondary school physical education experience to foster the development of motor skills with enduring serviceability.

College and University

Movement experiences at the college and university level are broad and varied. In many institutions, the broad spectrum of individual needs are served by the basic instructional programs, professional degree programs including the opportunity to major in physical education or to minor in the field as a second teaching area, and coaching certification programs. In addition to these, the college or university student may participate in club level athletics, intramurals, and intercollegiate athletics.

THE BASIC INSTRUCTIONAL PROGRAM

The basic instructional program is typically a program for all students, although colleges and universities vary in regard to requiring the program

Intramural and intercollegiate athletic programs along with the club sports must be considered integral parts of any college or university curriculum that has as an objective the fostering of human potential through movement experiences.

for all. In many instances, the basic instructional program is an elective option offering academic credit. The emphasis in the basic instructional program tends to be at beginning levels of instruction in the various activities offered. Opportunities are frequently available for intermediate and advanced instruction as indicated by student needs and interests. Basic instructional courses are in general activity-centered, concentrating on the learning of skills, rules, and strategies of the various activities. Successful completion of a beginning level basic instructional program should provide the individual with the fundamentals for continued and enjoyable participation in that activity at least on a recreational basis.

Some basic instructional programs are now beginning to include learning experiences in their curriculums that focus upon the "know why" of physical activity. Rather than the traditional "know how" approach and its emphasis upon skill development, the "know why" approach seeks to help the student understand the rationale for physical activity and to appreciate the scientific bases upon which physical education is founded. The basic premise of the foundations approach suggests that the individual who is able to intellectualize the "know why" of physical education will be more likely to incorporate regular physical activity into his permanent life-style.

Extra-Class Programs

Sport programs, including club, intramural and intercollegiate programs, are the means through which many students pursue skill refinement beyond the scope of the emphases in the basic instructional program. Intramural and intercollegiate athletic programs along with the club sports must be considered integral parts of any college or university curriculum that has as an objective the fostering of human potential through movement experiences. Participation in club, intramural, or intercollegiate programs is, almost without exception, entirely voluntary on the part of the student. To this extent, participation in these programs would seem to epitomize the desired outcome of all formal education: the continued pursuit of excellence beyond the bounds of formal curriculum requirements.

PROFESSIONAL PHYSICAL EDUCATION

Should the individual choose to pursue a career as a professional physical educator, there are several options. Majors and minors in professional physical education study to become teachers both of and through movement. A major course of study, with physical education as the primary teaching field of expertise, implies more intensive preparation throughout the collegiate career. Those individuals who minor in physical education will not have so intensive or comprehensive a curriculum in physical education because some other area of teaching will have been selected as the primary emphasis. The choice of a major or minor emphasis is an entirely personal matter, and the final decision depends upon the individual's preferences, motivations, and career aspirations. In addition, some colleges and universities offer concentrations in the area of dance. Depending upon the school, dance may be contained within the physical education degree structure, or may be a separate degree program that is not allied with physical education.

The coaching certificate is a relatively new concept in professional preparation curriculums. Coaching is a course of study which endeavors to prepare individuals who wish to coach but who may not intend to also teach physical education. Teachers wishing to coach athletic teams, but who are not professionally prepared as physical educators are now being required by law in some states to have earned a coaching certificate. This requirement appears to be an emerging trend.

Physical education and movement program emphases in colleges and universities tend to be rather diverse because of the varied nature of student interests and career aspirations. There are many specific areas of expertise within the general field of physical education. All physical educators should have had courses in each of these areas during their years of undergraduate preparation, and should have gained at least a working knowledge of each of the areas. These individual areas are discussed briefly but comprehensively within the following sections.

Motor Learning

Motor learning involves the study of skill acquisition. It is an area of scholarly emphasis in which we attempt to discover the most efficient ways through which people may be taught to move well. By definition the study of motor learning:

> ... is concerned with the factors that influence motor behavior, with the design of experiences that will result in desirable changes in this behavior, and with the influence of this learning on the capacity of the individual for future development.[10]

All teachers of movement must be students of motor learning. Knowledge of the skill acquisition process enables the teacher to present instruction in ways which are both complementary to and compatible with the ways in which people learn.

Motor learning experts try to determine whether or not time-honored teaching procedures and methods are in fact the best ways to teach and to learn. Motor learning research attempts to determine whether young children should be introduced to certain skills first by using over-sized or otherwise modified equipment, such as larger balls when ball-handling skills are first introduced; whether throwing a ball sidearm will serve as a lead-up skill for the forehand drive in tennis; whether learning to throw a ball overhand will in some way help the child to learn to cast with a fishing rod; whether or not skills are retained, and if so, the extent of retention; whether or not practice periods should be long or short; and whether speed or accuracy or both should be the primary emphasis when throwing skills are being practiced.

While this list is not exhaustive, it is indicative of the role motor learning expertise plays in guiding skill acquisition. In seeking answers to such problems of procedure and method, motor learning researchers have begun to find that not all of the traditional physical education teaching

10. Loretta M. Stallings, *Motor Skills: Development and Learning.* (Dubuque, Iowa: Wm. C. Brown Co., 1973), p. 5.

practices can be justified in the light of scholarly inquiry. All individuals who teach movement would do well to remain abreast of current motor learning research findings in order to afford their students maximum opportunities for achieving their potential in movement activities.

Tests and Measurements

Expertise in tests and measurements is a most valuable tool for the teacher. Too often, the evaluation of student performance has served either solely or primarily as the means by which teachers have assigned grades. Perhaps for this reason, many undergraduate students majoring in physical education have tended to look upon courses in tests and measurements in a narrow and sometimes threatening context.

A program of tests and measurements should render direct benefits to students, and these benefits should be totally unrelated to the grading process. A comprehensive program of tests and measurements is designed in a logical way, and should have as its primary objective the yielding of information that will help the physical educator to design a better instructional program for the students involved. When a tests and measurements program is properly designed, the student will receive continual knowledge of his performance levels. Students tend to remain interested in learning experiences only as long as they receive feedback that keeps them informed of their progress. Without feedback, there is little else of an extrinsic nature that will help to motivate the learner.

By testing and measuring their students, physical educators determine the effectiveness of their programs. Perceptive teachers who are concerned with the humanistic aspect of physical education will use tests and measurements expertise not merely for the purpose of assigning grades, but also to help the learner to understand his abilities and needs better. There can be little justification for designing a program of tests and measurements unless the student is the prime beneficiary of the evaluation process.

Research

"Research is used to designate those careful investigations conducted to extend knowledge, or to further explore and verify that which has already been explored."[11] Research is a scholarly undertaking which attempts to bring new knowledge to practioners so that they will be better able to help

11. Barry L. Johnson and Jack K. Nelson, *Practical Measurements for Evaluation in Physical Education.* (Minneapolis: Burgess Publishing Co., 1974), p. 2.

Primary level physical education should focus on the refinement of the basic motor skills engaged in during the preschool years.

their profession progress. As consumers of current research, or even as those engaged in research themselves, physical educators can contribute to their profession and to their students by incorporating new ideas and new innovations that come about as a result of careful and scholarly research.

Research can and must be undertaken at all educational levels and in each of the subfields of physical education discussed in this chapter. Research put into use by the instructor represents a major way by which physical education remains viable, credible, and progressive. One major challenge facing physical education at present is the need to bridge the gap between the researcher and the teacher. While researchers should endeavor to present their research with the reader in mind, the reader in turn must make a commitment to becoming a critical and intelligent user of the results of research reports and studies. The physical educator who keeps abreast of the latest research in the field, and who then attempts to use that research for the benefit of students is making a major contribution to the goals of physical education.

Exercise Physiology

Exercise physiology " . . . is the study of human functions under the stress of muscular activity."[12] The exercise physiologist studies many of the facets of human performance. He may, for example, be interested in determining the kinds of physical training which will yield maximum performance results. In studying performance, the exercise physiologist considers many variables: do certain body types exhibit greater physiological capacity in certain sports or activities? In what ways can the heart, lungs, and circulatory system be conditioned to maximize endurance? In what ways should athletes train in order to become more proficient in the shortest possible time? What are the effects of high altitude on performance? What are the effects of heat or cold on performance? What kinds of strength training are most appropriate for any given activity? The exercise physiologist attempts to answer these and other questions through research. His results, in turn, are used by physical educators to benefit their students.

Exercise physiology in humanistic perspective means that the exercise physiologist is engaged in discovering ways through which human beings may reach maximum performance levels in accordance with their individual potential. Thus, through the study of exercise physiology, knowledge is discovered and used that helps people reach fulfillment through the medium of movement.

Kinesiology

The word kinesiology is derived from two Greek words: *kine,* meaning movement, and *ology* meaning study of. Kinesiology, then, is the scientific study of locomotion, and it derives input from both the life sciences and the physical sciences. From the life sciences, the kinesiologist draws upon the disciplines of anatomy, neurology, and physiology. From the physical sciences, the kinesiologist learns of the physical laws which govern all movement, and to which all moving bodies must conform.

In order to analyze the basic components of skilled movement, kinesiologists have relied on cinematography as one of the most effective tools. By using slow motion photography and applying mathematical expertise, the kinesiologist may readily determine body-segment angles, body-segment movement sequences, body-segment velocities, and the placement of the body's center of gravity throughout the performance of any given motor skill. A knowledge of kinesiology enables the physical educator to approach the teaching of movement with an understanding of the principles of movement. In this way, the physical educator may better

12. Daryl Siedentop, *Physical Education: Introductory Analysis.* (Dubuque, Iowa: Wm C. Brown Co., 1972), p. 46.

guide and instruct students as they attempt to gain an ever wider variety of movement skills and understandings.

Perceptual Motor Development

Perception is generally defined as, " . . . knowledge through the senses of the existence and properties of matter and the external world."[13] Thus, perception is the interpretation of information monitored by the senses and the nervous system. Theories which attempt to explain the development of perceptual awareness often suggest that movement is a major developmental component. Such theories further suggest that perceptual awareness develops during infancy and early childhood. These theories also note that during the years when perceptual development occurs most intensely, movement seems to be the primary means through which the child gains needed experiences. Thus, there is the implication that perceptual awareness may in large measure result from the many and varied opportunities to move and, moreover, from the ability to learn to move well.

Professionals who have made an intensive study into the area of perceptual motor development are attempting to determine the kinds of movement experiences which most effectively enhance perceptual awareness. Further, they are also attempting to determine at what age the benefits from movement experiences are most highly correlated with the development of perceptual motor awareness.

The preceding paragraphs have been devoted to discussions of selected courses important in the professional preparation of every physical educator. The remainder of this chapter will highlight some of the career fields that are allied with physical education, but which require additional intensive preparation before expertise can be acquired.

PROGRAMMING FOR INDIVIDUALS WITH SPECIAL NEEDS

Many states have laws designed to protect the atypical student from the possible negative effects derived from participation in programs that are geared to only the needs of the so-called typical student. As they generally relate to physical education, such laws usually state that any student who cannot safely or successfully participate in the regular physical education program must be provided with a program in accordance with individual needs. Such laws, unfortunately, are often open to many local interpretations, and as such leave relatively little assurance that the spirit of the law is

13. Robert N. Singer, *Motor Learning and Human Performance.* (New York: The Macmillan Co., 1971), p. 82.

being fulfilled. Where schools are truly humane, and where physical education is conducted as a human service, atypical students find genuine enrichment and fulfillment through movement experiences.

In programming physical education for the individual with special needs, a differentiation must be made between the terms "corrective physical education" and "adaptive physical education." Programs termed "corrective" are those programs intended to correct or remedy a temporary handicapping condition. Helping in the rehabilitation of a fractured arm is one example of corrective physical education. Programs that are "adaptive" are those designed for individuals whose handicapping conditions are permanent. Creating meaningful movement experiences for amputees, or for partially sighted or blinded individuals exemplifies programming in an adaptive vein. Where a corrective program, then, is intended to remedy a temporary problem, an adaptive program is intended to enable the individual to achieve his fullest movement potential within the limitations set by the permanent nature of the handicap.

In programming for individuals with special needs, the physical educator or specialist in this field functions as but one member of a multi-talented team. The team, all of whom provide input to help facilitate the development of a meaningful learning experience, should include the handicapped individual's physician, the school psychologist, school nurse, classroom teacher, and the physical education teacher. The team approach helps to assure that the special needs individual is regarded as being something more than his handicap. Often, the physical educator or specialist is the school professional who works most closely with the individual's physician. Where the physician suggests certain activity experiences, the physical educator's efforts assure that these recommendations are implemented for the benefit and enjoyment of the individual.

Personal fulfillment through movement is vastly important for virtually all young people. For the special needs individual, whose movement needs are no less important, there should be a rededication by all physical educators to serve individuals through the medium of movement.

ATHLETIC TRAINING

The care and prevention of athletic injuries is the primary task of athletic trainers. Athletic training is a most significant speciality given the inherent risks in physical education and sports activities. While physical education and sports are not inherently unsafe, the quality and quantity of some movements tends to heighten the probability of accident or injury.

Athletic trainers endeavor to prevent athletic injuries by helping to assure that participants have been properly conditioned. Trainers are skilled in caring for injuries, and often take complete charge under the supervision of the participant's physician. The athletic trainer is often the only qualified person available to render emergency assistance immediately after an athletic injury occurs. Recent years have brought significant improvements in the professional preparation of individuals functioning as athletic trainers. There is currently a mounting tend toward in-depth specialization in this field. Today, an individual wishing to become an athletic trainer must enrol in many intensive courses, and will emerge well qualified in the care and prevention of athletic injuries.

Concern for the best interests and well-being of students engaged in movement experiences mandates that the physical educator also be knowledgable in the prevention and care of athletic injuries. Where courses in athletic training are offered, every future professional physical educator should pursue as many as possible so that the best interests of students will be served.

ATHLETIC COACHING

The desire to coach often leads many college students to decide to major in physical education. Many people who have experienced the joy of skilled movement through sport tend to want to become teachers of others who also move well. Previously, a college major in physical education was the sole vehicle through which an individual could become a coach. However, some institutions are now beginning to offer coaching certification programs for individuals who wish to coach, but do not wish to teach physical education. If an individual is interested solely in athletic coaching, the possibility of a major in some field other than physical education should be considered. The intent of coaching certification programs is to provide the coaching-oriented individual with an opportunity to become competent in coaching without requiring that the person also pursue a major in physical education. The individual is thus free to choose a major in a discipline that best meets his noncoaching needs and interests.

Athletics is an area that is committed to serving students who are gifted in movement. Students who move well, like students who excel in virtually any curricular area, deserve further education commensurate with their potential and desire for achievement. Coaches are movement experts, either in a given sport, or in a particular aspect of a sport. It is no longer uncommon for secondary schools with strong commitments to athletic programs to boast of one or more special coaches for any given athletic team. Athletics can become a vehicle through which participants develop a wider variety of physical, social, and psychological outlooks. Much, however, depends upon the training and dedication of the coach to serving the needs and interests of student athletes before even considering any other facets of the athletic program of which the coach is a key part.

ADMINISTRATION

Administration is that phase of any program that is responsible for coordinating the many aspects of personnel, facilities, and equipment. In their own unique ways, each teacher is an administrator at one time or another. A teacher is carrying on administrative duties whenever records are being developed, maintained, or updated. A teacher engaged in preparing a program budget, or involved in purchasing equipment and supplies is carrying out administrative responsibilities. Administration is, however, generally thought of as a larger umbrella under the direction of a single individual who is charged with supervising an entire program or school system.

The administration of a program or school exists specifically to facilitate effective teaching. Physical education department chairpersons are administrators. Other administrative personnel within a school may include those individuals with the job titles of intramural director, interscholastic athletics director, or intercollegiate athletics director. Depending upon the individual institution, such persons may or may not also teach and/or coach. An educational administrator is really an executive functioning in much the same manner as would an executive in any large corporation. A profound difference, however, is the way in which executive success is measured. In the world of business, success is often predicated on the size of profits. On the other hand, administrative success within physical education and its allied fields is measured in terms of human achievement through movement, and the fulfillment of human movement potential.

INTRAMURAL MANAGEMENT

Intramural management is involved with motivating students into wanting to participate in physical activities beyond their basic instructional class experiences. Intramural management involves the creation and implementation of individual sport experiences, team sport experiences, leagues, and tournaments. The development of a comprehensive intramural program helps assure that all students who so desire can have an opportunity to find fulfillment through sport.

Unlike interscholastic or intercollegiate athletic programs where often only a highly skilled few find opportunity and enrichment, intramurals exist to serve all students regardless of ability level. Intramural programming lends credibility to the concept of humanism in physical education because intramurals exist solely to afford students the opportunity for participation in only those experiences they have chosen to meet their own unique need and interests.

Sport psychology is the study of human behavior as it relates to participation in physical activity and sport. Sport psychology endeavors to understand the behavioral phenomena which cause people to succeed or fail, and it also attempts to try to understand why individuals act and react as they do within the context of sports. Further, sport psychology seeks to understand why people are motivated to participate in movement activites. Beyond this, sport psychology attempts to understand why athletes of superior ability sometimes are defeated by their lesser skilled opponents.

Sports psychology recognizes the principle of the whole man, and is therefore humanistically oriented as an allied field of physical education. Physical educators should be familiar with the field of sport psychology so that they can gain a better understanding of their students as active, moving individuals.

SPORT SOCIOLOGY

Because sport is of profound social significance throughout most of the world, the study of sport as a social phenomenon is most relevant. According to Barrow:

Sports and games are a part of basic human behavior and are among the most effective means of socialization of man.[14]

Sport sociologists are interested in the ways individuals interact with other individuals in game situations. It is no longer uncommon for professional athletic teams to retain the services of sport sociologists who specialize in group dynamics. The group dynamics expert attempts to manipulate the group and/or the environment in order to improve the performance of the group and the individuals within the group. Sport sociologists also study how changing values of a social nature affect both the participant and the spectator during the sport experience. Further, racism in sport is the subject of intense study by many sport sociologists, and recent events have made the status of women in sport a relevant issue for sport sociologists.

Sport sociology, along with the previously discussed area of sport psychology, are two of the most rapidly growing subfields of physical education. They are both highly worthy of pursuit and study by physical educators, since the results of ongoing research within both fields will have profound effect upon the conduct of physical education classes in the future.

14. Harold M. Barrow, *Man and His Movement: Principles of His Physical Education.* (Philadelphia: Lea and Febiger, 1973), p. 204.

While this book is not intended to be a book of activities, and while dance may certainly be classified as an activity as well as a movement-centered experience, dance is nevertheless surrounded by circumstances and issues which warrant its mention here. In many respects, dance represents a significant departure from other movement experiences, because dance is not only movement, but art as well. Few other forms of movement may legitimately make this claim.

Where dance is art, dance also approaches aesthetic experience. The art and aesthetics of dance, perhaps more than any other consideration, cause dance to be viewed apart from most other domains of movement. Perhaps it might be best perceived as an alternative movement experience for those who choose not to identify with sports. Dance tends to be experienced and pursued apart from sports. The dance experience pursued as art tends to be a highly personal, intrinsically satisfying experience. Extrinsic reward systems which traditionally include winners and losers, trophies, medals, most valuable player awards, letter jackets and the like, seem not to be an integral or desired part of the dance experience. There should be little denial that dance is a precise and demanding athletic pursuit. Dance as a mode of human achievement through movement will likely become an increasingly exciting and relevant speciality to growing numbers of movement professionals during the coming decade.

SUMMARY

This chapter has focused upon the broad aspects of physical education, and has attempted to show how physical education strives to fill the human need for movement activities. It was pointed out that it is the physical educator who is ultimately responsible for providing enjoyable opportunities for movement experiences on each of the educational levels. Carefully planned movement experiences must begin on the preschool level, for it is at this age that children begin to comprehensively explore the many varieties of movement available, and it is at this age that the fundamental motor skills can be presented in a logical fashion so that they will serve as building blocks for future movement experiences and ultimate skill refinement. Throughout the school experience, including the college level, movement opportunities must remain important if the child is to grow into a physically educated adult who has developed a habit of participation in joyful movement.

This chapter has also briefly presented discussions of the subfields of physical education. While most professional physical education students are required to study such subfields as kinesiology and physiology of exercise, it is demonstrated that it is no less important to gain familiarization with additional subfields such as the psychology and sociology of sport, motor learning, and programming for people with special needs. Also, if a physical educator is to be truly conversant with his field, and competent in it, he must also garner knowledge of methods of evaluation, research, motor learning, extra-school sports programs, and administration.

SUGGESTIONS FOR FURTHER READING

Cratty, Bryant J. *Social Dimensions of Physical Activity.* Englewood Cliffs, N.J.: Prentice-Hall, 1967.

Helleson, Donald R. *Humanistic Physical Education.* Englewood Cliffs, N.J.: Prentice-Hall, 1973.

McGlynn, George, ed., *Issues in Physical Education and Sports.* Palo Alto, Calif.: National Press Books, 1974.

Ogilvie, B. and Thomas Tutko, "If You Want to Build Character Try Something Else." *Psychology Today* (October 1971).

"Perspectives for Sport." *Quest* (January 1973).

Singer, Robert N. *Motor Learning and Human Performance.* New York: The Macmillan Co., 1968.

Singer, Robert N., *Readings in Motor Learning.* Philadelphia: Lea and Febiger, 1972.

"Teaching Teachers." *Quest* (June 1972).

Toffler, Alvin. *Future Shock.* New York: Bantam Books, 1970.

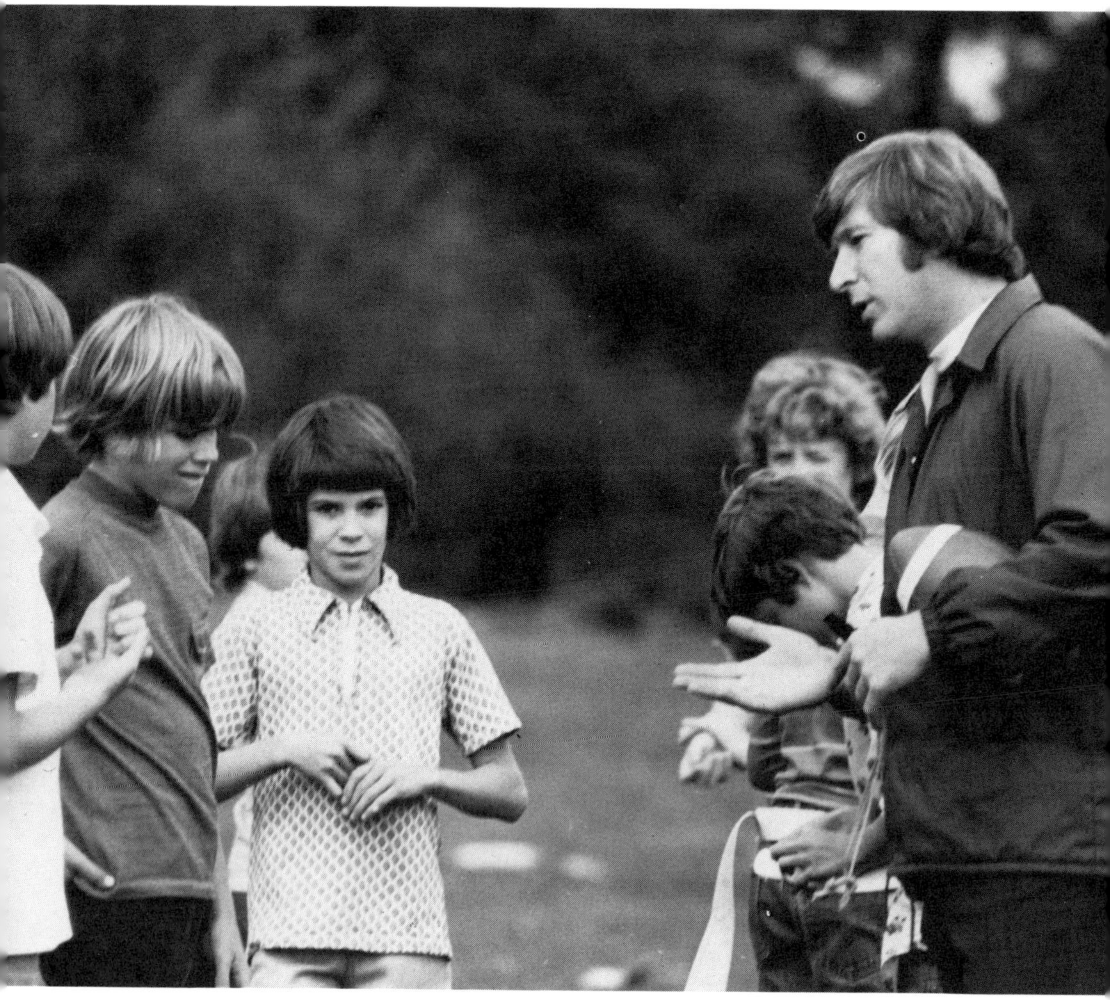

10

The Student as Consumer

In a straight business sense, a consumer is a person who purchases goods, services, or both, and then uses the goods or services to fill some personal need. Producers are those who manufacutre the goods or provide the services which they then make available to the consumer. The consumer is almost wholly dependent upon the producers to make the needed or wanted goods and services obtainable. In turn, the producer relies on the consumer to keep him in operation. Many educators, and an increasing number of students, are beginning to conceptualize the process of education as a consumer-producer relationship, and this analogy has proven disturbing to some educators.

The consumer-producer relationship is viewed as a veiled threat to the traditional concept of education because it seems to many educators that education is being likened to the business world, where the consumer is the one who determines what goods and services will survive in the market. A system of free enterprise is in operation when consumer preference and demand determine the viability of a product or a business concern. In the free enterprise system, when a consumer makes a purchase, he is, in effect, voting for continued availability of his purchase. Sufficient votes for a product or service help to assure survival, and conversely, those products and services shunned by consumers gradually disappear from the market.

THE CONCEPT OF STUDENT CONSUMERISM

The concession is often made, even by critics of the concept, that students do, in fact, "consume" the services rendered by teachers. However, the critics are quick to point out that most students do not possess adequate wisdom to intelligently select those learning experiences, from among the many choices available, which will prove to be of greatest value to them. The critics suggest that students are really educational neophytes, and that they will be better served by benevolent leadership rather than by free choice. Thus, the most ardent critics of student consumerism are really advocating what has been called "lock step" education, a system in which the student's education is programmed for him and in which elective course choices are very limited or nonexistent.

Further, where students are regarded as total neophytes, there is little or no opportunity given them to provide input into curriculum development, to evaluate the curriculum, or to evaluate their teachers. Many educators contend that the student, who is young in both age and experience, is not qualified to make such judgments and evaluations. The critics of student consumerism say that educational expertise rests with the educators, and that these are the individuals who can best make educational assessments and decisions.

On the other hand, advocates of increased student educational input suggest that students should have at least some say about the process of their education since the schools could not exist without the students, and in fact exist specifically to provide a service for their student consumers. The advocates of student consumerism prefer that education become more of a dialogue between students and educators. At present, they say, education is a monologue involving only the educators, and the student is left out. According to the proponents of student consumerism, student input into curriculum development, curriculum appraisal, and teacher evaluation will help to assure that student needs and interests are made known and served.

Implications of Student Consumerism

The schools need to know what parts of the curriculum students feel are relevant, what parts irrelevant, and most of all, why students feel that way. It is doubtful that learning really occurs when students consider their curriculum to be irrelevant to their needs and interests. The concept of the student as consumer may suggest that schools should consider undertaking marketing research among students in order to determine what students are thinking, what they need, and what they want from education. This type of research has been effective in business and industry, and has helped to provide invaluable insights into the desires of the consumers. It might also help educators to understand the desires of students.

No matter how tempting such research may seem for education, there will, as Bronson points out, be strong opposition to such a move among many educators who will feel threatened:

> It is difficult to imagine any system other than the one we have been raised and trained in, in which the teacher or authority determines the boundaries of the course. Our whole administrative structure is based on the validity of curricula and the departments which are responsible for them.[1]

Advocates of student consumerism say that the learner must share in curriculum design in order for the curriculum to be valid. This does not imply that students are to be regarded as curriculum experts but rather that student input is vitally important if the learning experience is to be appropriate and meaningful.

Student Consumerism and Accountability

The current "in" word in education today is "accountability." When accountability is demanded in education, the schools and its teachers are expected to be answerable to parents and other tax payers who help to support the school system. But unfortunately, accountability often stops before it reaches the student, and the student is the one for whom the schools exist.

Accountability asks the schools and their teachers to set goals, tell how they will go about reaching them, and then to demonstrate that they have really done what they said they were going to do by achieving measurable results. According to Siedentop:

> The concept of accountability reflects the fact that responsibility for learning gradually is being shifted from the student to the school. Increasingly, the input of public resources into educational systems will be determined by the measurable output of the systems.[2]

The concept of accountability seems to pose a treat to those teachers who feel that individuals less qualified than themselves, or less knowledgable about the educational process, will ultimately be given the responsibility for making judgments in regard to accountability. Though there is probably some logic in this view, it would be equally as bad if teachers were given

---

1. David B. Bronson, "Thinking and Teaching," *The Educational Forum* 39 (March 1975): 349.
2. Daryl Siedentop, "Behavior Analysis and Teacher Training," *Quest* 18 (June 1972): 27.

the sole responsibility for sitting in judgment on themselves. This would deny the system of checks and balances, and would create further chaos in education. Educators who fear accountability the most seem to be those who also fear the possibility of student input into the evaluative process. Yet if student consumerism is to move forward as a real force in education, then students must have a voice into all of the phases of their educations.

Student input into teacher accountability does, in fact, present some problems. Teachers who oppose student input are concerned that a vocal and dissident minority may be perceived as speaking for a more silent, yet more supportive majority of students. This is a legitimate concern whose resolution lies in the student sampling techniques used. In cases where the majority does not speak out, the polling process must be designed to draw out the attitudes and opinions of this group. Critics of student input also suggest that transient students may have an undue effect on any evaluative process, particularly since our society is becoming more and more mobile. Student populations in schools now turn over at an alarming rate, and educators say that transient students often do not have to live with the consequences arising out of the choices and decisions they have helped to make. This could create some difficult problems, since as Crockenberg points out:

> Teachers are the least-ranking members of a far-flung educational establishment that diffuses educational decision-making powers so broadly that accountability and responsibility are difficult to locate precisely.[3]

Still other critics of student input worry that student opinion tends toward faddism, and that students might be highly motivated about something one day, and totally negative toward it the next. These critics are concerned that students lack the foresight to understand which experiences will prove to be of more lasting value and use. To many then, where long-term curricular validity is desired and important, student consumerism may prove to be a contradiction. Yet the futurists contend that long-term curricular validity is a relic of the past, and that students should concentrate on those experiences which are relevant at any given point in time, and which have immediacy of use. Taggart reminds us that:

> In the minds of parents, success in the outside world has become so dependent upon school success that schools are thought of as the prime instruments of social mobility.[4]

3. Vincent Crockenberg, "Poor Teachers Are Made Not Born," *The Educational Forum* 39 (January 1975): 192.
4. Robert J. Taggart, "Accountability and the American Dream," *The Educational Forum* 39 (November 1974): 34.

The comment is often heard that a particular child is not motivated by school or school work. This statement is at various times made by both educators and parents. The word "work" is, in itself, reflective of the attitude some individuals hold toward learning. Yet it is doubtful that young children consider learning to be work—this is an attitude they seem to acquire when they reach school age.

From birth on, the child experiences countless learning situations and these stimulate the child to continue to explore and learn about the environment. In the preschool years, learning seems to occur almost naturally, and there is little perceptible boredom because these experiences, which are largely self-guided, are meaningful and pleasant, and are, moreover, fun for the child. Once formal schooling begins, much of the pleasure and fun seems to be drained away and the learning experience becomes "work." In the words of Galloway:

> It may be a sad commentary on life that people play games or that students need to learn behavioral games to fulfill the requirements of schooling . . .[5]

Perhaps, then, problems of motivation in learning rest not so much with the student, but with the schools, which tend to foster learning in less than natural, and inherently unmotivating ways. Just as successful businesses seek to more fully understand their customers in order to make their products and services more appealing, so must education come to know students in ways which will enable education to be a process that is more compatible with the ways in which students learn and want to learn.

The Student as Captive Audience

One basic difference between business and education is that businesses must compete with each other in order to win satisfied customers. Our educational systems typically operate as monopolies, and the customer has relatively few choices. This makes the student a virtual captive audience. Whenever the audience is a captive one, there are not very many efforts made to elicit opinions or to offer alternatives. Particularly in the case of education, this leads to complacency and a tight rein on the status quo, since the student really has nowhere else to go.

A classic example of how such a system operates is illustrated by the legendary story about the late Henry Ford, who pioneered the mass prod-

5. Charles M. Galloway, "Teaching Is More Than Words," Quest 15 (January 1971): 69.

uction of the automobile. In the early years of production of the Model T, Ford informed his customers that they could have their cars in any color they wished so long as it was black. When there are no alternatives, the consumer cannot be given a choice, and consumer input need not be sought. In today's automobile market competition is so keen that the customer literally can select from thousands of alternatives and options to the basic models. The automobile manufacturers know that different people have different needs, and that no two people are alike, and so they offer a multitude of options to satisfy the customers and to compete for their car-buying dollars. Education has managed to remain in the era of the Model T.

Under its present structure, education cannot endeavor to be all things to all people. Perhaps such an attempt would be a foolish undertaking with any conceivable future structure. However, because education does function as a monopoly, it is highly insensitive to consumer input. Education must seek out a middle ground somewhere between its monopolistic posture and the competitive madness which has stricken the auto industry. The schools must find a way to become more responsive to the needs and desires of students than is now typically the case. Scott has suggested that the counter-culture ethic looks for schools in which:

> Cooperation replaces competition, an emphasis on process replaces an emphasis on product, sport as a coeducational activity replaces a concern for excellence, and an opportunity for spontaneity and self-expression replaces authoritarianism.[6]

Student consumerism does not mean that students will run the schools. It does mean that those who are responsible for the schools will have to become sensitized to the feelings and opinions of their students. Attendance laws place the students into the educational framework, but such laws do not take away the academic freedoms of students, nor do they dictate that students must accept the role of captive audience. Educators must become sensitive to the student's frame of reference, and begin to empathize more fully with the student. Educators must be willing to take a critical look at education from the students' point of view. Educators must make a real effort to understand how the student feels, why he feels the way he does, and then determine how this input can be used most effectively to revitalize the learning process.

Communication between the schools and their students must become a two-way street. Students must be liberated from their uncomfortable status as captive audience in order to free education to become a real learning process.

6. Jack Scott, "Sport and the Radical Ethic," *Quest* 19 (January 1973): 74.

What specifically, does the student-as-consumer concept imply for physical education? As a part of general education, physical education will feel the same basic effects of student consumerism, but with certain applications that will help physical education to also become more meaningful and valid. Modifications in the consumerism concept will have to be made in order to bring each of the separate academic areas into line with the general concept. Rather than being a delivery system concentrating on skill learning, physical education will have to become much more responsive to the affective expectations and needs of students. Clarke wrote:

> The physical educator should consider boys and girls as total integrated beings. Each child brings more than his body to the gymnasium, the playground and the athletic field; he also brings his mind, his emotions and his unique personal and social traits.[7]

Student consumers in physical education will expect to receive consumer information in the form of the "whys" of physical education. Only with this kind of information in hand will students be able to make intelligent decisions about their personal need for physical activity. Student consumers will demand that physical education present its body of knowledge in a clear and meaningful way. The AAHPER has described the body of knowledge unique to physical education in this way:

> In addition to the scientific facts and principles underlying the acquisition and performance of motor skills and organized activities, this body of knowledge logically includes an understanding of the organic requirements for power, skill, and endurance, the values and hazards inherent in physical activity, procedures for proper and safe participation, and the understanding essential for the individual's assuming responsibility in personal planning for good health and well-being.[8]

When students become consumer-oriented in physical education, they will not be merely arbitrarily directed to participate in activities which may or may not hold relevance for them. Instead, the cognitive and affective aspects of activities will be presented in order to enhance and supplement the psychomotor aspects. Consumerism will demand that efforts be made to assure that students learn useful information and skills. This very strongly suggests that student consumerism will lead physical

7. H. Harrison Clarke, ed., "Individual Differences, Their Nature, Extent and Significance," *Physical Fitness Research Digest* (October 1973), p. 21.
8. American Association for Health, Physical Education, and Recreation, *Knowledge and Understanding in Physical Education*. (Washington, D.C.: AAHPER, 1969), p. viii.

education further away from team sports and closer to an emphasis on the lifetime sports. Berlin has observed that:

> The hope is that physical educators consider placing first priority on putting their own house in order by re-defining physical education, deriving its theories, improving upon its modes of measurement, and re-valuing the purposes which give it direction.[9]

When students are viewed as consumers, knowledge of student attitudes becomes very important to the teacher. Student attitudes toward the learning experience determine to a large extent to what use the student will put learning. Thus, the physical educator must not only provide a physical education program, but must provide something the student not only will enjoy, but will be unable to obtain or duplicate elsewhere. As Bucher warns:

> Many community residents have indicated they are not going to pay taxes, build swimming pools, pay high salaries, or have HPER programs unless some unique service is rendered.[10]

The physical educator is going to have to strive for satisfied clients who are satisfied with the value of their learning experience. Learner satisfaction should be one of physical education's major goals at all educational levels, but it is especially essential during the early elementary school years. It is during the formative period that positive attitudes toward physical activity can be instilled so that these attitudes will carry over throughout the life of the individual.

Physical educators must guard against the risks of becoming complacent in the knowledge that a captive audience of students will always be available. While physical education is still required of all students at many schools and colleges, the move has recently begun toward removing this requirement at some institutions. Even where such a requirement remains, physical educators cannot hide behind it and continue to offer programs that overlook the needs and interests of students. In describing the kind of physical education students need and want, and the kind of physical education that must be provided for them, Jewett said:

> In physical education concerned with persons in process, curricula will incorporate content-specific processes which need to be learned and internalized as an integral part of knowing and of understanding human movement phenomena . . . We will recognize that the best rationale for physical

9. Pearl Berlin, "Prologomena to the Study of Personality by Physical Educators," *Quest* 13 (January 1970): 61.
10. Charles A. Bucher, "What's Happening in Education Today?" *JOHPER* 45 (September 1974): 31.

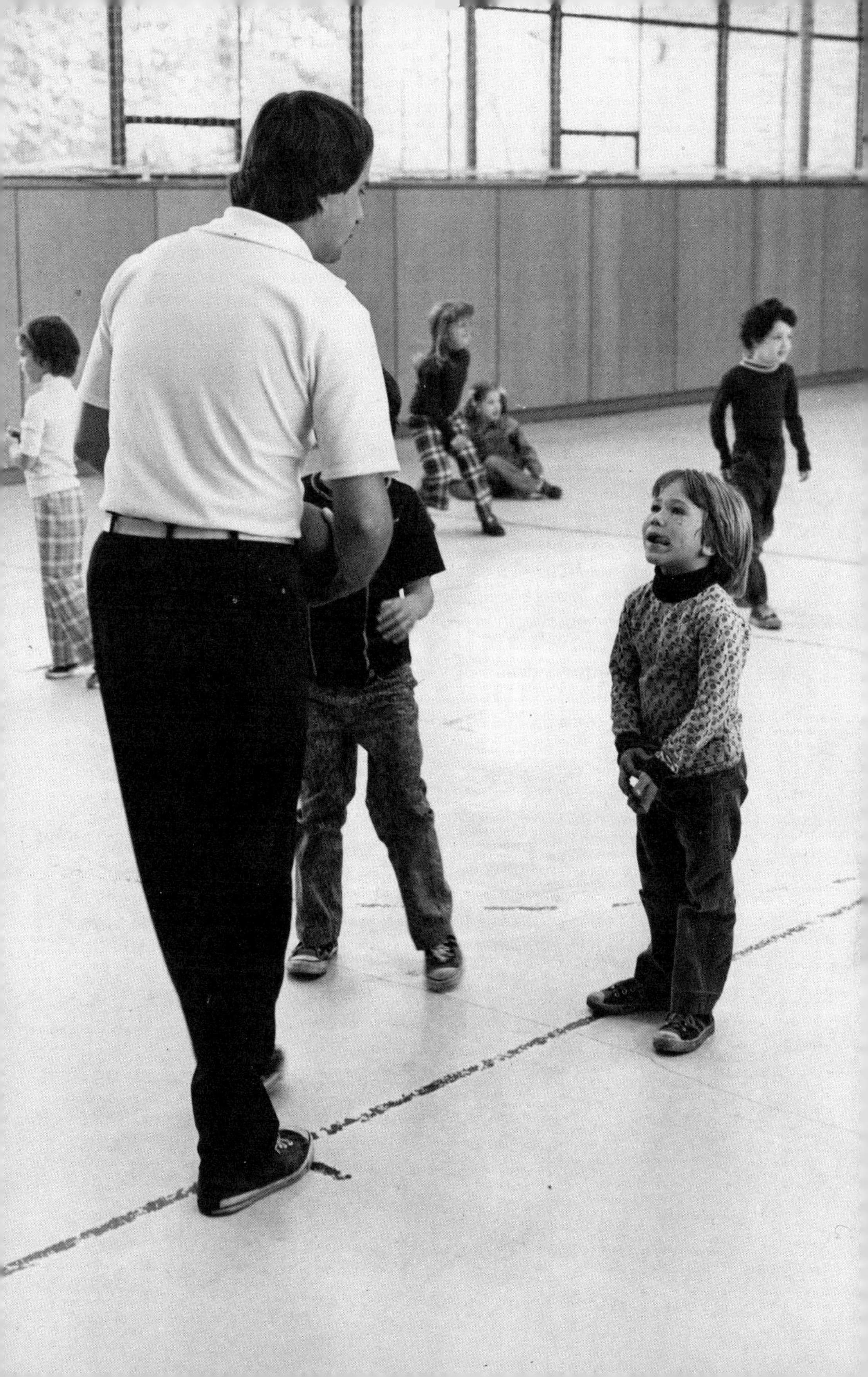

education for all in the school curriculum, the true significance of physical education as a part of an individual's general educational heritage, lies in its unique process content.[11]

The physical education curriculum will have lasting meaning for students when it provides them with a service that they need, want, and enjoy. Relating to students as affective beings and as consumers will help to assure that education will serve individuals in ways in which only education can serve them. Acceptance of student consumerism is eminently compatible with the philosophy of humanistically conceived learning experiences.

SUMMARY

It is highly probable that much of man's future rests with the kind and quality of education he receives today. The basic premise of this chapter is that education must begin to think in terms of the student as consumer, and therefore must begin to provide that very critical customer with high quality services.

The consumer concept as it relates to education was likened to the evolution of the Model T Ford of automotive fame. It was pointed out that the student consumer needs to be able to select alternatives so that education can become customized to the individual, and it was stressed that education can no longer afford to be complacent with the lock step system it has perpetuated.

Rather than concentrating on physical education in isolation, this chapter dealt with consumerism as a general educational concept and model. We have tried to show both the advantages and possible problems that could arise from student consumerism advocacy. Lastly, we devoted a brief section to physical education in particular, and outlined the ways in which student consumerism is very much in line with the humanistic perspective in physical education.

SUGGESTIONS FOR FURTHER READING

Ariel, Gideon B. "Physical Education: 2001?" *Quest* 21 (January 1974):49–52.

Berg, Kris. "Maintaining Enthusiasm in Teaching." *JOPER* 46 (April 1975):22.

11. Ann E. Jewett, "Who Knows What Tomorrow May Bring?" *Quest* 21 (January 1974): 70.

Giannangelo, Duane M. "Make Report Cards Meaningful." *The Educational Forum* 39 (May 1975):409–413.

Hoffman, Shirl James. "Traditional Methodology: Prospects for Change." *Quest* 15 (January 1971):51–57.

Siedentop, Daryl. "On Tilting at Windmills While Rome Burns." *Quest* 18 (June 1972):94–97.

Wittenauer, James L. "Voluntary Physical Education: A Sound Practice." *JOPER* (May 1975):23.

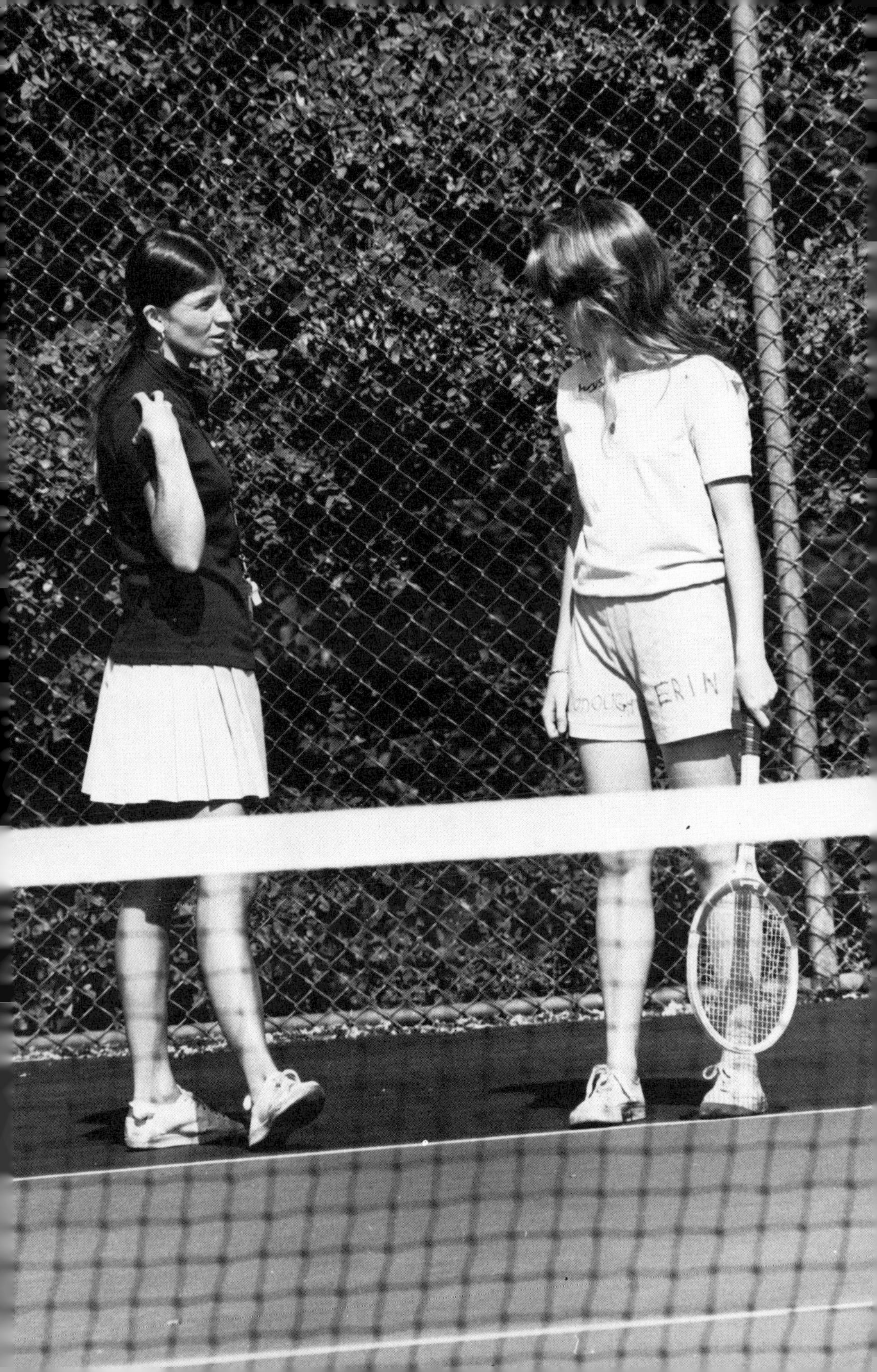
ERIN

11

Getting the Message
Across

What the public at large thinks about physical education, and whether or not the public is willing to accept physical education as a valid curriculum offering depends to a large extent on what physical education does to build its own image. Physical education exists solely to serve people, and it can have little validity or credibility unless it is sensitive to public opinion. Students, teachers in other disciplines, school administrators, school board members, and other tax payers who may or may not have children in the schools, are members of the public who will form opinions about physical education. Because each of these groups looks at physical education from a somewhat different vantage point, physical education must have a knowledge of group behavior and be aware of the many ways in which group attitudes are formed, so that each group can be communicated with by the most suitable means.

RELATING TO THE STUDENT

Often, the need to communicate with the student is overlooked. This is not done deliberately, but simply arises out of the tendency to consider students in paternalistic terms, because students are rather new to formalized educational processes. Education tends to take the position that since more experienced adults have designed learning, that it follows that what they have designed will of course be good for students. Education frequently errs in considering the student last in any listing of priority groups with regard to communication.

There are two primary, but closely related considerations in teacher-student communications in education and in physical education in particular. First, good communications will provide students with information that will assist them in becoming more understanding of the "whys" of physical education, and in turn more responsive to physical education and more supportive of it. Secondly, successful public relations with the learner help to assure that the learner will make a personal commitment to continued physical activity once the benefits of such activity are fully understood. When students become commited, they will be more apt to incorporate and integrate what they have learned into their lives.

It is doubtful whether learning which will not be incorporated, integrated, or used by the student is worth the time and effort expended on it by either the student or the teacher. Students must be helped to understand why a particular set of learnings will be of personal meaning to them. If valid analogies cannot be drawn, then it is pointless to waste valuable educational time on something that will be of no practical or personal use.

Students need to be treated as full partners in the educational process. They need, and in fact demand, to become convinced of the values of physical education. It is a fallacy to believe that the values of physical education are obvious to the uninitiated. If the values of physical education were in fact obvious, we probably would not have so many physically inactive adults in the general population. The time to begin "selling" physical education is in the earliest school years. Placing students into physical education classes, and then simply presenting skills is not enough. There must be much more offered in the way of useful learnings. Vodola has specified these additional cognitive learnings to be derived from physical education:

> The student must understand and be able to apply the scientific method to problems. He must be able to state a problem clearly, locate pertinent reference material, design an approach that makes a solution attainable, and be able to draw logical conclusions from the data available. Clearly, he must possess the ability to solve problems inductively . . .[1]

Yet, in our zeal to teach skills, we often overlook the cognitive aspect of physical education, and it is this cognitive aspect that holds the most potential for enhanced communications with students. Learners need to be "sold" the facts, which are vital information for any group of consumers. This is the foundation for establishing better communications and public relations with the student.

1. Thomas M. Vodola, *Individualized Physical Education Program for the Handicapped Child.* (Englewood Cliffs, N.J.: Prentice-Hall, Inc., 1975), p. 141.

Students need to be treated as full partners in the educational process.

RELATING TO OTHER EDUCATORS

Public relations efforts must be extended to teachers in other disciplines. They, too, need to receive physical education public information. Teachers outside of physical education help to form, within each school, the basis for in-house attitudes toward physical education and physical educators. Physical educators are often rightfully accused of becoming aloof; of not joining in with the mainstream of the faculty within a school; of isolating themselves in the confines of the physical education facility; of failing to contribute enough to joint faculty efforts within a school; in short, of considering themselves to be a breed apart. This is a serious error, since physical educators are members of a larger faculty sharing common educational interests, and physical education is but one area of study within a larger educational curriculum.

When physical educators become clannish, they increase the probability that physical education will be misunderstood. A failure to communicate with colleagues can result in misconceptions and stereotyping. Singer has written:

> Of the academic disciplines, physical education is one of the most controversial in terms of a place and function within the academic structure. Everyone outside of the field knows something about it. Many claim to be experts and will even decide our fate for us. Yet the ironical thing is that these same individuals do not really comprehend what physical education is all about.[2]

Coaching and Public Relations

In particular, physical educators who are also coaches must become astute in the management of good communications and public relations with faculty in other disciplines. The coach is often more highly visible in that role than as a general faculty member. Also, because athletic programs seem to be disproportionately expensive programs, a schism is sometimes opened or widened between the coach and other faculty who want increased equipment and expenditures for their own subject areas. Athletic programs are expensive, and physical educators and coaches must become aware of the resentment this can cause. Further, athletic programs are usually given great financial latitude by school boards and school administrators, and are widely supported by the general public as being worthwhile.

Athletics receive high educational priority, and occupy a major position of importance for the public. Athletics will remain an important educational priority only for as long as they continue in public favor. Thus, those engaged in coaching must remain very sensitive to the feelings of not only the public, but of their colleagues in education in particular. This requires a dedication to sincerity, honesty, integrity, and respect for the views of others, and is the hallmark of a good public relations program. Moreover, it warns against insensitivity to the views of others simply because the position of a particular curricular endeavor seems firm and secure.

True public relations must be realistic, and can never be used as a cover-up. Through public relations programs an attempt must be made to

2. Robert N. Singer, "Communicate or Perish," *JOHPER* 39 (February 1968): 40.

reach out to, and communicate with, individuals who are affected in any way by a program. Since all programs within a school have an effect on each other, good public relations among faculty members is critical if education is to be of service.

RELATING TO THE ADMINISTRATION

The school administration needs to be supportive of the physical education program or the program will not be a functional one. Just as each faculty member is responsible for education within each of the respective disciplines, so is the school administration responsible for the overall curricular offerings within a school. The maintainance of effective communications is a basic way in which the administrator is informed about the intentions and accomplishments of a given discipline.

It is particularly important that physical educators maintain effective public relations with school administrators because of the previously cited rather controversial nature of physical education among the various disciplines. Much of the controversy seems to stem from the fact that physical education bears a strong and overt "physical" connotation. Many individuals, school administrators among them, fail to recognize that physical education does have an academic and intellectual side as well. These individuals see the physical aspects but often are uninformed about the cognitive aspects of physical education.

At times, school administrators become concerned with the cost and with the equipment and facility needs of a sound physical education program, and tend to be nonsupportive on the basis of economics alone. School administrators depend on physical educators to communicate their needs to them based upon a sound and justifiable program. Physical educators need to take the initiative in communicating with administrators and must be able to articulate the goals, purposes, and values of the physical education curriculum.

COMMUNICATING WITH THE SCHOOL BOARD

It is imperative that the school board be fully aware of the nature of the physical education programs they sanction. Beyond state laws which govern school procedures and set policies on a state level, school boards are responsible for exercising local control over the schools and educators within their jurisdiction.

In many states, laws exist that require schools to offer physical education as a part of the curriculum. It is at the local level that the spirit of the law is carried out and supervised. Because support for school programs is the ultimate responsibility of the local school board itself, it is critical that members of such boards receive information that will help them to make valid judgments about physical education, and keep it in proper perspective as part of the total curriculum.

School boards seem at times to pay more attention to athletic programs than they do to the parent physical education programs, but this is often the case simply because of the high profile and visibility of athletics. Physical education instructional programs, which tend to be somewhat overshadowed by athletics, require support in the form of communications and public relations programs emanating from the physical educators themselves. School board members need to be informed about what is going on and what needs to be done. Without such direct information and input from physical educators they cannot act in behalf of any program.

In many instances, school boards must be shown how the good athletic programs in their schools are really outgrowths of an effective and contributory instructional program. While the basic instructional programs lack the glamour and visibility of athletic programs, they are in fact the springboard for athletics. Support for the basic instructional program on the part of school boards comes about when physical educators communicate the information that such programs serve all students in a necessary phase of their education. The basic instructional program will suffer and lose its impact when it is allowed to ride on the coattails of athletics. The distinction must be made between the two programs so that each can continue to serve in its own educational sphere. This need to differentiate the programs before school boards especially, is the responsibility of physical educators. As Singer has observed:

> Physical educators have taken a back seat too long. We must assume the responsibility of communicating with all those people who in one way or another, have some relationship to the program. This will, obviously, include everyone within the school and surrounding community.[3]

COMMUNICATING WITH TAXPAYERS

Taxpayers fall into two general groups: parents who have children in the schools, and other members of the community who may or may not have children whom the schools will at some time serve. Both groups do have one thing in common—it is their tax dollars that support the schools, and they want and deserve the best possible return for their investment.

3. Ibid. p. 41.

Parents whose children are already in a school system or close to school age, have probably the greatest vested interest in the quality of education available in the schools in their community. These parents can be very supportive provided that they receive adequate information on which to base judgments and conclusions. For such parents, the quality of education is a reality rather than an abstraction, and it is a reality that comes home with the child each school day. Parents will be supportive if they can see the observable and positive effects of education on their children. They need to know that the quality of education their child receives is the primary force in causing the child to grow and mature in ways the parents desire.

With regard to physical education in the public mind in particular, Bucher wrote:

> If we ever hope to render the greatest contribution to the community and to the larger society we must identify and prepare ourselves to render a unique and essential social service that is . . . valuable . . .[4]

Parents typically want what is good for their children. Parents will determine what is good about physical education based largely on their own experiences as students. If physical education was an enriching and enjoyable experience; if the parent-as-student was helped to understand the values and purposes of physical education; and if positive attitudes and a store of serviceable skills were outcomes of the physical education experience, then the parents will be more likely to be strong advocates of physical education for their children. Research in the realm of sports involvement seems to hold implications for physical education as well. For example, as a result of their research, Snyder and Spreitzer concluded, "For both sexes, the parents' interest in sports shows a consistent positive relationship with . . . sports involvement."[5] Satisfied parents are of profound importance because their opinions will have a high credibility among other parents, and a nucleus of satisfied parents can be an effective arm of any public relations program.

Effective channels for communicating with parents must be established, and there are several ways in which this can be done. Direct contact implies interpersonal communications between teachers and parents, and comes through such means as parent-teacher conferences, special programs where children demonstrate what they have learned, or through

4. Charles A. Bucher, "What's Happening in Education Today?" *JOHPER* 45 (September 1974): 32.
5. Eldon E. Snyder and Elmer A. Spreitzer, "Family Influence and Involvement in Sports," *Research Quarterly* 44 (October 1973): 252.

informal social contacts. The contact made during informal social situations may be the most invaluable, because teachers and parents can get to know each other as people, and can easily share common interests and goals.

In semidirect contact situations, another person or group serves as an intermediary between parents and teachers. This involves the passing along of information from person to person, generally by word of mouth, as when parents consult with each other about the schools and their programs. Such kinds of information relaying are vital because they can provide a basic means by which a program such as physical education can benefit from widespread exposure. Semidirect communications may approach the proportions of mass communications while still retaining a highly individualized and personal touch.

Indirect communications with parents tend to utilize the media of mass communications, including but not limited to, radio, television, newspapers, magazines, films, pamphlets and newsletters. Newsletters can be used very effectively by the physical educator, as described by Ziatz:

> For just the cost of duplication, a physical education newsletter can be sent to each set of parents . . . In a newsletter, physical educators can briefly explain the activities they are teaching, the objectives for which they are striving, and evaluation procedures. In other words, physical educators can just interpret their lesson plans to the parents . . . parents will realize that physical educators are making an effort to inform them of contemporary issues in their child's school.[6]

Any communications sent out by physical educators must be well written and dignified, and must project the desired image clearly and articulately. It must always be remembered that the use of any type of mass media reaches deeply into all parts of the community and may even be disseminated beyond the local level.

Nonparent Taxpayers

Taxpayers who are not also parents of school-age children nonetheless represent an important link in the public relations process. These individuals cannot be ignored, because their taxes also help to underwrite the cost of education. Soliciting support for education may be a more difficult proposition when dealing with nonparents. While such taxpayers help to pay for education on an equal basis with parents, they receive no direct benefits from the schools in terms of educational progress for their children. In this regard, the nonparent taxpayer is really being asked to invest in

6. Daniel H. Zaitz, "Practical-Realistic Public Relations," *JOPER* 46 (January 1975): 69.

society's future by investing in other people's children. For taxpayers who have no direct ties to the schools, the channels of semidirect and indirect communications become the primary public relations tools.

Often, public education is referred to as "free education." But this is, at best, a deceptive statement. Public education does not directly require payment in the form of taxes from those who rent houses or apartments, for example, but property taxes must be paid by those who own homes or rental units. It is these taxes that support education. It must be realized, though, that even the individual living in a rental unit will have his rent raised when property taxes are increased. Therefore, there are relatively few individuals who in some way are freed from the necessity of either directly or indirectly contributing to the costs of public education. Concerning the tax dollar Menzies wrote:

> Teachers' salaries are an explosive issue in suburbia as is the entire school budget. Salaries comprise about 80 to 85 percent of the average school budget and the school budget anywhere from 50 to 80 percent of the local property tax. What annoys voters most is that they have almost no power to alter school budgets . . .[7]

Education cannot take the public for granted, because it exists to serve the public, and in turn relies upon the public for the financing to continue its services. The public deserves the kinds of communications and public relations efforts which will let them know exactly what they are receiving for their money. The public also needs to know that their support is not only needed, but appreciated.

A FLAW IN PUBLIC RELATIONS EFFORTS

Many schools and educators have failed to take the need for public relations seriously. In some instances, this happens because there is a certain degree of complacency arising out of the knowledge that the public must pay for education in any case. Public education enjoys a virtual monopoly in the distribution of formal education. Private schools supported by private funding are relatively few in number compared to the number of tax supported public schools, and the private schools hardly have a recognizable effect on the monopolistic public sector.

On the other hand, private education has become highly skilled in the methodology of effective public relations. Parents who pay for a private education for their children bear a double burden, since they are still taxed

---

7. Ian Menzies, "The Touchy Teacher's Benefit Issue," *The Boston Evening Globe* 207 (June 16, 1975): 18.

to support the public schools. Thus, private education has had to learn how to compete for students. In so doing, the private schools have not taken the public for granted, but instead have kept the public well-informed about what they were doing and intended to do educationally. They have learned to utilize communications and public relations in a highly effective way, and public education would do well to develop similar methods.

The need to mount effective public relations programs becomes increasingly important in times of tight money and inflation. Moreover, there is a decline currently in the school-age population which gives all indications of continuing. Public education cannot afford to take the public for granted any longer, because in addition to all the other problems facing education today, there is an ever increasing number of other public services among which the income from taxes must be divided.

Physical education tries to offer a unique and essential service to students. While the instructional part of this service traditionally has been directed toward those in school, this instruction is really intended to be of use to the individual throughout life. That the public will, on its own, come to see physical education as being unique and essential cannot be assumed. An informed public will be the most supportive public. The public deserves the best public relations efforts which physical education can muster.

SUMMARY

Eventually, today's students will become members of the taxpaying public, and they will be asked to help finance the costs of education for the children of their future. While students are in the schools, education must speak to them in such a manner that they will come to understand why a community's educational system is a significant asset.

While in this chapter we were not concerned with the student alone, or the student in the future role of taxpayer alone, it is inevitable that the student of today will become the teacher, or the parent, or the school administrator, or the school board member, or perhaps simply the taxpayer, of tomorrow. Each of these groups and their individual members have a right to be fully informed about each of the programs within a school. Strong public relations programs are the information-delivery systems, and all educators must become aware of the techniques of communication on a community-wide level.

SUGGESTIONS FOR FURTHER READING

Giannangelo, Duane M. "Make Report Cards Meaningful." *The Educational Forum* 39 (May 1975):409–413.

Metzger, Paul A. "Our Other Job-Teaching Why." In George H. McGlynn, ed., *Issues in Physical Education and Sports*. Palo Alto, Calif.: National Press Books, 1974.

Singer, Robert N., David R. Lamb, John W. Loy, Jr., Robert M. Malina, and Seymour Kleinman. *Physical Education: An Inter-Disciplinary Approach*. New York: The Macmillan Co., 1972.

Slusher, Howard S. and Aileene S. Lockhart, *Anthology of Contemporary Readings: An Introduction to Physical Education*. Dubuque, Iowa: Wm. C. Brown Co., 1970. Several articles have to do with public relations.

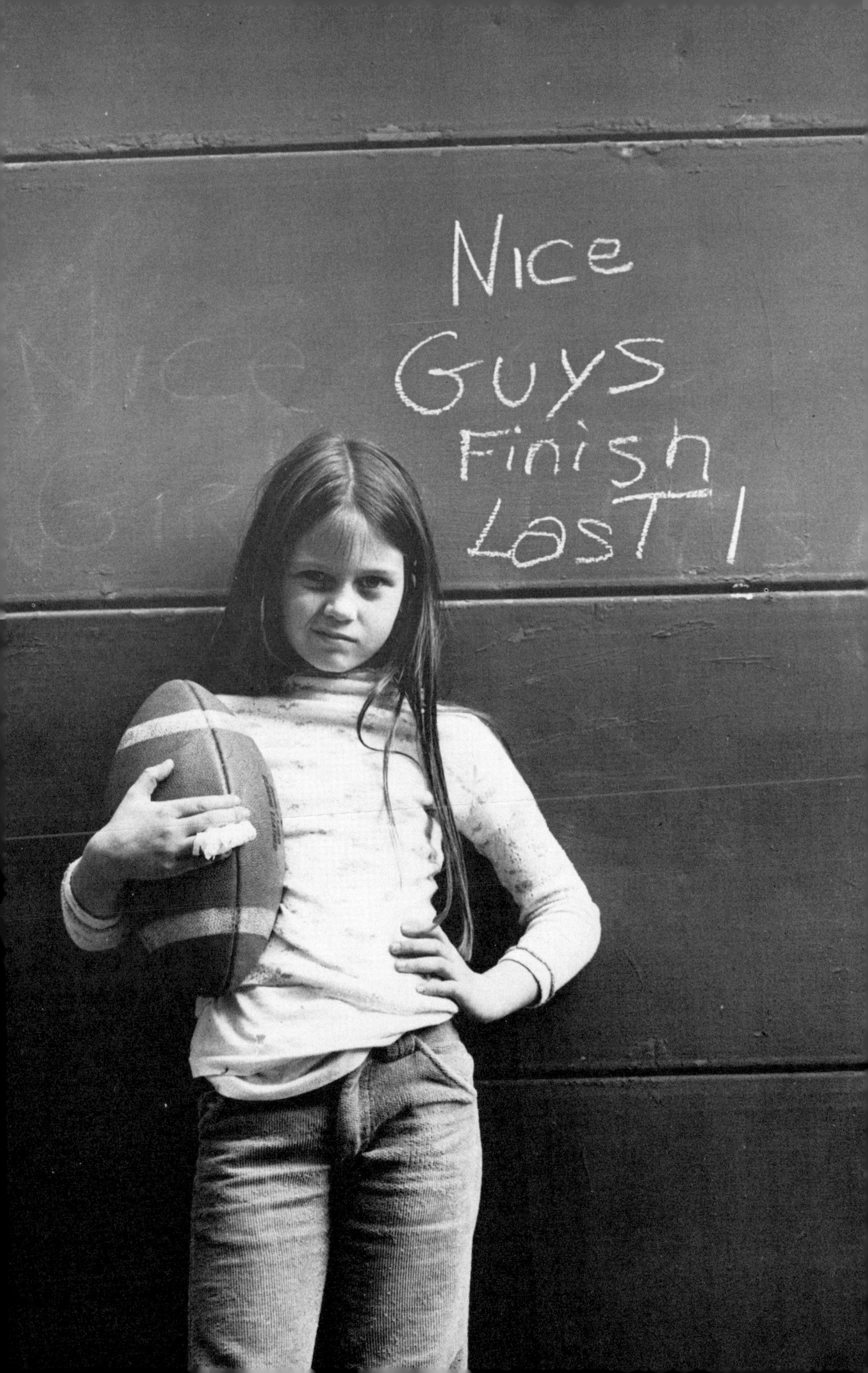
Nice
Guys
Finish
Last !

12

Athletics . . . A Case of Misplaced Priorities?

Most people look at the athlete as an individual who has reached the pinnacle of human achievement in movement. In general, athletics are one form of education in movement designed for the person who is gifted in movement. In this chapter we are concerned with athletics as a part of education, and we will investigate some of the controversies surrounding athletic programs in the schools.

ATHLETICS DEFINED

For the purpose of the discussions in this chapter, athletics refers to those competitive sport experiences which occur between and among the teams of various educational institutions. Intercollegiate athletic programs are those programs which function at the college or university level. When athletic programs are carried on at the secondary school level or below, they are called interscholastic athletics.

Intramural athletics, those programs which are open to all students who want to participate, are philosophically an extension of basic physical education instructional programs, regardless of educational level. Typically, there is little skill instruction given on the intramural level since these programs are basically of a recreational nature. On the other hand, interscholastic and intercollegiate athletics are philosophically extensions of the intramural programs, and are designed for only the most highly skilled performers. Because athletic programs are often equated on the basis of won-lost records, instruction in skills is frequently very intense on the most competitive level.

ATHLETICS AND THE TRADITIONAL PHILOSOPHIC FRAME OF REFERENCE

In traditional philosophic thought in physical education, athletics is the least important emphasis compared to the basic instructional program and the intramural program. Traditional philosophy, at least in regard to the interscholastic level of competition, dictates that the needs of the basic instructional program are to be satisfied before any expansion into intramurals, and especially into interscholastics, is attempted. The basic instructional program receives top priority because it is designed to serve all students. Intramurals receive second priority because while all students are welcome to participate, not all choose to do so. The athletic program is highly selective and serves relatively few students, and thus, in the traditional philosophic frame of reference, athletics comes last in any priority order.

ATHLETICS AND PHYSICAL EDUCATION

There is a point of view in physical education that considers athletic programs to be a natural outgrowth of sound basic instructional programs and well-run programs of intramurals. However, reality does not always reflect this philosophy. In some instances at least, priorities have been reversed so that athletic programs come first and relatively short shrift is given to the other two phases of the program. This is indeed a case of misplaced priorities, but it is also true that athletic programs, particularly if they are successful ones, are the glamour children of any physical education program, no matter what educational level they occur on.

Physical educators often become nearly totally engrossed running athletic programs because of the glamour, publicity, and recognition involved. Frequently physical educators are drawn to athletics inadvertantly rather than by design, but the end result is usually a deterioration of the quality of the basic instructional and intramural programs. In cases where the instructional program in particular is forced to stand in the shadow of an athletic program, the credibility of the entire physical education program, and the credibility of the people in charge of that program, must be questioned.

Whether or not athletics have been misplaced as a priority at any given institution can only be determined by an analysis of all of the physical education programs at that school. Athletic programs are neither inherently bad nor inherently good, and the effect of any program within a specific school system depends on the philosophy of the educators who have the ultimate responsibility for that program and its operation.

It is not the intent here to be hypercritical of athletics, nor to condemn such programs out of hand. The intent is rather to suggest how and why athletics, which hold so much educational potential, sometimes become the primary focus that seems to overshadow and diminish the basic instructional and intramural programs. Perhaps in the final analysis the reader will arrive at a personal philosophy of athletics that agrees with Locke's statement that:

> Sport is not education of or through the physical, because sport is not education. Sport is just what it is.[1]

Athletics Are Reinforced by the Masses

People function largely as gregarious beings, and tend to congregate in groups. Further, people tend to exhibit individual patterns of behavior that conform to the expectations of the group. Behavioral psychologists suggest that people tend to behave in ways that are favored by a group and that give a measure of esteem, and that people tend to repeat these behaviors. Individuals learn very quickly about which behaviors are usually rewarded, and thus reinforced. On the other hand, inappropriate actions draw negative responses from the group, and the lack of reward and recognition results in a diminishing and gradual extinction of the behavior. Athletics are a primary motivator for the behaviors of many individuals.

Throughout much of Western culture, participation and interest in athletics and sport is massively reinforced by public opinion. As Vanderzwaag expressed it:

> Not only do Americans use the concepts of sport and athletics synonymously; they would probably prefer it that way even though it is done rather unconsciously. Competition is the name of the game in this country. Therefore, both sport and athletics symbolize something 'good' because they offer a media for wholesome competition.[2]

Individuals who are seeking personal fulfillment and acceptance are very likely to be drawn to athletics as a vehicle for achievement. People tend to participate in activities which will give them a measure of esteem and which will draw positive reactions from others. Athletes and coaches,

1. L. F. Locke, "Are Sports Education?" *Quest* 19 (January 1973): 90.
2. Harold J. Vanderzwaag, *Toward a Philosophy of Sport.* (Reading, Mass.: Addison-Wesley Publishing Co., 1972), p. 67.

and even the spectator, can achieve a degree of recognition from their participation, knowledge, and interest in athletics.

It is unfortunate that the physical educator who is assigned coaching responsibilities sometimes unwittingly becomes a coach primarily and shortchanges physical education responsibilities. This is, however, part of the acceptance-recognition syndrome. Because there is only so much time and energy which any one person can devote to any one endeavor, and because athletics are so much in the public eye, the physical educator-turned-coach tends to devote more time and energy to the more immediately rewarding of the two educational careers.

The Implications of a Misplaced Priority

What will result if athletic programs are permitted to dominate physical education curriculums? Athletic programs demand enormous amounts of money, and they require the best of facilities and equipment. Further, much time must be allotted to practices, games and travel, and coaches, trainers, and other support staff must be assigned. All of this puts a strain on the available resources, and encroachment on the operation of physical education and intramural programs is almost unavoidable.

Moreover, there is often community pressure for the continuance, upgrading, and expansion of athletic programs. Members of the community seem to frequently be more vocal about athletic programs than about any other single phase of the school curriculum. Parents and other spectators seem to see within athletics the fulfillment of what has been called the "American Dream." They tend to see athletics as embodying much of what America is all about, and they tend to endow athletics with an almost mystical ability to promote discipline, character, physical fitness, religion, and patriotism. Smith has written that:

> As a child grows up he sees his older male models attending sporting events, watching games on television and reading about sports in magazines and newspapers. With so much attention devoted to sport the child soon learns that sport is important and worthwhile.[3]

THE OBSESSION WITH WINNING

Very often, the conduct of athletic programs centers around an all-encompassing need to win. This obsession with winning is one of the basic issues which concerns many people who are close observers of interscholastic athletic programs. This phenomenon is not restricted to the

3. Garry Smith, "The Sport Hero: An Endangered Species," *Quest* 19 (January 1973): 63.

interscholastic level, but is common throughout the world of athletics. However, its effect on the athlete is highly questionable, particularly at the interscholastic level of competition.

Many common axioms have grown out of the "win at any cost" philosophy. Leo Durocher, who for many years has been associated with professional baseball, is creditied with first saying, "Nice guys finish last." Durocher's recently published autobiography even carries that phrase as its title.[4] That phrase is a byword today with coaches on all levels. Probably the most famous axiom came from the late Vince Lombardi, who is still revered by football coaches as a premier example of what a coach ought to do and be. Lombardi coached and lived by the axiom he made famous, "Winning isn't everything, it's the only thing."

Coaches, athletes, and even spectators sometimes are excessively desirous of victory, and this ethic often serves only to distort the sport experience for everyone involved. Morford reinforces the negative aspects of the need to win no matter what the price of victory by observing that:

Surely it is a tragedy if, in modern sport, the applied pressure of the need to win is so great that the athlete is deprived of that moment of recognition in achieving his maximum performance or of even the realization of having attained his potential.[5]

The desire to win is frequently so great the common values become blown out of proportion. For example, drugs are used to dull the pain of an injury; stimulants are taken in an attempt to enhance performance; an injured athlete is put into a game in spite of his injury, because even handicapped, his performance will be superior to that of a substitute; athletes' academic grades are altered, sometimes without the players' knowledge, in order to maintain eligibility. These are but a few of many such examples of the methods used to insure victory. All of them are unfortunate, because they are negative educational examples that succeed only in distorting the world of athletics. Further, such practices pervert the intention of the competitive athletic experience. As Scott reminds us:

The Lombardian ethic views sport as a masculinity rite from which women are excluded. Lombardi often motivated his players by indicating none too subtly that to lose a game was to lose one's manhood.[6]

Athletics and Elitism

An athletic program becomes elitist when its primary goal is winning. Such a program becomes even more highly selective in regard to players it

4. Leo Durocher with Ed Linn, Nice Guys Finish Last. (New York: Simon and Schuster, 1975).
5. W.R. Morford, "Is Sport the Struggle or the Triumph?" Quest 19 (January 1973): 85.
6. Jack Scott, "Sport and the Radical Ethic," Quest 19 (January 1973): 73.

retains on teams, cutting those who are regarded as less than superstar caliber. While many athletes who are good, but not quite good enough, may accept the role of team manager, assistant manager, or, at the very least, spectator, such an elitist philosophy must be questioned. This type of comparatively ruthless selection process does little to promote the educational goals of an athletic program.

Athletic programs designed around an elitist philosophy create in the public mind the impression that the superstar, or sports hero, is the most important focus. According to Smith:

> To be a sports hero the athlete must have a high level of physical ability. Sometimes this ability in itself is enough to make the athlete a hero.[7]

Participation on a team or in a specific game becomes, in the elitist system, secondary in importance to the stellar performances of a relatively few, but highly talented athletes. This kind of system becomes so pervasive that many athletes will not even try out for a team because they realize that their chances of ever playing range from slim to none. These individuals, then, frequently sublimate their competitive drive by joining the ranks of spectators.

"Win or Else" vs. Winning

The desire to win, should, of course, be a part of any athletic contest. The determination to win is not the crux of the issue here, because it would be foolish to suggest that any individual or team striving for excellence would play to lose. The crux of the issue is the "win or else" or "win at any cost" frame of reference, which rejects any performance as unsatisfactory unless the performance has culminated in victory.

There is an obsession with winning in American sport that has created the attitude that athletes or teams who finish second are losers. Frequently, those who fail to win are stigmatized as being losers, and even future winning streaks make this stigma difficult to erase. American society has had a very difficult time coping with the philosophy that "winning is everything." Physical educators, coaches, athletes, fans, alumni, teachers, school administrators, businessmen and women, summer softball teams, bowling leagues, church teams, and even "pee wee" football players, among many other such groups, exhibit at one time or another the symptoms of the "win or else" ethic. As Sadler has written:

> One of the tragedies of our era is that the spirit of competition, which has been a stimulating element in progress and individual development, has

7. Smith, op. cit., p. 65.

*become so widespread and intense as to go out of control; many organized
sports function to keep it out of control.*[8]

"Win or Else" and Finances

Winning is much more than the outcome of a contest or event in which teams or individuals pit their respective talents against each other. In fact, the more important issue is the effect of participation, win or lose, on the athlete or athletes involved. In the school setting, athletics are supposed to have a desirable and positive educational outcome, the purpose of which is to serve the needs of the student participant. This primary objective of school athletic programs is what is so often perverted.

Where winning is the basic criterion on which the success and/or worth of an athletic program is judged, then a serious and critical question must be asked: For whom, or for what purpose, does the athletic program really exist? Athletic programs that function as a part of an educational institution must exist, before any other considerations, for the benefit of the participant. Sadly, some programs exist to serve the needs of fans and alumni, and as such, the athletes are nothing more than entertainers. In such cases, which are only too prevalent, the relevance of a school being in the entertainment business must be questioned. However, the ulterior motive for pleasing the spectator at the expense of the athlete is very obvious: a winning team brings fans through the turnstiles, and many school athletic programs depend upon gate receipts as their major source of financing. Thus, winning teams become important to program administrators because of the financial implications. A balanced budget may depend upon a winning season, and in such situations the athletic talents of students become a source of income for the school.

In the vast majority of instances, gate receipts offset only a relatively small percentage of the total cost of an athletic program. However, the premise remains that sports are a money-making proposition for many schools, and that athletes are frequently exploited for reasons that are not only not in their best interests, but are noneducational as well.

Winners and Losers

In a society where winning is so highly exalted, it is ironic that many athletic programs appear designed to generate more losers than winners. Single and double elimination tournaments and organized league play are but two examples of how a system can be designed, although inadvertently

8. William A. Sadler, Jr., "Competition Out of Bounds: Sport in American Life," *Quest* 19 (January 1973): 129.

it is true, so that a second place finish is often the cause for embarrassment. In these types of tournaments, there is room for only one winner, and the consolation champions are often stigmatized as losers. Athletes and spectators have adopted the ethic of first place being the only place, and a second place finish isn't quite good enough.

The "Winning Is Everything" Ethic May Be Declining

The credo that "winning is everything," and the need to be number one seems to be in decline as far as *some* athletic participants are concerned. Some competitive athletic programs on a few college campuses have been dropped lately not only because of budgetary and other internal institutional problems, but also because many good athletes seem to be turning away from intense competition. Some individuals have attributed this phenomenon to a backlash against the "winning is everything" ethic.

In the place of formal, intensely competitive programs, there is presently a tremendous growth in intramural and club sports. This interest in a more informal and low-key type of competition is even reflected in the sudden spurt of interest in such relatively new activities as floor hockey, frisbee, and coed volleyball. At schools where such sports activities are gaining in popularity, coaches are beginning to find pockets of resistance to high-pressure recruitment of athletes, accompanied by a gradual decline in attendance at certain games. The major exception to this newly emerging phenomenon seems to be the increase in women competitors who are now seeking out more intensive levels of competition.

Throughout the period of emergence of women's sports programs there have been admonitions from male and female leaders alike that the women must be on constant guard in order to avoid the ills which have existed in men's programs. There is wisdom in this admonition, but only time will tell whether or not the warning has been heeded. Not too many years ago, The Pennsylvania State University hosted a series of lectures entitled *Women and Sport: A National Research Conference*. A speech by Michael D. Smith included this telling commentary:

> *Comparisons with males aside, aggressive violence appears to be more in evidence in women's sport than in most other sectors of female life, a function, perhaps, of the psychological characteristics of females who persist in sport. It has been reported, for instance, that female athletes tend to be achievement-oriented and aggressive, traits ordinarily associated with the male sex-role . . .*[9]

9. Michael D. Smith, "Aggression and the Female Athlete," The Pennsylvania State University, Penn. State HPER series no. 2 (1972), p. 105.

Some people have commented that the all-pervasive need to win takes much of the fun out of participation in athletics. These same individuals contend that the pressure to win has caused some athletic programs to become rigid and authoritarian in nature and philosophy. Rigidity and authoritarianism have a direct effect upon the athlete, and tend to be dehumanizing. Further, programs operated in this manner tend to stifle individuality because it is thought that the best team is one that conforms, or is, in effect, a group of individuals cast from the same mold.

The authoritarians believe that individuality is not conducive to the best possible team effort. In such an environment, players tend to look upon the coach as a benevolent dictator whose actions and words are not unlike those of the stereotyped image of the drill sargeant. The athletic experience in such an atmosphere is rigorous and highly disciplined, and the coach demands rather than commands total allegiance and obedience from the athletes. Sport experiences are supposed to instill at least some democratic principles, yet both male and female coaches sometimes function as complete autocrats. This curious inconsistency between theory and practice does not help to establish the credibility of competitive athletics, and is a common criticism made by many observers who are knowledgeable about athletics. As Sage observed:

> . . . athletic coaches are being forced into reassessing their current beliefs concerning interpersonal relations, especially in a leadership context, and many are seeking ways of developing more effective personal relationships with the young athletes on their teams.[10]

The most vocal critics of interscholastic athletic programs contend that the programs are not fun, that too much emphasis is placed on spectator appeal, that winning is over-emphasized, and that too much time and attention is given over to printing programs, solving parking problems, and achieving effective crowd control. Instead, the critics call for an emphasis on increased student participation, on eliciting the best performance possible from the athletes even if the effort is a losing one, and upon seeing that the athletes achieve some measure of personal satisfaction from a program that has sound and solid educational goals and objectives. This latter emphasis can be achieved providing that all of the individuals involved in a program are willing to redefine and redirect their philosophies of athletics, and are further willing and committed to taking positive action.

10. George H. Sage, "The Coach as Management: Organizational Leadership in American Sport," *Quest* 19 (January 1973): 35.

THE EMULATION OF PROFESSIONAL ATHLETICS

Interscholastic athletic programs have come under fire for attempting to emulate the world of professional athletics. Professional athletics are designed to be profit-making business enterprises, while interscholastic athletics are supposed to be educational. Professional athletes are businessmen who sell their skills and perform before a paying audience. Interscholastic athletes are amateurs who are in the business of learning, and they should be using their skills to please themselves.

In professional sport, the profit motive is a primary motivator. The use of sport as a socializing force, as fun, as a method of enhancing physical and emotional well-being, as an aesthetic experience, and as a mode of human expression must take a back seat. For the interscholastic athlete, all of the uses of sport except for the profit motive are of vital and critical importance and necessity. Yet only too often we find the motives of professional athletics being used as the criteria for the design of interscholastic athletic programs. Felshin has written:

> Sport has symbolic power because essential testing and refinement of skill and mastery are clarified as human challenges. Sport has aesthetic and thematic compulsion because expressive modes of performing and contesting are significant and valued.[11]

WINNING AND THE COACH

Many coaches live by the Lombardian ethic that winning is everything, and when outsiders raise questions about this philosophy, coaches tend to feel threatened and they assume a defensive attitude. Some coaches believe that their primary goal is to field a consistently successful team, and they devote themselves to defending this aspect of what is really their vocation as well as their avocation.

Coaches who come under fire constantly for their "win or else" posture are not really tuned-in to the educational objectives of athletic programs. School boards and school administrators frequently are guilty of being obsessed with winning also, because coaches who fail to win often enough are usually relieved of their positions. Those who place excessive pressures on the coach to consistently produce winning or championship teams must bear equal guilt for perverting the athletic experience. It is unfortunate that sometimes coaches who have done everything right except for winning, are also summarily dismissed. Because this is a coaching fact of life in all too many communities, some coaches are intimidated into

11. Jan Felshin, "Sport Style and Social Modes," *JOPER* 46 (March 1975): 31.

abandoning their personal philosophies and adopting the one of "winning is everything," since the public value system seems to be so intolerant of losing no matter how well the athletes perform, or how well-run the athletic program may be.

The athletic coach, then, is often an individual faced with what seems to be an almost insurmountable ethical decision, and the choice made is frequently the criterion used for retaining or releasing the coach. If winning is all-important in a particular coaching situation, then it frequently makes little difference to those who cry for victory whether or not the athletes in a program have received the very best experience possible.

Concerning the loss of integrity on the part of some coaches, Morford has written:

> The modern coach, instead of being the man who encourages and guides others to struggle to do their thing, has instead become that person who manipulates and controls others and their environment so as to do his thing. [13]

The foregoing is in no way intended to be an indictment of all, or even a majority of coaches who are currently active, be they male or female. Rather, this discussion was intended to enlighten the reader concerning some of the dilemmas facing many coaches. It is also true that there is a large number of coaches who have followed the dictates of their conscience and training, and chose to produce good teams who have learned to lose as well as win. These coaches, in numerous instances, have become highly respected individuals and revered leaders.

THE OUTCOMES OF PARTICIPATION IN ATHLETICS

Part of the mystique of athletics has been the claim that the experience builds character, prepares the individual for life, and stimulates the development of desirable personality traits. There is currently no literature that supports such claims per se, and in fact, the literature tends to question such claims as being highly speculative. To begin with, Berlin tells us that we really cannot explain what personality is—"To define personality in a meaningful and functional way poses a challenge to even the ablest scholars."[13] If it is so difficult to define personality, it then becomes ludicrous to try to claim that a particular experience, namely athletics, can mold individuals so that they will have better, more acceptable personalities.

12. Morford, op. cit., p. 86.
13. Pearl Berlin, "Prologomena to the Study of Personality by Physical Educators," *Quest* 13 (January 1970): 55.

The claim that athletics builds character is also open to some question, especially if we note this pertinent observation by Ingham and Loy:

> Performers are always on stage and just become adept at the techniques of impression management since they are required to present a front which does not affront popular conceptions. Thus, the athlete's performance on and off the field becomes typically stereotyped . . .[14]

Many individuals who study the psychology and sociology of athletics suggest that such experiences are neither inherently good nor inherently bad for the athlete. Rather, they suggest that the outcomes of sport are determined by the quality of the leadership, the integrity and principles of the leadership, and the kinds of pressures brought to bear on both the coach and the athletes.

In particular, the win or else ethic tends to severely restrict any outstanding social or psychological outcomes. Perhaps because this ethic is so common in American athletics today, team rosters may in fact be filled with only those athletes who are also obsessed with victory. Just possibly, the less intense, less victory-oriented athlete is the backbone of the increasing club sport movement. These latter activities, along with intramurals, are established and run solely for the participants, and a deep concern for the participant seems to be lacking in much of athletics today. Perhaps, then, competitive sports truly do have the potential for positive social and psychological development, but this potential has not been exploited. In this respect, the issue of what athletics can do for the participant remains a wide-open question. We must know more about athletics and much more about the athlete before the issue can be resolved. As Singer has noted:

> . . . one cannot comfortably conclude anything about the effect of participation in sport and changes in the athlete's personality. Common sense suggests that the athlete decides to experience a given activity and then becomes competent due, at least in part, to the personality he brings to the situation. Sport and fulfillment must be somewhat compatible with an individual's personality.[15]

THE ROLE OF THE SPECTATOR

There are those who welcome the role of spectator over the role of athlete, and freely choose to participate in sport by vicarious means. Some indi-

14. Alan G. Ingham and John W. Loy, Jr., "The Social System of Sport: A Humanistic Perspective," *Quest* 19 (January 1973): 5.
15. Robert N. Singer, *Myths and Truths in Sports Psychology.* (New York: Harper & Row, 1975), p. 97.

The spectator is one of the most interesting social and psychological phenomena in the world of sports, and the importance of the spectator is often overlooked.

viduals, of course, are not highly skilled enough to join a team in any case, or are of an inappropriate age to compete, or simply do not like exercise or the rigors of practice. The role of the spectator is a somewhat curious one, because spectators develop team loyalties and become ardent fans. In an indirect manner, the spectator who is intensely loyal becomes an extension of the team. Yet the spectator need not worry about being benched or dropped from the team entirely because of a poor performance.

When the favored team is losing, and the spectator becomes disgusted or bored, there are options open that are not available to the athlete who is performing. The spectator can leave the game and go home, or if the game is being watched on television or heard on the radio, the set can be switched off or dial changed to another program. Moreover, the spectator can influence the operation of a team by failing to purchase tickets, or by being openly critical by phoning radio talk-shows devoted to sports or by writing letters to newspapers or to the management of the team itself. Fan displeasure has at times dictated the release of players, managers and coaches, and fan approval has sometimes meant the retention of individuals whose release was being considered. The fan is a very dominant force in professional athletics in particular, but spectator influence is beginning to become greater and greater on the interscholastic level. The spectator is one of the most interesting social and psychological phenomena in the world of sports, and the importance of the spectator is often overlooked.

Heinold has remarked that not very much research has been done on the spectator, or on the reasons for certain behaviors by spectators, but he has observed that in general:

> ... given individuals consume sports through all media and that generally the non-watcher is also the non-participator ... There are those who seek relaxation, others who seek stimulation and still others who seek information and so forth.[16]

THE NEED FOR AN ALTERNATIVE TO INTENSITY

There is currently a growing awareness that there can be success in sports, even in the most competitive sense, without the necessity of an over-emphasis on the need to win. This is a social comment upon a system of education which has for years helped to produce more losers than winners. The world of athletics would do well to heed the words of Sadler:

> To rescue sports from the madness of unbounded competition we can begin by recognizing the range, intensiveness, and consequences of competition in sports and in society. To be faithful to humanistic values within the world of sport will require taking a stand that will run counter to powerful forces in modern American life.[17]

There are many individuals who want to participate in athletics in a capacity other than that of spectator, yet they are turned-off and turned away because they realize that athletics are not now truly participant-oriented. Only a real concern for what is good for the participant can bring athletic programs into a more proper educational perspective.

The problems abounding in sport today are not unique to sport alone, but are observable problems of our society as a whole. Because sport cannot exist apart from society, we cannot expect sport to be totally immune from societal influences and priorities. However, coaches, athletes and spectators alike—in fact anyone who has any interest in the world of sport—must make a concerted effort to set the world of athletics in

16. William D. Heinold, "Motive Typology for Female Sports Spectators: A Comparison With Male Types," The Pennsylvania State University, Penn. State HPER series no. 2, (1972), p. 316.
17. Sadler, op. cit., p. 132.

proper perspective so that it begins to fulfill more satisfactorily its humanistic and educational roles.

SUMMARY

The contention of this chapter has been that while athletics are certainly worthy of pursuit, that the emphasis in athletics has been misdirected. Where athletics should be designed to serve the participant, there is instead a pervasive obsession with winning and being able to claim the title of "Number One." To achieve this goal, the athlete is not served, but exploited. The authors have come down hard on the conduct of athletics, especially in the area of interscholastics, and many coaches will no doubt cry "Foul." But there can be no compromise with ethics where the high school athlete, in particular, is concerned.

We have defined athletics and attempted to show how athletics are meant to be encompassed within the educational framework of the schools. We have discussed the contributions athletics make that are of a positive nature, and have contrasted these with the obsession for producing championship caliber teams by exploiting the talents of the participants.

Intramural and club programs have been considered, and their use as alternative outlets for the competitive urge has been discussed. Finally, we have shown the serious problems faced by coaches, and have outlined the influencial role played by spectators.

SUGGESTIONS FOR FURTHER READING

Scott, Jack, *The Athletic Revolution*. New York: Free Press, 1971.

Shecter, Leonard, *The Jocks*. New York: Paperback Library, 1970.

Tutko, Thomas and Jack W. Richards, *Psychology of Coaching*. Boston: Allyn and Bacon, Inc., 1971.

Weiss, Paul, *Sport: A Philosophic Inquiry*. Carbondale, Ill. Southern Illinois University Press, 1969.

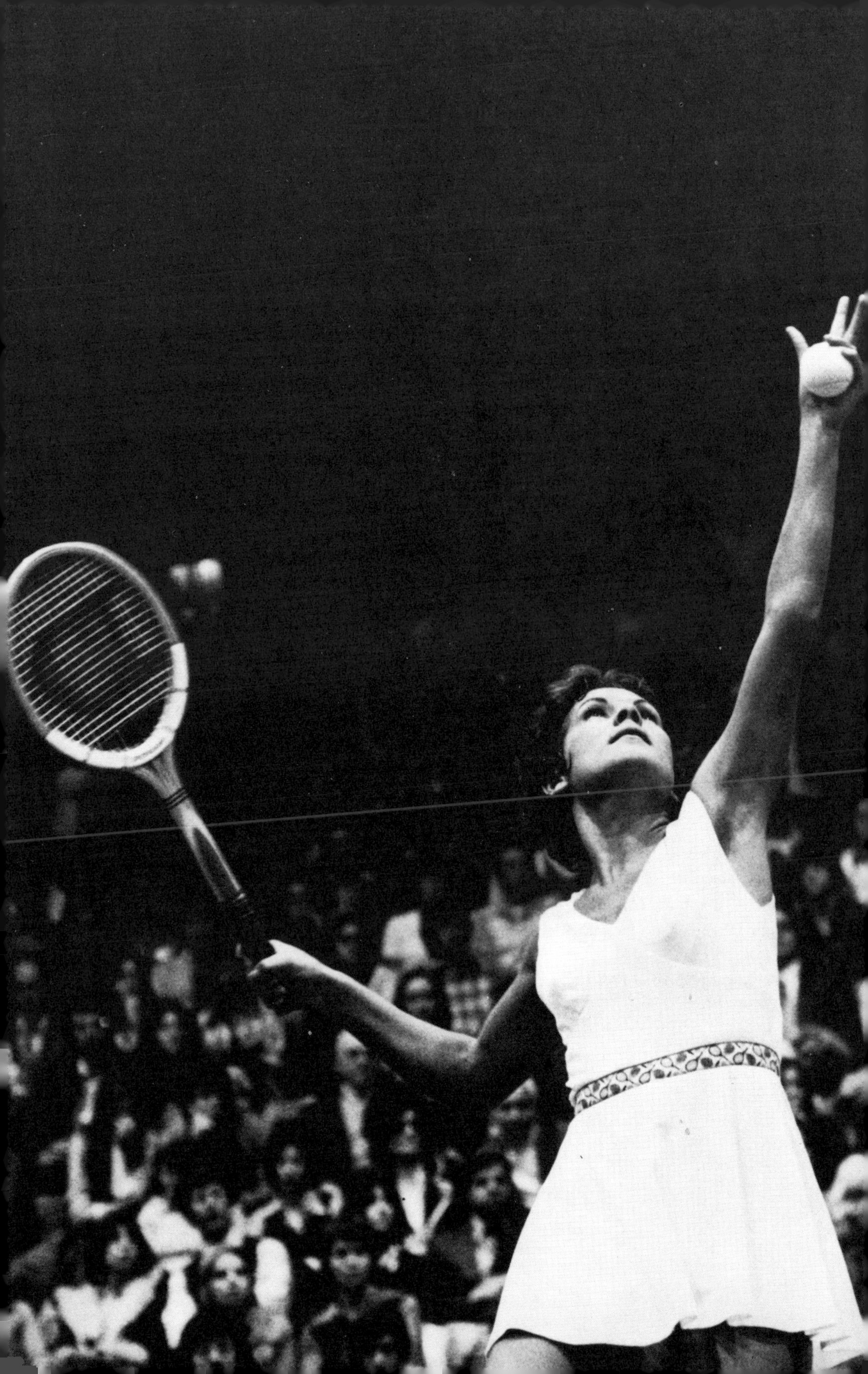

13

Women in Sport: A Quest for Equality

The quest for equal opportunity for women in sport has only just begun. The current women's movement in sport denies gender as a valid determinant of the availability of opportunities for full participation. Traditionally, women as a group have been assigned their roles by a male-dominated society, and wide participation in sports has not been one of these assigned roles. Historically, achievement in accordance with potential has not been an alternative open to women, particularly in aspects of life thought to be male oriented. Participation in sports, and achievement in sports has carried a masculine connotation that effectively barred women from much of the wide spectrum of enrichment opportunities available to men. In this chapter we will look closely at the female as a sports-minded person, and as an athlete.

THE THREAT OF FEMALE ACHIEVEMENT

There are some situations in which both men and women feel threatened by the achievements of a woman. Because sport has traditionally been associated with such masculine sex roles as domination, competitiveness, aggressiveness, and ruggedness, the female athlete is frequently considered a threat to the male and the male ego. Other women tend at times to denigrate the female athlete, feeling that such an individual is a threat to femininity simply because the female athlete has stepped outside her assigned sex role. In fact, there seems to be a nonachievement syndrome permeating many cultures, and thus affecting many women. Within such cultures, women are limited to the roles of housewife and mother, and achievement beyond this is unacceptable. This is a powerful deterrent to many women who have not only the desire, but also the ability, to achieve not only in athletics, but in many other aspects of life as well. On this latter issue, Harris has taken the stand that:

> ... those females who are insecure in their own sense of femininity are not willing to take the risk of doing anything that might threaten their selfhood. These are generally the females who avoid vigorous activity and competitive sport because it is unladylike. Perhaps we need to examine the reasons for the fears that produce the threats. If the standard for feminine behavior is that dissonant from behavior in athletics, maybe we need to change the standard for appropriate behavior in athletics.[1]

Roles which are acceptable for women have largely been assigned to women by men, because most cultures are male-dominated. This phenomenon is often called by the term "sexism," which has an equally negative effect on both sexes. Any sexist ideology tends to take opportunities away from one sex, and thus makes both sexes less free to pick and choose from the many options available. For example, behavior which has been designated as "masculine" implies also that there are behaviors which are "feminine." Conversely, the concept of "feminine" behavior indicates that there is behavior uniquely "masculine," and which is therefore limited to males only.

Those individuals or groups who adhere to the concept of sexism attempt to restrict male or female behavior to those activities designated as being uniquely masculine or feminine. Males or females who cross over the lines of accepted behavior become threats to those individuals who firmly believe in the sexist ideology of assigned sex role behavior. On this theme Roberts has said:

> It has been argued that humans are basically psychosexually neutral at birth and that gender roles are learned through the socialization process ... Sex differences in interests, values, roles, and personality emerge and result in well-defined conceptions of appropriate behaviors for men and women.[2]

The attitude that governs and attempts to dictate appropriate human sex-role behaviors seems curiously out of step with our modern era.

---

1. Dorothy V. Harris, "The Female Athlete: Psychosocial Considerations," *JOPER* 46 (January 1975): 34.
2. Glyn C. Roberts, "Sex and Achievement Effects on Risk Taking," *Research Quarterly* 46 (March 1975): 58.

Though we are, perhaps, in an age of unprecedented enlightenment, irrelevant traditions and vestiges of the past seem to die hard. Many people become very insecure when changes in traditions are made, and they tend to seek the comfort and security of familiar traditions by adopting an attitude of strict conservatism. Sometimes, however, conservatism only serves as a deterrent to needed and meaningful change.

Of late, women have begun to assert themselves in order to gain equal rights in all aspects of life. This pursuit of equality will lead to a significant advancement of humanism in societies that traditionally operated on a philosophy of sexist supremacy. While it would be naive to even remotely suggest that gains in equality for women, particularly in sport, will quash sexism, any gains in equality by women will help to gain more equality and freedom of opportunity for all groups. As Kane has said:

Women in sport may well need to be considered primarily as human beings with special abilities and needs, and secondarily as being of a particular sex. The personality supports that are needed by men for achievement, are those broadly needed by women in the same kind of situation. [3]

Equality for women in sport is one of the most significant issues to which the field of movement must currently address itself. The demands by women are unprecedented, yet they are legitimate, because what is sought is equal consideration, recognition, and opportunity to participate fully in all the domains of skilled movement. Women are asserting their right to achieve fulfillment and self-actualization in movement through avenues that traditionally have been extremely limited or open only to men. The limitation of opportunities for women seems to be derived from traditional psychological and sociological sex-role assignments rather than from any legitimate biological or physiological restrictions.

Contrived Value Systems

The psychological and sociological pressures which discourage women from full participation in movement activities are largely outgrowths of contrived and learned human value systems. Where values and mores seem to facilitate the perpetuation of arbitrarily designated sex roles, women have been victimized more often than not. Research seems to indicate that much of this sex-role typing is, in fact, psychologically and

3. J. E. Kane, "Psychology of Sport with Special Reference to the Female Athlete," The Pennsylvania State University, HPER series no. 2, 1972, p. 31.

sociologically based. For example, on the basis of their research, Wilmore and Brown noted that:

> ... the results suggest that the large differences observed between normal males and females ... at all ages beyond the age of 12 years are at least partially socioculturally determined as opposed to being strictly of biological origin.[14]

Sexist values have tended to stereotype women in sport as being less than feminine, and have stereotyped many women athletes as being "masculinized," or "muscle women." Yet these criticisms and stereotypes have no foundation in fact. Sports participation does not masculinize the female participant, as this policy statement by the American Medical Association indicates:

> The Committee on the Medical Aspects of Sports reiterates the beneficial aspects of sports and exercise participation for girls and women. Female participation in such programs previously was discouraged due to societal and cultural stereotypes that considered such participation a departure from the 'traditional role.' Much to the contrary, physiological and social benefits are to be gained by girls and women through physical activity and sports competition. In many cases, vigorous physical activity improves the distinctive biological functions of the female.[5]

WOMEN AND MILITANCY

Presently, women are pressing for equality in sport and such other aspects of life as employment, through the courts and through pressure for the passage of equal rights legislation. Until recent years, women were more willing to go along with the system that dictated their role in society, and they sought change through less militant tactics. However, low-pressure, subtle attempts to effect change in order to achieve equality brought about few real changes in the system. Thus, rebuked in their less forceful attempts to achieve equality, women were forced to adopt a posture of assertiveness and militancy. This has caused a great deal of controversy not only because of the threat posed to male dominance, but also because many women are themselves afraid to upset the status quo.

The fight for equal rights for women is opposed very strongly by many women who do not understand the true nature of the new militancy,

4. Jack H. Wilmore and C. Harmon Brown, "Physiological Profiles of Women Distance Runners," *Medicine and Science in Sports* 6 (Fall 1974): 178.
5. Committee on the Medical Aspects of Sports of the American Medical Association, "Female Athletics," *JOPER* 46 (January 1975): 45.

Women are asserting their rights to achieve fulfillment and self-actualization in movement through avenues that traditionally have been extremely limited or open only to men.

and thus fear its consequences. One possible explanation for this opposition by the women themselves has been brought out by Zoble:

> *The achievement orientation of the female seems to involve both a fear of failure and a fear of success. This lessens the motive to achieve and perpetuates passive dependence . . . In our society competitiveness is a valued trait for the male, but not for the female.*[6]

5. Judith E. Zoble, "Femininity and Achievement in Sports," The Pennsylvania State University, HPER series no 2, (1972), p. 213.

Whether or not these militant means of achieving equality and civil rights will create factions not only within society, but more specifically within physical education and sport, is perhaps not really the relevant question. More relevant seems to be the question of how the changes may actually be brought about so that equality becomes a fact. Given the priority of the need for social change, no matter how distasteful the current militancy is to some segments of society, the end may more than justify the means. The legislation that is being sought is designed to benefit not only women, but any individual or group whose opportunities for equality have been limited by traditionally and arbitrarily assigned roles.

Should the attempts at legislating equality be an effective vehicle toward that goal, then opportunities for achievement will be based more firmly on potential rather than on gender. Physical educators are just now beginning to witness an era in which females will be welcome as full participants, skilled performers, and as athletes. Physical educators and others in the movement fields must assist this emergence by providing programs that will become true vehicles for the fulfillment of human potential for all individuals alike.

> By the twenty-first century women will have liberated sport both as a male domain and from its contemporary models. Without the assumption of sport as a singular male preserve and the corollary of male superiority, new perspectives must emerge.[7]

As more women grow to find satisfaction through skilled movement in physical education and sport experiences, no doubt many more women will follow their example. Women who today are physically active as full participants are taming a frontier that is replete with archaic misconceptions about what ought or ought not to be desirable human experiences.

Women seem to be particularly affected by the socialization process within sports participation. Many women still feel threatened by the idea of female athletes. This fear is based upon the social criticisms that seem to arise when women step out of their stereotyped sex role activities. Women will achieve full freedom and equality as athletically-oriented individuals when culturally induced inhibitions linked to sex-role expectations are abolished. Those women who are in the forefront of the equality movement are bucking centuries of sex-role traditions and stereotypes. As long-standing social attitudes toward women in sport fade into irrelevance, sports participation will finally be recognized as a human, rather than a sex-linked need.

The Changing Face of Power

Over the years, sports programs for women have largely been controlled by men. At times, the men exercised an oppressive, and perhaps even tyranni-

7. Jan Felshin, "The Triple Option . . . For Women in Sport," Quest 21 (January 1974): 40.

cal, influence. As the women's movement continues to gather momentum, control over sports for women will gradually transfer from the men to the women, but the transfer will in no way be easy, and it may, at times, be less than amicable.

How the women's sports leaders handle their new power will be of interest to all students of human behavior. Hopefully, one set of tyrannical leaders will not have been replaced with yet another set of oppressive leaders who differ only in gender. The women's movement in sports needs the kind of leadership that will emphasize, along with the competitive ends, the human aspects of sports. However, any shift in power or control is usually plagued by problems that can only be resolved gradually. The shift in leadership from male to female domination will not bring about immediate changes that will be satisfactory to all of the critics of sports for women. It will be many years before solutions can be found to many of the problems now rampant not only the realm of women's sports, but in men's athletics as well. As Felshin noted:

> As the 'men only' nature of sport is challenged successfully, and as budgets and facilities are shared by legal sanction, men and women will have to learn to co-exist in sport. [8]

WOMEN AND COMPETITION

It was only relatively recently that female physical educators began to recognize that competitive athletics for girls and women had any educational benefit. Historically, female physical educators tended to deny that competition could be reconciled with any educational philosophy. In fact, the prevailing attitude of many women physical educators toward sport was closely aligned with their philosophy of physical education: opportunities to participate in any and all movement experiences should be open to every female who desired to participate. These women were especially adamant about the exclusionary nature of athletics, since athletics are necessarily limited to a relatively few highly-skilled individuals. These women also felt that athletic programs tended to exploit the athletes and thus were noneducational.

For these and other similar reasons, the philosophy of women physical educators toward athletics was generally negative, especially where intensely competitive sports were concerned. However, the need was recognized for a level of competition beyond intramural programs. Also, a need was recognized for sports-oriented contacts outside of a single school. Interschool sports days and play days were an outgrowth of these needs, and helped serve as a balm to those girls and women who wanted

8. Ibid., p. 40.

some form of competition. The sports day and the play day do not emphasize winning, but instead are based upon the premise that everyone who wants to participate is welcome to do so. Rather than being intensely competitive encounters, the sports day and the play day were used as methods of educating through movement in a way that it was felt that athletics per se could not.

The sports day and the play day still have their places as supplements to any athletic program. Unlike varsity teams, participants are not excluded on the basis of their skill level. Instead, allowances are built in to account for a variety of skill levels among the participants. However, such days are not an adequate substitute for a properly run athletic program designed to serve the individual who does have a greater need for competition, and the ability to become a member of an athletic team. Yet there are many who still are philosophically opposed to any type of intensive athletic competition for girls and women. Smith has keyed-in on one of the stumbling blocks to the full acceptance of the women athlete and athletics for women in general:

> Impelled by the increasing importance of winning and as the value-climate in sport subtly changes in the direction of the legitimation of female violence ... female sport may be moving toward the male model ... On the other hand, the fact that females have avoided, thus far, many of the problems rife in male sport argues well for the view that women's sports will resist becoming scaled-down replicas of sports for men.[9]

CRITICS OF COMPETITION FOR WOMEN

There are many individuals who are vehemently opposed to any expansion of athletic programs for women. These critics seem to fall into three general groups: (1) men who fear that any gains by the women will harm their programs; (2) women who see an ulterior motive on the part of feminists in general; and (3) those who contend that women are not physiologically capable of intensive competition. Let us look at each of these viewpoints individually.

Men vs. the Women's Movement

Chief among the problems facing athletics for women is the question of financing for the programs. In an era of tight money, men feel, and often rightly so, that the financing for women's programs will come from the budgets for their own already well-established programs. Caught in a

9. Michael D. Smith, "Aggression and the Female Athlete," The Pennsylvania State University, HPER series no. 2 (1972), p. 197.

financial bind to begin with, the necessity of releasing funds to promote programs for girls and women may result in forced curtailment of programs for boys and men. The financing of women's athletics is at the core of almost all male opposition to these programs. Most male physical educators and coaches fully support the women's movement in athletics, until the question of financing is raised. Title IX of the Education Amendments of 1972 calls for the provision of facilities, equipment, and financial support for programs for girls and women, and Title IX has many vocal and powerful male opponents.

Title IX of the Education Amendments of 1972 is intended to eradicate sex discrimination so that arbitrary bases will no longer exist for allocating funds and other necessities for physical education and athletic programs. While such legislation is a bench mark, it still leaves some important questions unanswered, particularly with regard to financing. For example, it does not determine whether expenditures for women's programs will be elevated to the level of expenditures for men's programs, or whether the expenditures for both programs must converge toward an equal but more conservative ground.

The proponents of women's programs see either alternative as a significant improvement over present practices. Quite naturally, women would seem to prefer as much equality as possible. On the other hand, the men remain apprehensive because they believe equality, if legislated, will not help to hold budgets in line. Thus, they see their own programs sliding backwards, and contend that their budgets ought not to be reduced in order to accommodate the programs for women. The men feel that if both programs must converge toward some middle ground that it will be a victory for mediocrity only, and they forecast a dim future for any continued pursuit of excellence. This particular problem, however, will be resolved by the courts, and men and women alike will have to abide by the rulings and operate their programs accordingly.

Women vs. the Women's Movement

Many, many women are violently opposed to the women's movement in general, and to the women's movement in athletics in particular. They suggest that the overall feminist movement is looking for high profile vantage points from which to put its cause across, and that the world of sport is thus being exploited because it is so widely known and admired by the public. The critics contend that the feminists are only seeking to move ahead in women's athletics because they have no real objective in mind except to dilute the men's programs and thus put another sizable dent in male domination.

A dissection of the female vs. female criticism seems to reveal that it is based on a familiar philosophy. Traditionally, womens' physical education and athletic programs have reflected society's expectations of the female sex role. Perhaps more than any other single phenomenon, the sheer weight of public opinion about women's role in society has molded the principles which for years guided women's physical education programs. For years, women in physical education opposed competitive sport experiences for their students because they themselves had been taught that competitive sports fell well beyond the bounds of behavior expected of women. For example, men and women alike have rigidly adhered to the philosophy defined by Harris:

> Masculinity and femininity, as culturally defined, have been extremely resistant to change; this has been especially true where sport and athletic competition have been concerned. The traditional role of the male has allowed him to determine the range of behavior he will condone as being feminine—and this does not include those behaviors that appear essential for success in competitive sport.[10]

The proponents of the women's sport movement assert that the fallacies of the old ideas about competition for women have been exposed, and that the time has come to pursue the wide spectrum of experiences that were previously arbitrarily denied women. That women have taken such a stance ought to be praised rather than condemned, especially by other women.

Physiology vs. the Women's Movement

Aside from sex-role assignments, many opponents of athletics for women have contended over the years that competition is physically detrimental to women. This view seemed to cross over sex lines, so that both men and women alike used this argument to support their negative attitudes toward athletics for women. While these negativists brought forth many objections to athletics, including the familiar point that women athletes would develop a masculine musculature, they were unable to cite any research to give credence to their side of the debate. Many opinion papers were in fact developed by respected leaders in physical education, but these authoritative opinions still lacked for hard evidence.

In recent years, both male and female researchers have published the results of investigations that tend to refute the opinion that physiology alone should prevent girls and women from full participation in intense athletic competition. Also, there is no evidence to suggest that women are masculinized, or made any the less feminine, by such participation. In fact, much of the research seems to indicate that participation in athletics can be

10. Dorothy V. Harris, "The Female Athlete: Psychosocial Considerations," *JOPER* 46 (January 1975): 32.

of benefit physiologically as well as psychologically. While space does not permit a comprehensive survey of all of the research concerned with the effects of athletics and athletic competition on women, the following will serve as examples of the literature that is currently available, and helping to shed light on this aspect of athletics for women.

Jack H. Wilmore has been either the sole researcher or the co-experimenter in a series of recent studies dealing with the physiology of the female athlete. In two similar studies, carried out in collaboration with C. Harmon Brown, a key point of the first study was that women were capable of achieving high levels of strength, but that muscular development would be effectively held in check by the female hormonal structure.[11] In the second study, which was limited to female runners as subjects, the researchers concluded that:

> ... there still appears to be basic physiological differences between the male and the female, although ... these differences are not as great as one might expect ... With further training, better coaching, better equipment and facilities and a greater emphasis on women in sport, the gap between the sexes will close.[12]

In two studies specifically designed to study strength, Wilmore made the point that women use their lower bodies more than their upper bodies, and therefore have developed greater lower body strength. This strength is proportionately similar to the lower body strength development of males. Wilmore wrote:

> ... similarities in lower body strength are likely the result of similarities in use. The female walks, climbs stairs, bicycles, etc., and therefore maintains her leg strength at a level comparable to that of a male of similar size.[13]

Further, Wilmore advocates, on the basis of his research, similar if not identical training programs for both male and female athletes. He says:

> It is apparent that there are few differences between the female athlete and her male counterpart, other than in actual performance. Therefore, there is little reason to advocate different training or conditioning programs on the basis of sex since their needs are essentially identical.[14]

11. Harmon Brown and Jack H. Wilmore, "The Effects of Maximal Resistance Training on the Strength and Body Composition of Women Athletes," *Medicine and Science in Sports* 6 (Fall 1974):174–177.

12. Jack H. Wilmore and C. Harmon Brown, "Physiological Profiles of Women Distance Runners,"*Medicine and Science in Sports* 6 (Fall 1974): 180.

13. Jack H. Wilmore, "Inferiority of the Female Athlete: Myth or Reality?" *Sports Medicine Bulletin* 10 (April 1975): 7.

14. Jack H. Wilmore, "Body Composition and Strength Development," *JOPER* 46 (January 1975): 39.

On the psychological side, Alderman conducted an attitude study involving male and female Pan-American Games participants, and found a remarkable similarity of attitudes toward sport among athletes of both sexes. In fact, Alderman stated that, " . . . the strongest attitude of the athletes toward physical activity was as an aesthetic experience . . ."[15] In a more recent study, Snyder and Kivlin concluded that stereotypes concerned with female athletes were highly questionable. These researchers pointed out that female athletes enjoyed participating and were able to develop more satisfactory self-concepts than comparable groups of nonathletes. Snyder and Kivlin wrote that, " . . . even though women athletes have frequently received negative sanctions, their participation in sports has apparently been psychologically satisfying and rewarding."[16]

THE ROLE OF THE COURTS

Observers of human behavior are going to find very fertile ground for analysis as more and more sex discrimination cases are brought before the courts for resolution. As the law now reads, no individual can be barred from an athletic team on the basis of sex alone. While this law is meant to apply equally to both males and females, women have been the plaintiffs in most sex discrimination cases brought to trial so far, and in the majority of cases the courts have ruled in favor of the female complainant. The cases most often in the public eye are those such as the one involving the Little League, where females have sued for the right to participate on what were, until court action, exclusively male teams.

The Problem of Single-Sex and Mixed Teams

It is becoming increasingly more common to find females competing against and with men in such sports as swimming, diving, track, bowling, golf, and tennis. In fewer cases, female athletes have won places on male teams in such contact sports as basketball and football. The issue of women's involvement in contact sports on mixed teams or against all men's teams is a vital and critical issue. While the American Medical Association strongly supports athletics for women, it has made an unequivocal statement concerning the vigorous contact sports such as basketball, football, and ice hockey:

15. Richard B. Alderman, "A Sociopsychological Assessment of Attitude Toward Physical Activity in Champion Athletes," *Research Quarterly* 41 (March 1970): 1.
16. Eldon E. Snyder and Joseph E. Kivlin, "Women Athletes and Aspects of Psychological Well-Being and Body Image," *Research Quarterly* 46 (May 1975): 197.

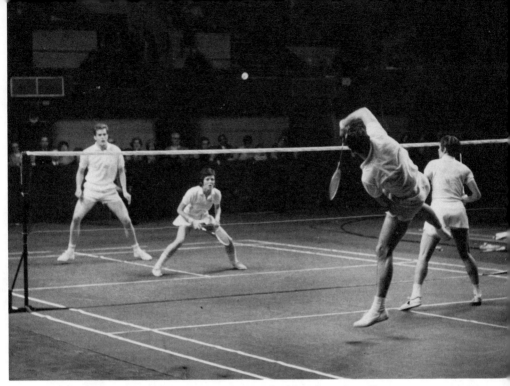

It is becoming increasingly more common to find females competing against and with men.

Since girls are at a distinct disadvantage to boys in such sports because of their lesser muscle-mass per unit of body weight and bone density, it is advisable on medical grounds that they not participate in such programs. The differential between the weight of boys and girls opposing each other would be substantial. Even if competitors are matched according to weight, girls are still exposed to potentially greater injury, since the ratio of adipose tissue to lean-body weight varies considerably between the two sexes, to the disadvantage of girls.[17]

The question of mixed teams in contact sports with the possibility of participant injury is not the only critical issue. As the sex lines drawn for sports begin to fade, new issues will continue to arise and demand solutions. Two current problems with as yet obscure answers are: (1) will the entry of women onto men's teams have a negative impact on the development of sports programs for women?; and, (2) will budget-conscious schools and school boards use the newly sex-integrated teams as justification for holding back budget allocations for separate programs for women in some sports? Where the courts have ruled that women have the right to compete on men's teams, some questions are already being raised concerning the need for any kind of separate program for women alone. The

17. Committee on the Medical Aspects of Sports, op. cit., p. 46.

term "women's teams" seems to imply a kind of reverse sex discrimination. In fact, recent federal court rulings have indicated that since girls and women may join teams that were once exclusively male, that boys and men have the same rights with regard to teams that are exclusively female. This seems to threaten the dualistic concept of separate teams and athletic programs for males and females.

The concept of dualism states that there must be two separate sports programs. This would require twice the expenditures, twice the facilities, twice the scheduling problems, and twice the coaching staff. Total dualism seems to be impractical because teams now exclusively for males or females seem to be in violation of federal law. Moreover, everyone now has equal opportunity, by law, to try out for any team because no one can be excluded from participation on the basis of sex alone. Some female sports leaders have expressed the concern that federal law has unwittingly paved the way for the eventual elimination of women's programs and that this will in turn force women out of any controlling role over women in athletics.

Also, some individuals have observed that women's teams may, in effect, be relegated to the role of a men's B team or junior varsity. They suggest that men who are unable to make a varsity team will gravitate toward women's sport programs in order to be able to compete on an interscholastic or intercollegiate basis. Such a development could effectively turn women away from participation unless they are able to develop their skills to a level that will insure them a spot on their own teams. While this particular issue may never grow to critical proportions, it is within the realm of probability, especially if the letter rather than the spirit of the law is carried out.

It will be some time before the quest for equality can be resolved. The problems are complex, and simple solutions will not appear overnight. Certainly, answers will not be forthcoming as long as the spokespersons for each side continue to polarize their colleagues along sexist lines. Only a coalition of reasonable people can join together to resolve the conflicts. The longer the conflict continues, the more harm will be done not only to sports programs, but to physical education programs as well.

SUMMARY

This chapter was concerned with women in sport and the many current critical issues surrounding athletic programs for women. We have discussed the attitudes of both males and females toward the woman athlete, and have attempted to show how negativism arises from both sides. We have looked at some of the possible effects, both positive and negative, that have been brought about by legislation, and we have tried to show

how value systems are contrived, at times, to suit an issue or point of view, rather than being based on concrete evidence.

The increasing militancy of women, and its effect, has been traced. Further, we have summarized some of the most recent research on women athletes and have shown that this research seems to indicate that a woman does not dilute her feminity by becoming an athlete.

SUGGESTIONS FOR FURTHER READING

Drinkwater, Barbara L. "Aerobic Power in Females." *JOPER* 46 (January 1975):36–38.

Harris, Dorothy V., ed., *DGWS Research Reports: Women In Sports*. Washington, D.C.: AAHPER, 1971.

Hawley, Edward T. and Mary Edna Glover. "The Caloric Costs of Running and Walking One Mile for Men and Women." *Medicine and Science in Sports*. 6 (Winter 1974):235–237.

Johnson, Patricia Ann. "A Comparison of Personality Traits of Superior Skilled Women Athletes in Basketball, Bowling, Field Hockey, and Golf." *Research Quarterly* 43 (December 1972):409–415.

Ryan, Allan J. "Gynecological Considerations." *JOPER* 46 (January 1975):40–44.

Sherif, Carolyn Wood. "Females in the Competitive Process." The Pennsylvania State University, HPER series no. 2 (1972): 115–139.

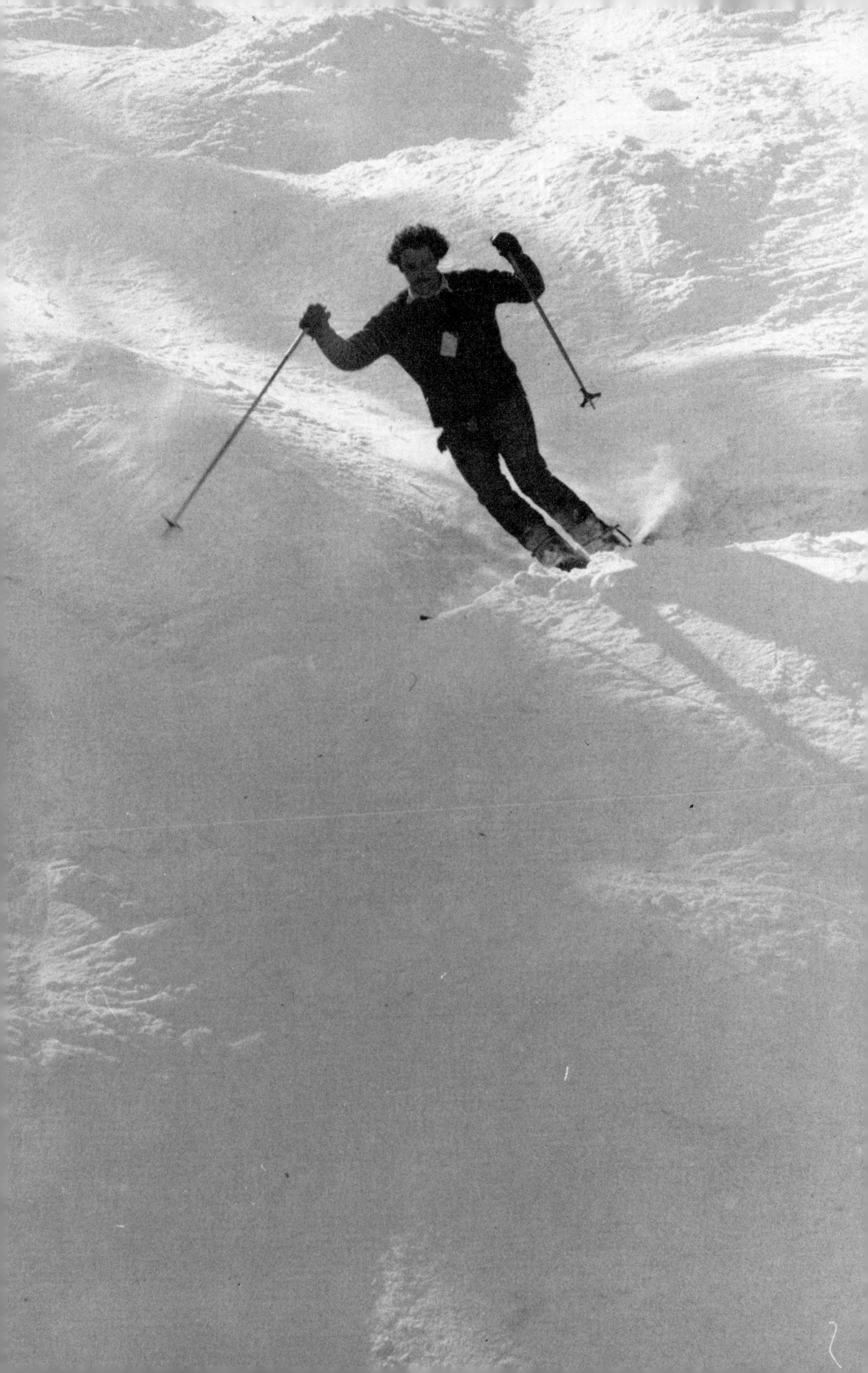

14

Physical Education and Movement Experiences in Futuristic Perspective

The past represents an immense repository of experiences which are, in effect, the core of human knowledge. In preparing students for the present and the future, education has, out of necessity, drawn on the past. It was not so very long ago that the lessons of the past could serve as adequate preparation for the future. Because of this, education at times unwittingly dwelled rather heavily on the past without doing a real disservice to students. In that not too distant era, the past was a rather accurate reflection of the future. Since the dawn of the twentieth century however, life has begun to move at a much faster pace, and it can no longer be comfortably assumed that the future will be nothing more than an evolutionary, linear projection of the past. One hundred years ago, life held relatively few surprises, so that sociocultural systems and educational curriculums tended to remain viable and relevant from decade to decade.

We are now at the doorstep of the twenty-first century, and we have witnessed a multitude of sociocultural and technological advances. In spite of the distances we have traveled, it is education alone that is seemingly reluctant to keep pace. Education seems slow to break its ties with the past, and instead seems almost eager to remain behind. Many of the educational models which characterize the schools of today were first formulated during the Industrial Revolution of over one hundred years ago.

There has, of course, been a mounting concern for the future course of education, but no significant alternatives have as yet been proposed or tested out. Longo has pointed out education's failure to keep up with the times by noting that:

> Innovative approaches in education have for too long been victimized by uninformed attempts at implementation. Once an idea has been popularized, we appear to abandon it step by step until it dies of neglect.[1]

Alvin Toffler, author of *Future Shock,* has described society's and education's response to the need for modernizing education as being a good deal of talk but very little action:

> Yet for all this rhetoric about the future, our schools face backward toward a dying system, rather than forward to the emerging new society. Their vast energies are applied to cranking out Industrial Men—people tooled for survival in a system that will be dead before they are.[2]

A number of other authorities agree with Longo and Toffler that education has failed to respond to the demands of the future. The futurists warn us that education must project itself into the future, and must select a series of alternatives by which it can become a meaningful and potent force for serving man's needs in the fast-approaching tomorrow. Will physical education be relevant as a part of all of education in the twenty-first century?

IRRELEVANCE AND THE CURRICULUM

If we take note of the rapidity with which social and environmental changes are occuring today, it becomes more and more difficult to justify our educational systems and curriculums. Today's commonly used curriculums are an outgrowth of a less dynamic and less complex era, and most have outlived their usefulness. Because the future will be significantly different from the present, education today must become an avenue of preparation for tomorrow. Schools must reflect the realities of the future rather than of the past. In education, as in many social institutions that are founded upon traditional ways of doing things, change often is characterized by a long and tortuous process marked by inertia and deliberateness. Education cannot afford any longer the luxury of resistance to change:

> It is the focus and organization of curricula which need to change. Teachers need to be guided by a theoretically conceptual framework in order to guide students . . .[3]

1. Paul Longo, "Opening the Door to the Open Classroom," Kappa Delta Pi *Record* 11 (April 1975): 98.
2. Alvin Toffler, *Future Shock*. (New York: Bantam Books, 1970), p. 399.
3. Ann E. Jewett and Marie R. Mullan, "A Conceptual Model for Teacher Education," *Quest* 18 (June 1972): 87.

The futurists tell us that the twenty-first century will be characterized by rapid and unprecedented change. In fact, some futurists suggest that change itself will be a constant. The schools, they contend, will not be immune to change, but will cease to exist as we now know them because they will have failed to keep up with significant social and environmental changes. Education, then, would continue to occur even perhaps more effectively within the context of a "deschooled" society.

A deschooled society would not mean that teachers would be eliminated, only that teachers would become guides for the learning process as more of the responsibility for learning shifts to the student. As Hall has noted:

> Children's time today, in many cases, is too highly structured in and out of school; thus, there is a need for time and space for children to use their own resources to develop self-direction and creativity.[4]

In a deschooled society, a dynamic "real world" rather than the traditional world of the school house might more effectively become the child's teacher and might provide the more appropriate setting for an education of the future. This seems to be a logical assumption, since the futurists insist that schools in their present form simply will not be able to adapt to a world characterized by constant change. The schools are even now too slow to adopt new ideas and new methodologies. There is even now an increasing time lag between the development of new ideas and their testing by the schools, and as the years move along this time lag will increase until the point is reached where it no longer will be possible to catch up. At that point, the schools will cease to be a relevant educational force.

In order to remain viable social and educational institutions, schools of the future will have to teach students how to learn. If the schools do not begin to change their focus, they will find it increasingly difficult to deliver a useful service. The schools must increasingly approach education as a process rather than a product. There is every evidence to support the contention that in the twenty-first century, ongoing education will become the first line of defense against human obsolescence. The schools, then, will have to treat learning as a dynamic, ongoing experience. Process-oriented learning will become increasingly more relevant. In this vein, Toffler has strongly suggested that tomorrow's students," . . .must, in short, learn how to learn."[5]

---

4. Sue M. Hall ed., *Children and Fitness.* (Washington, D.C.: AAHPER, 1962), p. 13.
5. Toffler, op. cit., p. 414.

EDUCATION AND LIFELONG LEARNING

There will probably be widespread acceptance of the concept of continuing education as society continues to change and grow. Even now there is a growing awareness of the need for education to continue beyond the end of the formal school years. This represents at least some evidence to support the contention that we are beginning to take the first steps toward becoming a truly learning-oriented society.

The concept of a learning-oriented society will have a positive impact upon the schools. Schools of the future will probably disavow the traditional ideology that education must occur in heavily concentrated doses administered particularly during the early school years. This traditional concept is largely the outgrowth of an era marked by relatively gradual change; an era in which it was considered advantageous to complete an education as quickly as possible so that the individual could more quickly enter the job market. The benefits from such an education come not in terms of learning or the longevity of learning, but instead are derived from the ready marketability of skills.

Since the twenty-first century is going to bring about a rapidly changing and expanding lifestyle, the practice of requiring students to memorize vast quantities of facts early in life will be increasingly questioned. Instead, students might be better served by open-ended types of educational systems which they can enter and leave and re-enter again in a continuing cycle as long as there are new learning experiences to be sampled. This would, of course, do away with our traditional kindergarten through grade twelve systems, but it would, in turn, set no arbitrary limits on the completion of an education. Education would then become a continuing and lifelong experience, with its boundaries set by each individual. This is but one alternative to meeting the challenge of the future.

THE FUTURE AND LEISURE

Economists and environmentalists as well as technologists and futurists tell us that people living in the future will have significantly more leisure time than people enjoy now. What new functions and purposes is education going to have to fulfill in order to meet this additional challenge? There is a rapid, if not rampant, growth of industries whose primary purpose is to devise, develop, manufacture, and sell to the public a variety of goods classified as recreational equipment. If the ecologists and environmentalists can exert their influence, recreation and leisure will take on a "doing" rather than a "having" frame of reference.

For example, two currently popular recreational-leisure time pursuits are backpacking and camping. However, the increased number of people backpacking into and camping in ecologically fragile areas has caused tight restrictions to be placed on the number of people who may use these areas at any given time. These restrictions will become more, rather than less, rigid as more and more people seek out remote areas that give life a quality not available in urban areas. This creates a paradoxical situation that will not be easily resolved.

It is conceivable that in the future, recreational pursuits which require elaborate equipment such as motor homes and power boats will begin to fall into social disfavor. Where recreation is becoming more people-powered, such as with bicycling, skiing, rock climbing, swimming, and the like, the emphasis will certainly be on "doing" rather than "having" in order to be able to participate. Such movement-centered pursuits will be more compatible with a future social order that will value living in harmony with the environment rather than holding mastery over the environment. However, steps must be taken now to preserve the environment so that it will be intact and available for the recreational needs and pursuits of the future.

THE FUTURE AND MOVEMENT EXPERIENCES

It is reasonable to assume that in the future there will be much more time available to be expended in movement-centered experiences. This linear projection from the recent past and the present into the future seems relatively sound and assured. People will continue to need certain kinds and quantities of physical activity to maintain minimum levels of physical well-being. Physical activity is likely to remain the most effective method of maintaining fitness unless science can develop viable alternative non-physical methods. In fact, in a future that will be characterized by "doing," physical activity seems likely to become a major force for the enrichment of life.

THE FUTURE AND PHYSICAL EDUCATION

The teaching of motor skills through physical education may assume an unprecedented importance in curriculums of the future. Schools may eventually free students to study and participate only in those subjects which seem to guarantee future usefulness. Where relevance becomes the major criterion for the inclusion of a subject in a curriculum, then curriculums will of necessity be far more flexible as old subject areas disappear and new ones emerge to meet shifting priorities.

In schools of the future, those subject areas which facilitate "doing" meaningful things will probably receive top priority and emphasis. Physical education programs that teach students to "do" activities and to achieve their potential through movement will become vitally important. What kinds of skills and experiences might physical education programs of the future offer? Before attempting to develop an answer to such a question, we must first look at two additional factors that will greatly affect the society of the future.

Mobility

When they are no longer locked into a single career or to the desire to accumulate wealth and material goods, people will become significantly more mobile. There is even now an ever-increasing trend toward mobility. In the not too distant past, people did not generally move very great distances from the place of their birth. Life, values, employment, and surroundings remained rather stable, and there was little motivation to migrate from one geographic area to another. Today, we have already seen men landed on the moon. It is any wonder, then, that ordinary individuals are becoming less and less satisfied with geographically limited existences?

Perhaps in the future, lasting relationships with people and places will be unknown simply because people will be so highly mobile that no firm and lasting commitments and attachments will be practical. This kind of society will hold profound significance for all of education. What kinds of things should be taught to students who may just be in a particular school for a brief period of time? Lengthy courses or sequences of courses may be an impossibility if students cannot or will not remain in a school long enough to complete them.

Several alternatives do present themselves, however: self-paced instruction, individualized instruction, and the use of educational media are but a few examples. Also, educators might consider putting courses into concentrated blocks of time so that students could be assured of completing any course once it has been started. Such adjustments to the traditional system we now have would help education to meet the needs of a highly mobile society. While this is, of course, highly speculative, education must become more accountable so that is can move into the future with some degree of respectability. Feingold made the telling point that:

> Educators everywhere are being forced to examine what they do in classes. In the past it was possible to make the comfortable assumption that the activities of the teacher had a generally positive effect upon student learning.[6]

Educators and educational systems must begin now to meet the new challenges that the future and all of its unknowns will bring.

6. Ronald S. Feingold, "The Evaluation of Teacher Education Programs in Physical Education," *Quest* 18 (June 1972): 33.

Individual-type sports require relatively little dependance on others, and are thus eminently suited to a more mobile style of living.

Socialization

The school as a social experience will probably be drastically altered in the future. Many social experiences as we know them now, depend upon knowing other people, sharing experiences with others, and developing allegiances. Should life become as fast-paced and as highly mobile as has been predicted, then interpersonal relationships will be vastly altered. Moreover, the social concepts involved in school loyalty, school spirit, or allegiance to school teams will also be greatly modified if they continue to exist at all.

What will become of what we now call "team sports" if the future is characterized by a transcient society? Will a physical educator still teach the team sports? Indeed, will students want to learn, or will they have any need for team sports? If team sports are no longer taught, what viable alternatives are there through which physical educators will teach such concepts as team work, cooperation, and group effort toward a common objective? And what will become of coaches who may not be able to field an intact or complete team from one game to the next?

Where transience becomes the new way of life, team loyalties or school loyalties simply will not have time to develop. In fact, there may no longer be loyal fans to cheer any team on. Perhaps team sports, for the players and the spectator alike, are destined to become a drastically less significant part of life when measured against today's standards. Yet, there may be some good in all of this. Felshin has written that:

> In the sense of its use of movement, sport is the effect of man's biological technology on the environment. And on that level, sport is inherently meaningful ... Why would man develop and impose structure, except that something was initially and inherently meaningful? Structure and meaning are, thus, interactive, and sport, based on man's inherent power to act, embodies his modes of meaning in its structure.[7]

It is probably likely that team sports will stay with us into the future, but the focus and direction will have changed. People will probably form teams in order to meet social needs rather than for purely competitive reasons. Should team sports of the future lose their spectator appeal, then a re-emphasis on the participant may emerge. This change would be welcomed even now by many who feel that the trend toward mass spectatorism is in direct opposition to the real aims of team sports.

THE FUTURE AND LIFETIME SKILLS

Lifetime individual sports may be the sports of the future. In an increasingly mobile society, people will need to be able to obtain opportunities to be physically active wherever they are. Individual-type sports require relatively little dependence on others, and are thus eminently suited to a more mobile style of living. Where team sports require relatively large numbers of people plus officials and other necessities, most individual-type sports even today demand little in the way of preplanning, logistics, and the coordination of various individuals and groups. These sports are likely to be just as uncomplicated in the future.

In the future, as is true in the present, participation in sports other than the team type can and will occur spontaneously. The lifetime, individual-type sports are truly future-oriented because the spontaneity that makes them operational seems to be highly compatible with the projected transient character of the society of the future. The lifetime sports will become but one significant means by which people of the future

7. Jan Felshin, "Sport and Modes of Meaning," *JOHPER* 40 (May 1969): 44.

Lifetime individual sports may be the sports of the future.

will pursue meaningful experiences and enrichment throughout their life spans. It is not enough for a sport merely to be individual in nature; it must ideally be of a type that can serve the person from youth through old age.

In a future that will be filled with many labor-saving devices and increased time for leisure, lifetime sports will be more credible and more essential than ever before. Lifetime sports will become an avenue not only of personal enrichment, but also a significant means by which health and fitness will be enhanced and maintained. Moreover, lifetime sports may become the basic theme for industries of the future that gear themselves toward providing services rather than products. Physical education, which has always delivered human services and taught skills necessary for life, may well become a major industry of the future.

Will future societies need the kind of physical education we have now? Will physical education be able to change in order to accomodate a new era, or will it cling to traditional ways, diminish in relevance, and eventually fade into obscurity? This is not really so speculative a set of questions when we realize how few steps physical education has taken even into the present era. If physical education is to give service, and if it is to become a major industry of the future, then change is needed now, no matter how difficult that prospect may seem. Not only must curriculums be revised and objectives brought into line with future needs, but so must we begin to prepare a new kind of physical educator:

> Professional preparation programs must change . . . The aim is not to identify all the specific skills which successful teachers have been observed to use and to implant them by some additive process into each new teacher, but to clarify a positive concept of the modern educator and create curricular alternatives which permit a young adult interested in the human movement professions to synthesize his unique talents into a way of working effectively with others.[8]

Among the ways in which man will adapt to the future will be by recognizing that the human body evolved over countless relatively stable millenia, and that in the future the body will essentially be an alien in a new world. The need to properly care for the human body as an evolutionary being in a revolutionary environment will have a tremendous impact on adaptation and survival. Physical education can and must become a significant factor in helping man to adapt to the future. Education through the physical will become essential. Jewett helps us to understand what course physical education must follow?

> Physical education will be a continuing educational process . . . A person's physical education will be a process, in that it is a continuing development, involving many changes. The physically educated person will have learned to perform crucial human movement operations; he will have developed volitional control over all key movement processes. He will be capable of somatic thinking. He will have learned to direct his own perceptual-motor learning; and he will have developed more skillful and more effective movements in relation to his personal purposes and goals.[9]

Physical education would do well to begin expending its energies toward the future right now. The future will very little resemble the past or the present, and the past really bears relevance only when it helps to prepare for the future. Physical education must recognize that the world is

8. Jewett and Mullan, op. cit., p. 87.
9. Ann E. Jewett, "Who Knows What Tomorrow May Bring?" Quest 21 (January 1974): 69.

entering an era vastly different from any previously experienced. If physical education fails to meet the needs of the future, it will not be because it planned to fail, but because it failed to plan.

SUMMARY

In looking ahead to the twenty-first century, which is really not that far off, we have attempted to show what life may be like. While much of this chapter is highly speculative, it does little good to blindly assume that life will go on as we know it now.

We have drawn some implications from Alvin Toffler's book *Future Shock,* and strongly recommend that the reader of this text either read or re-read *Future Shock.* Much of what was speculative to the point of controversy in that book's original printing in 1970 is now confirmed fact. While in this chapter we have discussed the society of the future at length and have woven the future of movement only into the larger picture, we pointed out that it will be the societal changes that will dictate in which directions physical education must move.

Somewhat reluctantly, but we believe with some justification, we have criticized physical education for its propensity for sticking with tradition. We have, however, attempted to show how physical education must change, and have proposed some alternatives for coping with the challenges of the future.

SUGGESTIONS FOR FURTHER READING

Brunner, Burton C., "How Will Today's Physical Education Classes be Remembered in 1989?" *JOHPER* 40 (February, 1969):42.

Hoffman, Shirl James, "Traditional Methodology: Prospects for Change." *Quest* 15 (January 1971):51–57.

McGlynn, George, ed., *Issues in Physical Education and Sport* Palo Alto, Calif.: National Press Books, 1974.

Siedentop, Daryl, "Behavior Analysis and Teacher Training." *Quest* 18 (June 1972):26–32.

BIBLIOGRAPHY

Alderman, Richard B., "A Sociopsychological Assessment of Attitude Toward Physical Activity in Champion Athletes." *Research Quarterly* 41 (March 1970):1–9.

American Association for Health, Physical Education, and Recreation. *Knowledge and Understanding in Physical Education.* Washington, D.C.: American Association for Health, Physical Education, and Recreation, 1969.

Ariel, Gideon B., "Physical Education: 2001?" *Quest* 21 (January 1974):49–52.

Arnheim, Daniel D., David Auxter, and Walter C. Crowe. *Principles and Methods of Adapted Physical Education.* St. Louis: The C.V. Mosby Company, 1973.

_____, and Robert A. Pestolesi. *Developing Motor Behavior in Children.* St. Louis: The C.V. Mosby Co., 1973.

Baley, James A., and David A. Field. *Physical Education and the Physical Educator: An Introduction.* Boston: Allyn and Bacon, Inc., 1970.

Barrow, Harold M. *Man and His Movement: Principles of His Physical Education.* Philadelphia: Lea and Febiger, 1973.

Bates, Marston. *Man in Nature.* Englewood Cliffs, N.J.: Prentice-Hall, Inc., 1964.

Baumgartner, Ted A., and Andrew S. Jackson. *Measurement for Evaluation in Physical Education.* Boston: Houghton Mifflin Co., 1975.

Berg, Kris, "Maintaining Enthusiasm in Teaching." *Journal of Physical Education and Recreation* 46 (April 1975):22

Berlin, Pearl, "Prologomena to the Study of Personality by Physical Educators." *Quest,* 13 (January 1970):54–62.

Broadhead, Geoffrey D., "Gross Motor Performance in Minimally Brain Injured Children." *Journal of Motor Behavior* 4 (June 1972):103–111.

Bronson, David B., "Thinking and Teaching." *The Educational Forum* 39 (March 1975):347–353.

Brown, Harmon C., and Jack H. Wilmore, "The Effects of Maximal Resistance Training on the Strength and Body Composition of Women Athletes." *Medicine and Science in Sports* 6 (Fall 1974):174–177.

Bruner, Jerome S., Rose R. Oliver, Patricia M. Greenfield, Joan Rigney Hornsby, Helen J. Kenney, Michael Maccoby, Nancy Modiano, Frederic A. Mosher, David R. Olson, Mary C. Potter, Lee C. Reich, and Anne McKinnon Sonstroem. *Studies in Cognitive Growth.* New York: John Wiley and Sons, Inc., 1967.

Bucher, Charles A. *Foundations of Physical Education.* St. Louis: The C.V. Mosby Co., 1972.

_____, "What's Happening In Education Today?" *Journal of Health, Physical Education, and Recreation* 45 (September 1974):30–32.

Caldwell, Stratton, "Toward a Humanistic Physical Education." *Journal of Health, Physical Education, and Recreation* 43 (May 1972):31–32.

Chasey, William C., and Waneen Wyrick, "Effect of a Gross Motor Development Program on Form Perception Skills of Educable Mentally Retarded Children." *Research Quarterly* 41 (October 1970):345–352.

Clarke, H. Harrison, ed., "Individual Differences, Their Nature, Extent and Significance." *Physical Fitness Research Digest* (October 1973).

———, "Physical Fitness Testing in Schools." *Physical Fitness Research Digest* (January 1975).

Committee on the Medical Aspects of Sports of the American Medical Association, "Female Athletics." *Journal of Physical Education and Recreation* 46 (January 1975):45–46.

Corbin, Charles B. *A Textbook of Motor Development.* Dubuque, Iowa: Wm. C. Brown Co. Publishers, 1973.

Cowell, Charles C., "The Contributions of Physical Activity to Social Development." *Research Quarterly* 31 (May 1960, II):286–306.

Cratty, Bryant J. *Movement Behavior and Motor Learning.* Philadelphia: Lea and Febiger, 1967.

———. *Movement, Perception, and Thought.* Palo Alto, Calif. Peek Publications, 1970.

———. *Teaching Motor Skills.* Englewood Cliffs, N.J.: Prentice-Hall, Inc., 1973.

Crockenberg, Vincent, "Poor Teachers Are Made Not Born." *The Educational Forum* 39 (January, 1975):189–198.

Dillon, Stephen V., and David D. Franks, "Open Learning Environment: Self-Identity and Coping Ability." *The Educational Forum* 39 (January 1975):155–161.

Fait, Hollis F. *Physical Education for the Elementary School Child.* Philadelphia: W.B. Saunders Co., 1971.

Feingold, Ronald S., "The Evaluation of Teacher Education Programs in Physical Education." *Quest* 18 (June 1972):33–39.

Felshin, Jan, "Sport and Modes of Meaning." *Journal of Health, Physical Education, and Recreation,* 40 (May 1969):43–44.

———, "The Triple Option . . . For Women in Sport." *Quest* 21 (January 1974):36–40.

———, "Sport Style and Social Modes." *Journal of Physical Education and Recreation* 46 (March 1975):31–34.

Galloway, Charles M., "Teaching is More Than Words." *Quest* 15 (January 1971):67–71.

Gerber, Ellen W., "Learning and Play: Insights of Educational Protagonists." *Quest* 11 (December 1968):44–49.

Gibran, Kahlil. *The Prophet.* New York: Alfred A. Knopf, 1956.

Grabo, Carrol, "Teacher Education and Integrating the Humanities." *The Educational Forum* 39 (November 1974):17–25.

Hall, Sue M., ed., *Children and Fitness.* Washington, D.C.: American Association for Health, Physical Education, and Recreation, 1962.

Harper, William A., "Man Alone." *Quest* 12 (May 1969):57–60.

Harris, Dorothy V., "The Female Athlete: Psychosocial Considerations." *Journal of Physical Education and Recreation* 46 (January 1975):32–36.

Harrow, Anita J. *A Taxonomy of the Psychomotor Domain*. New York: David McKay Co., Inc., 1972.

Heinold, William D., "Motive Typology for Female Sports Spectators: A Comparison With Male Types." In Dorothy V. Harris, ed., *Women in Sport: A National Research Conference*. University Park, Penn.: The Pennsylvania State University, 1972, 307–319.

Hellison, Donald R., "Physical Education and the Self-Attitude." *Quest* 13 (January 1970):41–45.

Henry, Franklin M., "Physical Education: An Academic Discipline." *Journal of Health, Physical Education, and Recreation* 35 (September 1964):32–33.

Hoffman, Shirl James, "Traditional Methodology: Prospects for Change." *Quest* 15 (January 1971):51–57.

Ingham, Alan G., and John W. Loy, Jr., "The Social System of Sport: A Humanistic Perspective." *Quest* 19 (January 1973):3–23.

Ismail, A.H., John Kane, and D.R. Kirkendall, "Relationships Among Intellectual and Nonintellectual Variables." *Research Quarterly* 40 (March, 1969):82–92.

Jewett, Ann, L. Sue Jones, Sheryl M. Luneke, and Sarah M. Robinson, "Educational Change Through a Taxonomy for Writing Physical Education Objectives." *Quest* 15 (January 1971):32–38.

_____, and Marie R. Mullan, "A Conceptual Model for Teacher Education." *Quest* 18 (June 1972):76–87.

_____, "Who Knows What Tomorrow May Bring?" *Quest* 21 (January 1974):68–72.

Johnson, Barry L., and Jack K. Nelson. *Practical Measurements for Evaluation in Physical Education*. Minneapolis: Burgess Publishing Co., 1974.

Kane, J.E., "Psychology of Sport With Special Reference to the Female Athlete." In Dorothy V. Harris, ed., *Women in Sport: A National Research Conference*. University Park, Penn.: The Pennsylvania State University, 1972, 19–34.

Kephart, Newell C. *The Slow Learner in the Classroom*. Columbus, Ohio: Charles E. Merrill Publishing Co., 1960.

Kleine, Glen, "Let Freedom Really Ring in the Schools." Kappa Delta Pi *Record* 11 (April 1975):100–102, 118.

Kleinman, Matthew, "A Central Role for Physical Education in Early Childhood." New York University *Education Quarterly*, 6 (Spring 1975):22–28.

Kretchmar, R. Scott, and William A. Harper, "Must We Have a Rational Answer to the Question Why Does Man Play?" *Journal of Health, Physical Education, and Recreation* 40 (March, 1969):57–58.

Lawson, Hal A., "Physical Education and Sport: Alternatives for the Future." *Quest* 21 (January 1974):19–29.

Leithwood, Kenneth A., "Motor, Cognitive and Affective Relationships Among Advantaged Preschool Children." *Research Quarterly* 42 (March 1971):47–53.

Lipton, Edward D., "A Perceptual-Motor Development Program's Effect on Visual Perception and Reading Readiness of First-Grade Children." *Research Quarterly* 41 (October 1970):402–405.

Locke, L.F., "Are Sports Education?" *Quest* 19 (January 1973):87–90.

Longo, Paul, "Opening the Door to the Open Classroom." Kappa Delta Pi *Record* 11 (April 1975):98–99, 117.

Martens, Rainer. *Social Psychology and Physical Activity*. New York: Harper and Row, 1975.

Maslow, Abraham, "Psychological Data and Values Theory." In Abraham Maslow, ed., *New Knowledge in Human Values*. Chicago: Henry Regnery Co., 1971, 119–136.

Mathews, Donald K. *Measurement in Physical Education*. Philadelphia: W.B. Saunders Co., 1973.

Menzies, Ian, "The Touchy Teacher's Benefit Issue." *The Boston Evening Globe* 207 (June 16, 1975):18.

Merriman, Burton J., "Relationship of Personality Traits to Motor Ability." *Research Quarterly* 31 (May 1960, Part I):163–173.

Meyers, Edward J, "Exercise Physiology in Secondary Schools: A Three Dimensional Approach." *Journal of Physical Education, and Recreation* 46 (January 1975):30–31.

Montessori, Maria. *Spontaneous Activity in Education*. Cambridge, Mass.: Robert Bentley, Inc., 1964.

Morford, W.R., "Toward a Profession, Not a Craft." *Quest* 18 (June 1972):88–93.

_____, "Is Sport the Struggle of the Triumph?" *Quest* 19 (January 1973):83–87.

Nixon, John E., and Ann E. Jewett. *An Introduction to Physical Education*. Philadelphia: W.B. Saunders Co., 1969.

Olson, David R. *Cognitive Development: The Child's Acquisition of Diagonality*. New York: Academic Press, 1979.

Park, Roberta J, "Alternatives and Other Ways': How Might Physical Activity Be More Relevant to Human Needs in the Future?" *Quest* 21 (January 1974):30–35.

Piaget, Jean. *The Origins of Intelligence in Children*. New York: International Universities Press, Inc., 1952.

Riley, Marie, "Games and Humanism." *Journal of Physical Education and Recreation* 46 (February 1975):46–49.

Robb, Margaret D. *The Dynamics of Motor Skill Acquisition*. Englewood Cliffs, N.J.: Prentice-Hall, Inc., 1972.

Roberts, Glyn C., "Sex and Achievement Motivation Effects on Risk Taking." *Research Quarterly* 46 (March 1975):58–70.

Sadler, William A., Jr., "Competition Out of Bounds: Sport in American Life." *Quest* 19 (January 1973):124–132.

Safrit, Margaret J. *Evaluation in Physical Education*. Englewood Cliffs, N.J.: Prentice-Hall, Inc., 1973.

Sage, George H. *Introduction to Motor Behavior: A Neuropsychological Approach*. Reading, Mass.: Addison-Wesley Publishing Co., 1971.

_____, "The Coach as Management: Organizational Leadership in American Sport." *Quest* 19 (January 1973):35–40.

Sanborn, Marion Alice, and Betty G. Hartman. *Issues in Physical Education*. Philadelphia: Lea and Febiger, 1964.

Schendel, Jack, "Psychological Differences Between Athletes and Nonparticipants in Athletics at Three Educational Levels." *Research Quarterly* 36 (March 1965):52–67.

Schmidt, Richard A., and Warren R. Johnson, "A Note on Response Strategies in Children with Learning Difficulties." *Research Quarterly* 43 (December 1972):509–513.

Schurr, Evelyn L. *Movement Experiences for Children.* New York: Appleton-Century-Crofts, 1967.

Scott, Jack, "Sport and the Radical Ethic," *Quest* 19 (January 1973):71–77.

Scott, M. Gladys, "The Contributions of Physical Activity to Psychological Development." *Research Quarterly* 31 (May 1960, Part II):307–320.

Seidel, Beverly, and Matthew C. Resick. *Physical Education: An Overview.* Reading, Mass.: Addison-Wesley Publishing Co., 1972.

Siedentop, Daryl. *Physical Education: Introductory Analysis.* Dubuque, Iowa: Wm. C. Brown Co., 1972.

———, "Behavior Analysis and Teacher Training," *Quest* 18 (June 1972):26–32.

Singer, Robert N. *Motor Learning and Human Performance.* New York: The Macmillan Co., 1968.

———, "Communicate or Perish." *Journal of Health, Physical Education, and Recreation* 39 (February 1968):40–41.

———, "Introduction to the Psychomotor Domain." In Robert N. Singer, ed., *The Psychomotor Domain: Movement Behaviors.* Philadelphia: Lea and Febiger, 1972, 1–17.

———, *Myths and Truths in Sports Psychology.* New York: Harper and Row, 1975.

Smith, Garry, "The Sport Hero: An Endangered Species." *Quest* 19 (January 1973):59–70.

Smith, Michael D., "Aggression and the Female Athlete." In Dorothy V. Harris, ed., *Women and Sport: A National Research Conference.* University Park, Penn.: The Pennsylvania State University, 1972, 91–114.

Snyder, Eldon E., and Elmer A. Spreitzer, "Family Influence and Involvement in Sports." *Research Quarterly* 44 (October 1973):249–255.

———, and Joseph E. Kivlin, "Women Athletes and Aspects of Psychological Well-Being and Body Image." *Research Quarterly* 45 (May 1975):191–199.

Sonstroem, Robert J., "Attitude Testing Examining Certain Psychological Correlates of Physical Activity." *Research Quarterly* 45 (May 1974):93–103.

Stallings, Loretta M. *Motor Skills: Development and Learning.* Dubuque, Iowa: Wm. C. Brown Co. Publishers, 1973.

Studer, Ginny, "From Man Moving to Moving Man." *Quest* 20 (June 1973):104–107.

Taggart, Robert J., "Accountability and the American Dream." *The Educational Forum* 39 (November 1974):33–42.

Thomas, Jerry R., and Brad S. Chissom, "Relationships as Assessed by Canonical Correlation Between Perceptual-Motor and Intellectual Abilities for Pre-School and Early Elementary Age Children." *Journal of Motor Behavior* 4 (March 1972):23–29.

———, ———, "Prediction of First Grade Academic Performance from Kindergarten Perceptual-Motor Data." *Research Quarterly* 45 (May 1974):148–153.

Toffler, Alvin. *Future Shock.* New York: Bantam Books, 1970.

Ulrich, Celeste, "The Tomorrow Mind." *Journal of Health, Physical Education, and Recreation* 35 (October 1964):17–18.

Van Dalen, Deobold B., and Bruce L. Bennett. *A World History of Physical Education.* Englewood Cliffs, N.J.: Prentice-Hall, Inc., 1971.

Vanderzwaag, Harold J., *Toward a Philosophy of Sport.* Reading, Mass.: Addison-Wesley Publishing Co., 1972.

Vodola, Thomas M. *Individualized Physical Education Program for the Handicapped Child*. Englewood Cliffs, N.J.: Prentice-Hall, Inc., 1973.

Weston, Arthur. *The Making of American Physical Education*. New York: Meredith Publishing Co., 1962.

Williams, Jesse Feiring, and Clifford Lee Brownell. *The Administration of Health and Physical Education*. Philadelphia: W.B. Saunders Co., 1946.

Williams, William G., "Does the Educational Past Have a Future?" Kappa Delta Pi *Record* 11 (April 1975):103–104.

Wilmore, Jack H., "Body Composition and Strength Development." *Journal of Physical Education and Recreation* 46 (January 1975):38–40.

_____, "Inferiority of the Female Athlete: Myth or Reality?" *Sports Medicine Bulletin* 10 (April 1975):7–8.

_____, and C. Harmon Brown, "Physiological Profiles of Women Distance Runners." *Medicine and Science in Sports* 6 (Fall 1974):178–181.

Yee, Albert H., "Becoming a Teacher in America," *Quest* 18 (June 1972):67–75.

Ziatz, Daniel H., "Practical-Realistic Public Relations." *Journal of Physical Education and Recreation* 46 (January 1975):69

Zoble, Judith E., "Femininity and Achievement in Sports." In Dorothy V. Harris, ed., *Women and Sport: A National Research Conference*. University Park, Penn.: The Pennsylvania State University, 1972, 203–223.

Index

Date Due

BJJJ